THE TRANSFORMATION
OF ENGLAND

PETER MATHIAS

THE TRANSFORMATION
OF ENGLAND

ESSAYS IN THE
ECONOMIC AND SOCIAL HISTORY
OF ENGLAND
IN THE EIGHTEENTH CENTURY

COLUMBIA UNIVERSITY PRESS
NEW YORK

Library of Congress Cataloging in Publication Data

Mathias, Peter.
  The transformation of England.

  Includes bibliographical references and index.
  1. Great Britain—Economic conditions.
2. Great Britain—Social conditions. I. Title.
HC254.5.M37   1980   338.0941   80-10813
ISBN 0-231-05046-1

CONTENTS

ACKNOWLEDGEMENTS

The author and publishers would like to acknowledge the following publications in which the articles first appeared: ch. 1: *L'Industrialisation en Europe au XIXe Siècle* (C.N.R.S. Paris 1972); *Annales* XXVII (1972); ch. 2: *Trans. Royal Historical Society* XXV (1975); ch. 3: P. Mathias (ed.) (1972) *Science and Society, 1600-1800* (CUP); ch. 4: *Proceedings from the Sixth International Congress on Economic History* (1974, 1978); ch. 5: *J. European Economic History* II (1973); ch. 7: *Tijdschrift voor Geschiedenis* LXXXIX (1976); ch. 8: Istituto Internazionale di Storia Economica, Serie II, Florence (1978); ch. 9: *Economic History Review* X (1957); ch. 10: P. Mathias (1962) *English Trade Tokens: the Industrial Revolution Illustrated* (Abelard Schuman); ch. 11: *Explorations in Entrepreneurial History* V (1953); ch. 12: *Explorations in Entrepreneurial History*, special number (1957); ch. 13: *Economic History Review* V (1952); ch. 14: J.M. Winter (ed.) (1975) *War and Economic Development* (CUP); ch. 15: *Euromoney* (1976); ch. 16: S. Marriner (ed.) (1978) *Business and Businessmen: Studies in Business and Accounting History* (Liverpool UP).

PREFACE

Special justification is needed, perhaps, in these days of instant reproduction for publishing a set of essays, almost all of which have seen publication in one form or another. However, the number of specialized periodicals in economic and social history has been growing exponentially since I reached publishable age and, despite (it appears) the general hostility of publishers, that new *genre* of academic publication — collected conference papers — continues to increase. As conferences, large and small, multiply at home and abroad the pattern of scholarship is changing fast. More research time is being mortgaged for academic papers written for such occasions, destined to appear subsequently in specialized collections and journals, than in writing large coherent books. In the present collection seven chapters were originally published abroad in this way; six saw their conception, if not their birth, in lectures delivered at conferences overseas and one has appeared in a *festschrift* — all in their different ways quite outside the mainstream of British publications in the field and, for the most part, accessible to a series of different specialist audiences. As the diaspora of scholarship increases in this way the advantages of consolidating one's papers into a book are enhanced. In the one or two chapters where this is not the case blame must lie in a fatal combination of a lack of self-restraint in the author and the excessive kindness of his publisher.

The dangers of scholarship with this provenance are obvious. I hope, in the present case, that they may be mitigated when the wider themes and more specialized topics covered in the book are seen in juxtaposition with the text of *The First Industrial Nation* which was published almost exactly a decade ago. The subjects finding a place in this book, two thirds of which derive from research undertaken after 1969, amplify certain important themes discussed only briefly there (for example, capital accumulation, skills, taxation, the eighteenth-century entrepreneurs) while others (such as problems of leisure preference, coinage, diagnoses of poverty) seek to widen the dimensions of discussion about the process of economic and social change in eighteenth-century England. I have sought to limit the number and range of topics chosen to create a coherent and structured book, excluding papers which concern only later periods or methodological issues. Readers may be surprised, but not I hope disappointed, at the appearance of Samuel Johnson in these pages. Chapter 16 was written originally for the Johnson Club rather than for economic historians but I trust that the reflection of the burgeoning industrial growth of the time seen in the life of this great literary figure may give a wider insight into the contemporary consciousness of those changes.

Each chapter embodies obligations, whether to editors for their indulgence or to the organizers of conferences for their generosity, which cannot be separately acknowledged in a preface. For the book as a whole, however, the greatest debt — as all in my position will admit — is to my wife who has supported all these endeavours while not going to many of the meetings. I thank her now, once again, in retrospect and also Sam and Sophie (who did the index).

All Souls College, Oxford   Peter Mathias
20 July 1979

PART I

THEMES

1

BRITISH
INDUSTRIALIZATION:
UNIQUE OR NOT?

Some conceptual issues

The issues raised by such a provocative title deserve to be tackled operationally, rather than methodologically, in terms of the business of economic history. But certain conceptual problems do exist and merit prior discussion. Clearly in the strict sense every country's economic development has been a unique, one-off sequence, with distinguishing characteristics from all others. This will be true, in the absolute sense, of direct economic criteria — rates of inter-sectoral structural change, the exact mix of the constituents of industrial output, and the like — though the higher the degree of aggregation then the greater likelihood of statistical conformities existing between national case histories. The total rate of growth, or rate of investment or population growth may approximate in different instances; it is, however, much less likely that the disaggregated constituents of these conglomerate indices will conform: the share of industry, primary production, services, income from abroad which collectively make up an aggregate rate of growth; the exact mix of capital accumulation in different sectors which forms the aggregate investment rate; the balance of net migration and natural increase (itself a function of age-specific birth and death rates translated against age structures) which lies behind the rate of change of the aggregate population index. Tracking back a little further, we may rest even more assured that the more contextual aspects of economic growth have national specificity; and these, we are appreciating more and more clearly, are crucially important aspects — part and parcel — of the processes of economic change: institutional developments, political, legal, processes and the like; the extent and rapidity of urbanization, the pattern of resource endowment.

As historians concerned with processes of change and the dynamics of growth we should also be suspicious about statistical resemblances and correlations in the profile, or silhouette, of industrialization presented by different countries. Comparable rates of growth (for example, between the United States and Canada, or Norway and the United Kingdom, or Japan and Denmark between 1870-1913), or similar ratios, for values in foreign trade to national income (for example, Germany and Australia in 1911-13, France and Sweden, Japan and Italy) may conceal profound differences in the dynamics of the relationships which underlie these ratios. It would be even more true where similar ratios for two countries exist at widely different points in time (and therefore context). Comparable growth rates emanating from economies which have a markedly different balance between primary production and industrial output, or with a very different export dynamic (or great differences in the pattern of exports between highly processed goods or primary products) are similar masks hiding very different realities. The dynamics of growth, despite similar aggregate statistical contours to an economy, will also be profoundly different if the process of growth is mainly determined by expansion in the public sector, financed directly or indirectly by resources officially mobilized, rather than being primarily responsive to market forces and privately organized capital accumulation.

A further source of contrast in the dynamics of growth, despite statistical uniformities, is that of the differential size of economies, which strongly influences the *locus* of the forces for change or stagnation. A super-economy, covering half a continent, is more likely to have balanced resources and a large enough population to create a powerful internal market to make the main impetus for its growth indigenous — and the role of foreign trade in its development is consequently likely to prove less strategic. With micro-economies — the tax havens, oil sheikdoms, off-shore concession centres, gambling islands and the like — almost all the impetus for development must derive from the specialized services they provide for external demands. The same logic applies with lesser force but similar relevance to such economies as Holland and the Scandinavian countries who received much impetus for their own progress from demands made upon their resources by the heart-lands of European industrial development in Britain and Germany. Thus, even where the statistical profiles show comparable rates of growth of national income, industrialization or urbanization the sources of impetus may differ profoundly. Regional diversities within national aggregates can also complicate the pattern. Where great disparities lie on either side of a mean or average then the national aggregates may conceal more significance than they disclose about processes of growth.

One further logical trap in comparative history needs to be mentioned in relation to the uniqueness or otherwise of particular case histories. It is very common to see a comparison drawn between one particular aspect of the development process in different countries, which are then compared, and their effectiveness judged in isolation from other aspects of development. One looks at the role of agriculture, for example, in the development (or in the constraints upon the development) of Denmark and Russia in the mid-nineteenth century. One compares the role of banks in capital formation and entrepreneurial initiative in Germany and Britain in the later nineteenth century. Taking the last example in illustration, so often the lines of comparison run thus: German industrial banks were more active in these roles than British banks. British economic development was, in certain respects, more sluggish than development in Germany in these same years. Conclusion: (a) British development was being held back by — ? amongst other things — an unenterprising banking system; and/or (b) the British economy would have profited from the adoption of German banking organization and practices. Perhaps. But isolating the operations of a single factor, or institution, assessing performance in different contexts and then assuming that both efficiency and roles can be transferred to other contexts without 'frictions' is methodologically naive. Such inferred transplants contain heroic assumptions.

The Anglo-German example fails to recognize the very different organization of the capital markets in the two countries; that German banks were fulfilling functions of mobilizing capital which were institutionalized in Britain in a largely independent way through the stock market, with its own associated specialized intermediaries of brokers, jobbers, provincial stock exchanges with links of their own to the London money market, etc. This does not negate the point that, if capital accumulation is conducted through a handful of powerful industrial banks, there may be a greater propensity for more exacting standards of efficiency and initiative to be imposed upon management in the firms receiving capital and long-term credit through this mechanism, rather than through the stock exchange, but it does question the assumption that one banking system can adopt the role performed by another in a different context. The fact that the British banking system did not adopt these roles is not, *per se*, any demonstration of inefficiency or lack of initiative on the part of British banks. These roles were being performed in a different way in Britain; the criteria of judgement are therefore different. To put the point in a more general way: there is so much inter-relatedness in the institutional development of an economy, with role and structure so intimately linked, that it becomes difficult to compare and assess roles which relate to different structures, or structures which relate to different roles.

Even where identities are discovered, in such comparisons the significance of these identities is questionable. It appears, for example, that the average size of household in England, in numbers of persons per household, has not changed very much over several centuries, standing between 4 and 5 probably since the thirteenth century, and has been similar in many different countries. Such an identity, over such very different national and historical contexts, is important for refuting unwarranted assumptions, such as that industrialization broke up the 'extended family' in Europe, but it is difficult to see what positive implications it may have for comparative history.

One assumption has lain concealed beneath many discussions of the uniqueness of the Industrial Revolution in Britain. It is that of the potential, as distinct from the actual, specificity of the process of industrialization in the period 1700-1830 (the latter date being chosen to avoid complicating the issue by extending the assumptions to include the existence of railways). Do we assume that there was only one path possible towards effective, self-sustaining, ongoing industrial development in this period; one pattern for the structural combination of factors which allowed an industrial revolution, i.e. the pattern developed by Great Britain? Do we assume that no substitutability between factors and relationships was possible? Do we judge our historical logic by results; by the fact that only this combination of factors, with the pyramid of specific relationships upon which each main aspect of it rested, in fact paid off. If so, why? What are the criteria which have been implied to create and justify this assumption? Or is the potential logic more flexible, when in the perspective of later times and differences in context we see that other procedures, other combinations, other institutional frameworks, other strategic forces promoting industrialization could succeed?

In the later nineteenth century there is Professor Gerschenkron's typology showing exactly such different combinations, different modes of substitution of factors, combined with different institutional arrangements to promote industrialization in different European countries.[1] If this was possible and operative for that period of European economic development, why not for industrialization in the eighteenth century? In certain ways this methodology in interpreting the Industrial Revolution and the uniqueness of England is curiously reminiscent of an earlier assumption about the interpretation of political revolution in the eighteenth century and the uniqueness of France. Halévy, and radical historians more recently, for example, seemed to argue sometimes as follows: France had a political revolution at the end of the eighteenth century; hence, all respectable European nations ought to have had a revolution. There must therefore be a special, identifiable variable which prevented England from having one. Having thus predetermined the role, we can discover an actor — Methodism.

Transferring the assumption from political revolution in France to industrial revolution in England this line of argument prompts us to ask, not so much why England was unique, but the complementary enquiry into what constraints prevented equivalent industrial development elsewhere. If one accepts that a range of factors and relationships were required, as a syndrome, that each was necessary but not sufficient, then one can seek to identify that major constraints existed elsewhere in Europe. For example, Holland, so favoured in other ways, was without the crucial resource base for the technological pattern developing in an age when the logistics of transport and energy inputs gave major advantages in factor costs to the economy with easily exploitable coal and metal ores close to water carriage. Commercial priorities in Holland also acted against economic policies which might have counteracted this. A package of skills was intimately associated with this resource base in a long-developing industrial tradition. It is a commonplace to remark that Britain had been fortunate in her scarcities since the sixteenth century. Of course, the contents of the package of necessary conditions required to make it collectively sufficient changed over time and in accordance to context.

If, in seeking to establish typologies of industrialization, we give prominence to differences in the extent to which market forces and institutions developing spontaneously in response to market forces — institutionalizing such market forces in effect — were the carriers of the process of industrialization then a further general question arises. Clearly, in later times, industrialization has proceeded under 'command economies' with a spectrum of case histories showing different degrees of *dirigisme* by the state, with equivalently different institutional patterns. When so many states were so active in eighteenth-century Europe in seeking to capitalize upon the new industrial skills, what were the constraints operating against the success of promoting industrialization in this style in the eighteenth and early nineteenth centuries? There is no single cause explanation, I think. Unfavourable factor prices, of course, may well have made the new techniques uneconomic in a market setting so that they would not be tempted to escape from the enclaves of favoured state reception centres into which they had been transplanted — the state manufactures, national monopolies, and specially favoured firms. But there are institutional and administrative reasons also, which are currently rather unfashionable amongst economic historians. In the case of economic institutions controlled by European states in the eighteenth century, given the political processes of the day, functional efficiency was commonly not given the highest priority. It enjoined a rather higher priority in the case of the army and navy because there was a greater immediate premium on success and a greater direct penalty against functional inefficiency. But, in time of peace, functional efficiency was by no means a transcendent priority for the choice of generals in the British army. An efficient, ambitious, career-soldier could be dangerous politically. The dictates of political patronage and clientship, dynastic claims, family responsibilities and the like often meant that the priorities lay elsewhere. State patronage of economic institutions meant that they were tributary to the political process and that their role in the political cohesion of the state was often fulfilled at the expense of their functional efficiency. The Church and the judicature in England fall under this heading as well as economic and financial institutions.

The education of the market and the discipline of the market were absent in an age when modern administrative methods did not exist as alternatives. When the statement is made, therefore, that the crucial distinguishing mark of the Industrial Revolution in Britain was that of the 'market economy' or 'responsiveness to market forces' or 'institutionalizing market forces' or the 'smallness of the subsistence sector', we are making a positive statement about political decision-making in England, not simply implying the absence of political decision-making. A market is always politically determined in the sense of requiring a legal framework. A 'market', moreover, is itself a bundle of relationships; it implies physical relationships of production, resources, transport; it involves economic relationships in demand, costs and the like; it requires institutional relationships, of intermediaries and firms filling a related set of roles; it assumes legal and political relationships, allowing the necessary mobility of factors of production; the required freedoms. The discipline or education of the market is complemented by these wide pre-conditions required for the successful development of a market economy. Clearly, to a certain degree differing in time and place, European states were attempting to will the end of industrialization — the new technology — but not the means, as those means had developed in Britain.

In this wide sense, therefore, not just in the sense of being embodied in a particular *milieu* of skills which were intrinsically difficult to diffuse in this period, the new technology was embodied in a less tangible set of institutional relationships implied by its development within a market economy. In my view, these institutional assumptions were of profound importance as a distinguishing characteristic in the British case in the period 1660-1750.

The implications of such nihilistic reflections are to cast doubt upon the philosophical validity of speculating, in a more general sense of seeking to identify critical distinguishing features of the process of industrialization in Britain. Nor, in my view, can such methodological difficulties be resolved by invoking any single 'typology' of processes of industrialization. That advances the discussion a measure and shifts the problem of the 'degree of representativeness' of individual instances from a direct comparison between case histories to their assessment against categories. This procedure does not resolve the problem, even though it may clarify distinctions. In any case, one may object that the number of case histories that form the total population is fairly limited for purposes of basing a 'typology' upon a wide statistical base. In any case it may be imperative to speak of typologies rather than a single typology. Different criteria may need to be applied to typologies embracing different regional patterns of growth within a single economy, for example, than to those scheduling differences between national economies. To decline to accept a typology as an easy way out of the thickets of difficulties surrounding the quest for historical laws of development and growth is not to disparage the search for scheduling such ideal types; merely to claim that the typologies we seek to establish should be chosen according to the range of variables we seek to identify and assess, and that these will, in turn, vary according to the focus of our enquiries and the degree of difference between the case histories which are in question. A typology appropriate for scheduling the difference in the relationships involved in the process of industrialization between Britain and Russia, or Spain and Japan, will be too blunt an instrument to probe the differences between these processes in Britain, France, Sweden and Denmark. In other words, we should not treat our typologies, whether those of Rostow, Hoffman or whoever, like old friends and stick by them through thick and thin. When they have ceased to be useful to us we should drop them without compunction.

These abstract speculations may seem verbal flourishes but the implications of the methodological crux are to be seen in the likely result when attempting the exercise. One is driven either towards recounting the total economic history of the British Industrial Revolution or to selecting certain aspects of that process which seem to require heavier emphasis. Neither of these exercises is properly a direct answer to the question 'unique or not'. Let it be said also that current trends in theories of economic development are widening the range of variables that have to be brought into the analysis of the process of modernizing societies and economies, with greater emphasis being placed upon the non-economic dimensions of the changes than was previously the case. When social, political, administrative, legal, cultural, even the psychological and motivational characteristics of a society are seen to be integral influences upon the processes of economic growth (not just autonomous or dependent variables to that process) then the 'uniqueness' (or the probability of the 'uniqueness') of each national experience is much enhanced. Even the term 'economic growth' has given place to a more diffuse entity called 'modernization' and the search for an agreed set of variables, let alone a theory of their inter-relationships, is becoming more, rather than less, problematical.

It is not the purpose of this paper to offer new causes for the Industrial Revolution in Britain or to establish new criteria for its uniqueness. The spectrum of mono-causal, or the ingredients of multi-causal, explanation has been all embracing, including: a favourable natural resource position, population movements, social structure and a flexible social process, the growth of internal demand (particularly the rising demand of 'middling' income groups), a commercialized and progressive agriculture, a developing tradition of rural-based industries, foreign trade and colonies, the availability of capital, a native genius for inventing, or innovating or entrepreneurship, Protestant Nonconformity, a government system favouring intervention and *laissez-faire* in the most suitable mixture at different times, a legal process encouraging the efficiencies of competition and a market economy, scientific knowledge and scientific attitudes, psychological drives and motivations. New research is perhaps revealing important educational innovations, and other dimensions of the concept of 'human capital' are now being energetically explored by economic historians, having been instructed by economists and others that they are important.

The particular cocktail blending the particular mixture from such a list, with each ingredient influencing several others, being in part a dependent variable, in part a creative influence upon the process of growth, must also remain subjective. This chapter will, therefore, consider in a general sense the way in which being the first economy to develop an industrial base of high-productivity techniques, rapid industrial advance and cumulative innovation at an increasing pace made Britain 'unique' in relation to subsequent case histories; and the way in which the international context facing

that first industrializing base was itself unprecedented and unre-
peatable. A further chapter considers the problem of the diffusion
of technology and strategic technical skills in this period because
the logic of the argument about the 'uniqueness' of being first in
the field raises the question of lags in the spread of techniques.

First and, therefore, unique?

Britain's case history of industrialization was unique in being the
first in Europe and the world. Clearly Britain was not unique in
experiencing economic growth in the eighteenth century or before;
nor were many single features of the process of industrialization in
Britain unique. Certain other attributes of 'uniqueness' stem from
the fact that Britain's industrialization came first, rather than just
from the uniqueness of its characteristics. Once a single industrial
base existed, which had become a vigorous centre for innovation
and a flow of new technology for spreading higher-productivity
techniques, then, in a certain measure, the world context was
transformed. On the world scale, problems of initiating crucial
innovations became tempered in some degree to the problems of
diffusing innovations already extant and publicized. Such problems
of diffusion, which a further chapter considers, may prove as
formidable as those of initial innovation, but subsequent case
histories of industrialization are nevertheless set apart by the
success of a pre-existing industrial base.

This is for good and ill. On the one hand there are advantageous
techniques available for borrowing. Despite public regulations in
Britain against the export of certain techniques, skilled operatives
and the machines themselves, despite private efforts of industrialists to guard their secrets and invoke the laws against diffusing
strategic technology, other market mechanisms developed more
effective pressures to induce diffusion, where the context for its
reception was favourable. The laws were largely ineffective, ineffi-
ciently policed and never kept up-to-date, so that the flow of new
technology was continually adding new devices which escaped
entry on the schedule of prohibited exports. It was more difficult to
legislate against the diffusion of new processes than it was to
control the export of machines. It was even more difficult to
legislate against the diffusion of formal knowledge (although that
formal knowledge was not the only operative carrier of new skills

and techniques). In Britain, individuals, whether independent entrepreneurs or skilled workmen, accepted invitations to set up plants and work abroad without much reticence, although in many cases not the best or most responsible were attracted by such opportunities. Once mechanical engineering and machine-tool making had specialized out into firms engaged primarily in machine-making in their own right then a business interest group had come into existence pressing its claims for export markets for capital goods and invoking all the institutions and processes of established international trade for the export of such capital goods, embodying the fruits of the new technology, to flow to new countries. Even the patent system became an instrument for diffusing knowledge of new technology, partly because the registration of patents in Britain made public — for an international public if interested — formal knowledge of innovations, and partly because British engineers and innovators commonly took out patents in Paris as well as London.

Supplementing such 'push' mechanisms for diffusing new techniques from the leader economy were 'pull' forces from would-be recipient countries. Public favour, by offers of monopoly, the assurance of a market by sales to government establishments at favourable prices, fancy wages and fringe benefits, protective tariffs, in short the whole armoury of economic incentives, were offered at different times by continental states anxious to attract the practitioners of the new skills, ranging from steam-power technology, metal-working, mechanical engineering and machine-making to porter brewing. Prestigious chemists and engineers were pressed into the public service to travel overseas and report on the latest techniques, in the style of the productivity teams from British industry that toured overseas plants after 1945. A proliferation of official and private bodies sought to popularize the new techniques and transfer them across national frontiers. How effective all these endeavours were is another matter but their existence underlines the fact that the international context was fundamentally different when 'capital' in the form of a pool of advanced technology was potentially available to be drawn on by newly industrializing countries.

This new 'capital stock' was not, of course, confined to 'hardware' and industrial processes. The demonstration effect of successful industrialization could operate in a multitude of ways.

Most countries produced a band of proselytizers for the new economy (as they did a counter-suggestive lobby). Less tangible responses ranged from a demand for industrial tariff walls to encourage infant industries to a proliferation of translations of Adam Smith.

In other ways, of course, the international context facing all other economies once a major industrializing centre existed were less favourable — but it was certainly no different from that which faced Britain and other leading powers in the eighteenth century, when no single economy pre-eminent in industrial exports bestrode international trade and shipping. With the gap in prices between British exports of cheap cloth and iron and those of less technologically advanced countries, and with the proliferating engineering industry in Britain being able to offer a widening range of sophisticated products which could not often be matched in function, quite apart from price, the opportunities for other nations basing a major industrial impetus upon foreign markets were less than they were in Britain in the period 1780-1850. Thus, stemming from the implications of being the first industrial economy, to the extent that a technological gap had developed between the British economy and other advanced economies in this period, it can be claimed that in certain respects the processes of growth which determined British industrialization were set apart from those which conditioned all subsequent case histories.

Unique, therefore, first?

Many aspects of Britain's economic development in the eighteenth century were certainly not unique to herself. Equally, in my view, it is inadequate to conceive of the problem of identifying the causes of the Industrial Revolution in Britain in terms of a single-cause explanation. This implies, in consequence, that it is equally inadequate methodologically to seek to identify the operative variable which differentiates the British experience by comparative enquiry to discover the factor present in Britain but missing elsewhere. The numbers of possible influences are too large, and their mutual interactions too complex, to be able to use comparative history in this pseudo-scientific way. There are more paths to industrialization, with different combinations of factors, than that trodden by eighteenth- and nineteenth-century Britain. However, comparative enquiry is not robbed of utility by denying it scientific validity as a means of identifying the causes (or the cause) of industrialization. Perception about the significance of relationships involved in the process in different countries: and intimations (as distinct from demonstrable proof) about the relative importance of different aspects of the process may spring from cross-national comparisons more readily than from intensive study of a single case.

Common features in such cross-national comparisons stand out as prominently as so-called unique ones. In the growth of foreign trade and colonial expansion France marched step by step with Britain between 1713-80. In agricultural advance the United Provinces, Flanders and Northern France pioneered the innovations which characterized progressive farming in England during the eighteenth century. In their own way viticultural areas of France and certain areas in the Po valley were as efficient and as commercially orientated. Ireland experienced population growth at an equivalent pace to Great Britain. Protestantism, with minority Protestant and non-establishment sects, was a European-wide phenomenon. Moreover, if the classic Weberian thesis associating Calvinism with capitalism in the sixteenth century remains unresolved, but strongly challenged, it seems problematical, in this different debate, for the eighteenth century to place too much confidence in religious consciousness as a prime explanatory variable.

In commercial and financial sophistication, and the institutions associated with this, the United Provinces were more developed than London. Again, in the growth of shipbuilding, shipping, and foreign trade, with their complex of skills, Holland taught England her commercial arts; though by the mid-eighteenth century the Dutch were bemoaning their lost supremacy. Credit and capital remained more plentiful, and cheaper, in relation to investment opportunities in Holland than in Britain. In social structure, cultural attitudes and political processes accommodating the pursuit of worldly gain Holland was more truly a bourgeois society than any other in Europe, including Britain. More generally, the intellectual, scientific and cultural advance of north-western Europe was proceeding on a wide front, across national frontiers. The growth of scientific knowledge, in particular, was a European-wide phenomenon. In these cultural, intellectual and scientific fields France, in particular, developed the proudest heritage in

Europe. Economic growth in centres other than England had also come primarily from market responses rather than state action, although the implications of a market economy with all the political, legal and institutional developments which that involved had probably been carried further in England than in any other country except Holland. England's endowment of natural resources was not unique (though particularly favourable for the new technological base being established during the eighteenth and nineteenth centuries); nor was her facility for internal water carriage.

The list could be continued, and each item upon it elaborated at length. But the conclusion to be drawn appears inescapable, if commonplace: that if England's growth was not unique in most, if not all, particulars its uniqueness (unless precocity was mere accident) lay in the combination of relationships that focused within England during the eighteenth century but in no other European power. The general potentiality for economic growth and industrialization, bar certain constraints, existed far more widely in north-western Europe than just in England. Since the Middle Ages the essential apparatus of modernization — political, administrative, financial, cultural, intellectual as well as economic — was being developed in the nation states of this region of Europe. Advances in trade, shipping, colonial expansion and industrial techniques were phenomena common to them. Differences in economic growth between the regions of each country were greater than the differences between the most advanced regions of different countries. There was no great technological gap between such 'leader' economies; at least no preponderant technological advantage concentrated upon a single country. Levels of income (taking England, Holland and France at the end of the seventeenth century) do not appear to have differed widely. Transfer payments, particularly through taxation, probably accounted for more of the difference in levels of consumption per capita in the mass markets than differences in national income per capita. With the pace of technological change being relatively slow compared with later times, slow diffusion of innovations did not mean any significant cumulative gap widening between the most advanced economies, though specializations were developing between them, and in the narrow but strategic future sector of what Professor Harris has called a 'mineral-fuel technology' England was becoming pre-eminent at the end of the seventeenth and early eighteenth century.[2] This was confined to such a small sector of production, however, in the mid-eighteenth century that it did not affect aggregate rates of growth. In aggregate size, of course, by resources and population, the economy of France was several times larger than that of Britain, and *a fortiori* than all other nations of western Europe; while the mobilized resources available to the French government were similarly greater than those available to other states.

A century later perspectives had changed dramatically between Britain and all other nations, and there is an impressive list of the collective criteria, rather than single aspects of the process of industrialization by which Britain can claim to be 'unique by being first' in the mid-nineteenth century. Differential rates of population growth for over a century had brought British population much closer to that of France and Germany, and widened the population gap between Britain and other western European countries. When translated against a more rapidly growing economy it means that the scale of the British economy had become unrivalled in Europe, more particularly the growth and scale of its industrial output, the production of coal, cotton, iron, non-ferrous metals, and engineering products of all kinds. In rates of growth and in aggregate the gap in production in these modern sectors was now formidable. This reflected a technological gap in the same sectors: the net flow of innovations (if not of inventions) for mechanizing productive processes, machine and power technology went unmistakably from Britain outwards to other nations, with small reverse eddies in this current (to become of progressive significance as time passed) in such matters as wooden sailing ship design, woodworking equipment and interchangeable parts in firearms from the United States and certain lines of chemical technology from Germany and France.

Technological superiority, expressed both in technical leadership and in lower prices of industrial products, had led to even greater changes in the relative lead enjoyed by Britain in international trade and shipping. Taking certain structural indexes (none of which by themselves are necessarily indicators of relative precocity in industrialization), agriculture employed a much smaller proportion of the labour force in Britain than elsewhere (with the possible exception of Holland and Belgium) and contributed a much smaller proportion of the national income. The percentage of the population in Great Britain living in towns was well in advance of that in other countries; more particularly other countries with a large population. National income per capita in Great Britain in 1870, despite the faster population growth there than in many other countries, was higher than any other country in the world. Perhaps the clearest demonstration of this pre-eminence of the British economy in the mid-nineteenth century is to be seen in its progressive attrition, compared with other rising industrial economies, in the century since then.

In the broadest historical perspective we may therefore claim that the process which took Britain from being one of a group of most advanced 'pre-industrial' nations to international industrial and commercial pre-eminence in the world economy was unique. It was unique, using these criteria, in the extent of the dominance of a single national economy in the crucial matrix of cheap coal, cheap iron, cheap cloth, machine-making, power and mineral fuel technology, engineering skills, and was the product of a context unique in world history. It sprang from a very special combination of circumstances: the resources and logistics of energy and transport in a pre-railway age; the portentous initial leap in production and productivity, with the consequent dramatic fall in costs, as medieval handicraft techniques first gave way to factory and power production, translated against the very slow process of diffusion of skills grounded in an empirical tradition. The extent of the single economy's lead was unprecedented compared with the historical context before the springs of industrialization had been unleashed and such a gap has been unknown since industrialization has become diffused in the international economy. The unique historical phenomenon was the localization of these features in Britain to such a degree; not that which commentators have been seeking to explain ever since as somehow in need of special explanation — that other advanced nations subsequently caught up and surpassed.

The international context

The international context within which the early sequences of British industrialization took place also has claims under the assumptions of 'uniqueness' applied to the process as a whole. This is, in part, just the obverse of the arguments contained under the heading 'first, and therefore unique' but it has a more particular application. In the general sense we have argued that the advantages given to the British economy by being first in the field as an industrial economy were uniquely great because this represented the first giant gains of factory productivity beyond the very gradual gains in productivity and falling costs which had accrued from the slow improvements made with handicraft, artisan technology over the generations. Being the first to escape from the restraints of costs imposed by handicraft technology, the unprecedented fall in costs and prices of exports, particularly in the staple consumer goods of cheap textiles and the staple capital goods of cheap iron and cheap coal, gave unique opportunities in international trade, realized increasingly after 1783 (before which point the direct gains of the industrial revolution had not greatly boosted British exports of manufactured goods).

To this has to be added the, in part accidental, chronological coincidence of the Revolutionary and Napoleonic wars, which, for twenty-five years, imposed such great restraints upon the international trade of the continental economies. As Professor Crouzet has shown, particularly for the case of France, being cut off from the impetus for growth within the transatlantic trading area, the most strategic region for expansion in foreign trade at the time, crippled the momentum for expansion built up in the French economy during the eighteenth century through expanding trade.[3] This discontinuity imposed for so long, just at the time when the gains of industrialization were being first translated on a major scale into lower prices and a widening range of goods in Britain, meant that a critical gap developed which was, in many respects, consolidated during the ensuing century. Even more dramatic discontinuities were imposed upon Holland by war between 1780-1815.

The slow pace of the diffusion of strategic new skills in this period (which war further interrupted, though never prevented) also contributed to Britain seizing the unique economic opportunities presented by the international context after 1815.[4] The 'economic distance' created between Britain and other potential European industrial exporters was compounded by the expansion possible in third markets: the unprecedented growth of the United States' market in population and wealth; empty continents awaiting settlement and capital; many regions of the world potentially ready to supply primary produce but without long-distance shipping fleets, banking systems, or, in many cases the indigenous mercantile cadres to be able to structure such trade on their own account. Hence the consolidation of a British international commercial infrastructure in so many countries of the world, a complex of commercial, financial and shipping facilities; long-term capital, working credits and skills through which the complementarities between the primary produce suppliers and the workshop of the world could be so strongly developed.

Many countries shared in these international movements, of course, but none so fully or in so many of its aspects as the United Kingdom. Poland, Italy and Germany saw important migrations, as did Ireland; capital flowed from France (although more within Europe, and to Algeria, than worldwide); international trade levels rose in all advanced countries. But Britain was, again, unique in the degree to which her economic development was geared into the international economy in the course of the nineteenth century in *all* major aspects: by commodity trade, by shipping, by commercial and financial services, by migration, by the export of capital. This is doubly unique: the national response was unique in that century and it was a response to a unique historical context.

Notes

1 A. Gerschenkron (1968) *Continuity in History*, Cambridge, Mass., chapter 4.
2 Paper to International Economic History Conference, Leningrad, 1970; *Industry and Technology in the Eighteenth Century: Britain and France* (Inaugural lecture, Birmingham, 1971).
3 *Annales*, XXI (2), 1966; *Journal of Economic History*, XXIV (4), 1964.
4 See chapter 2.

2

SKILLS AND THE DIFFUSION OF INNOVATIONS FROM BRITAIN IN THE EIGHTEENTH CENTURY

I

This inquiry stems from an initial interest in the relationships between science and technology in the eighteenth century.[1] Hence its concern lies principally with the nature of technical innovation and the sources of technical change during the Industrial Revolution. Exploring the ways in which new technology is diffused can shed light on the nature of technical change itself, which is a complex amalgam of influences governing invention, innovation (the bringing of inventions into productive use) and the diffusion of new techniques. Taking as a topic the diffusion of technology, particularly in machine-making and engineering, between Britain and Europe in the late eighteenth century is thus not meant to be a peg on which to hang wide-ranging animadversions on the differing economic fortunes and pace of advance of Britain and Europe, or a discussion of why industrialization came first and fastest to Britain and lagged elsewhere: it is a much narrower enquiry into seeing what light the processes and difficulties of diffusing new technology cast upon technical change itself at this time.

Such a limiting proviso is important because any enquiry into the general reasons for the failure of new technology on a wide front to get indigenized in a country other than that of its birth does lead into the widest realms of explanation, invoking the whole range of possible reasons for lags in rates of economic growth and industrialization in different countries, the net result of which collectively leads to a failure to adopt modern technology, at once the symbol, the measure and the means of modernization. Secondly, there is in-built bias in setting up an enquiry to look at the diffusion of such technology from Britain to Europe which isolates a principally one-way flow in what was, in fact, a very turbulent stream of change moving in different directions. The view from Russia in 1815, for example, shows French and German entrepreneurs more prominent than British in many fields (save in machine-making and cotton textiles) with Dutch and French skilled artisans present in large numbers.[2] Estonia was largely a technological and business dependency of German groups. Germans were most prominent in the Russian Academy and as technical advisers to the government (with notable exceptions like Sir Samuel Bentham and General Wilson).

A similar picture is drawn in the Spanish royal manufactories during the eighteenth century: French artisans and entrepreneurs (with some Italians) dominated the transfers of technology in the silk industry, as they did throughout Europe (not just as a consequence of Huguenot persecution); Germans and French in linen; English and Irish in fine woollens and cotton; the Dutch in some other cloths.[3] The Guadalaxara woollen mill, for example, was principally worked by English, Irish, French and Dutch artisans (sought in integrated groups with complementary skills), but others came from Poland, Prussia, Switzerland and Italy. France was a principal source of new inventions and technology in Europe during the century, leading a counterpoint between French inventions and English development in the basic development of branches of the chemical industry, in paper-making and in the glass industry, amongst others.[4] During the Revolutionary and Napoleonic wars French scientific administrators and civil engineers vigorously set about surveying for minerals and promoting mining techniques throughout the territories they controlled or influenced, in a European-wide endeavour to develop materials, skills and productive capacity for the armament industries.[5] Professor Rondo Cameron's study, *France and the Economic Development of Europe, 1815-1914*, which isolates a different flow, shows the extent of French technological influence, tightly packaged with French capital and business initiative. The closer technology depended upon formal scientific training at the end of the eighteenth century, the greater the influence of France as the mentor of Europe.

But with the basic mechanization of the textile industry after 1770, the growth of deep mines and large-scale metal fabrication, and the associated growth of engineering, it was principally British engineers and artisans who sponsored diffusion of these new techniques abroad. This was particularly true of machine-making and mechanical engineering generally (although not of civil engineering) — technologies that were to have the widest influence in the spread of mechanization and the engineering industries during the nineteenth century.[6] British technology also spread indirectly; when direct exports of machinery were prohibited (if never prevented), Russian textile factories drew on French and Belgian machines, much dependent on British expertise. In the 1840s, after repeal of the laws, a much more direct invasion of British textile technology took place.[7] As will be apparent, individual examples of best-practice technology — particularly dramatic new machines like the steam engine, installed in state-promoted or state-favoured plants — were transferred relatively rapidly in continental Europe, but they failed so often to become adopted more generally so that a much larger gap existed between best practice and the representative level of diffused techniques in such industries than was the case in Britain.

There was also a significant gap between the record of invention and development in many fields. The English had long been known as the perfecters of other people's ideas, but this continued in many fields. A Swiss calico printer remarked in 1766 of the English: 'they cannot boast of many inventions, but only of having perfected the inventions of others; whence comes the proverb that for a thing to be perfect it must be invented in France and worked out in England.'[8] All this is significant evidence that the general economic and commercial context was not so favourable in these countries.[9] In such an economic climate single swallows do not make a summer.

Doubtless a principal explanation for such lack of momentum in adopting new technology was the absence of the requisite extent of demand. A cumulative extension of demand for the products of these industries in continental countries would have put the necessary strain upon the inputs of conventional resources, threatened the traditional balance between techniques, materials and skills, forced up prices of the scarce factors and created the requisite incentives for adopting new technology. Britain was fortunate in her shortages in this period. These seem to have underpinned the diffusion of innovations such as coke-smelting in England and explained their timing in a commercial context.[10] Pointing to insufficient demand as one general explanation, of course, is to identify not a single relationship but a large bundle of economic and social, institutional, legal, political and motivational factors which underlie a highly abstract and conceptualized entity such as 'the level of effective demand'. An equivalent bundle of relationships lies at the back of the 'single' entity called a 'market economy'.

Of course the resource position with factor costs for cheap coal and iron was more favourable in the United Kingdom and in certain ways the commercial context less favourable in France and other continental states further east. The state willed certain of the ends of industrialization, such as the acquisition of new skills, but opposed (consciously or through the effect of other policies and positions supported by government) many of the general means to attain those ends and other pre-conditions of the process, such as general mobility of labour, growth of commercial institutions and the like.

There is also the question of economic or commercial rationality about the adoption, or absence of adoption, of such innovations.[11] If the relative prices of labour (in different grades, skill for skill), capital and materials were very different from what they were in the region where these devices were developed and adopted, then strict economic rationality of maximizing returns from a 'minimum cost' mix of inputs might have dictated that they be not adopted. There can be a sharp contrast (as we are still forcibly reminded from time to time) between the most technically advanced methods and the most commercially effective and most economic arrangements. There would have been, in the areas of these economies subject to market pressures and where changing price levels acted meaningfully as signals for action, a lower incentive to move along a production function substituting expensive capital equipment for labour, or adopting devices making large demands on scarce resources (whether skills or materials); and, doubtless, less commercial incentive also for wider reasons to move to new combinations of factors through technical progress and new innovation. Technical and economic criteria merge in such an analysis. The costs of getting the exactly suitable fuel, or the precise grade of labour required to maintain and operate new machines, for example, could prove too high, although expressed in terms of local shortages of suitable resources or suitable skills. These problems of relative shortages and differential factor prices are not to be conceived as offering an infinity of choices smoothly phased over a spectrum from highly capitalistic to highly labour-intensive techniques. Shortages of particular kinds of skills and particular sorts of material can be, in practical terms, absolute: differentiation in price would not reflect the degree of shortage, save that no supply would be forthcoming in the short-term at any price. In much technology the choice is set by such barriers. And for many techniques, particularly those involving new products, there is, in practice, not much choice; in others new techniques are so superior on all counts, in saving labour and capital and in the quality of product relative to price, that they offer no graduated choice according to differential prices of inputs.[12]

Technical problems of diffusing skills and technology still apply, particularly in situations where economic incentives are not of major relevance, or in the enclaves of technology where the imperatives for diffusion do not depend directly upon criteria of profitability — as in militarily useful technology, or other technology sought by the public sector, not subject to cost-effective decision making. Mechanisms for the diffusion of skills and the ways in which the production of skills have been institutionalized at the very least also affect the length of the time-lags involved in the diffusion process; and here, as in so many other fields, there is no clear-cut division between the short and the longer run. Economic history, like any other sort of history, is essentially concerned with time-lags. Technical problems and skills have so often been assumed as a dependent variable in theoretical formulations about processes of economic development, but theoretically any other single constraint can be wished away from the analysis as a 'dependent' variable on the argument that if demand, or capital, or resources are there then the skills will surely follow. Questions of technical change and the diffusion of new techniques were (and are) much more complex than the application of neo-classical models and the logic of relative factor prices might suggest.[13] In the continental economies the reception points for new technology and development were often outside the market sector, as they are in much of the world in our own day, either formally within the state sector, where prices do not have a direct significance in market terms, or sheltered from market forces in the private sector.[14] It is for this reason, amongst others, that the *technical* problems of the diffusion of new technology can be considered meaningfully outside strictly commercial criteria of relative prices, costs and profits, determined in a competitive market with freely moving prices.

Continental governments made systematic efforts to promote technical change, new industrial skills and modernized technology into their countries.[15] Encouragement came partly from tariff walls or physical restrictions on competing imports, behind which monopolies could flourish undisturbed. There were royal monopolies, directly promoted state arsenals, shipyards, gun-foundries, manufactories, some with research laboratories and scientists in attendance. Most continental governments had established departments of state which were virtually ministries of industrial progress deploying a whole range of economic policy weaponry: public subsidies and direct financing of investment; purchasing by the public sector focused upon the publicly favoured plants or the state monopoly at lavish prices; public finance to attract entrepreneurs and workmen possessing new and scarce skills from other lands with fancy offers of reward in monopolies, guaranteed profits, high wages and other benefits in kind; ambassadors mobilized as recruiting agents. Jean Rulière, the French entrepreneur in Spain, had the foresight to negotiate with the king in advance: noble status, a very large salary, free house and living expenses, all travel costs for his family, an assured pension and a fixed percentage of the profits of the mill. The latter provision alone proved superfluous. Such state promotional agencies and inspectorates employed some of the most distinguished scientists and publicists of the new technology on their payrolls — as Réamur, Gabriel Jars, Chaptal and Faujas de St Fond in France. Academies of Science had obligations to apply scientific knowledge to the advance of technique. There was nothing in England like the *Seehandlung* of Prussia, the Corps des Ponts et Chaussées (from which came the École Polytechnique in 1795), the École des Mines, the Conservatoire des Arts et Métiers, or the royal factories in the public sector of France. Institutionally, by public endeavour and by aspiration, all was orchestrated to the grand design of promoting new industrial techniques in these lands; more particularly because governments were conscious that ranges of new techniques were being developed more progressively elsewhere and that normal commercial processes did not produce sufficient incentives for their diffusion.

Such policies of direct and indirect state promotion for the attraction of new technologies had certain counter-productive effects, quite apart from the more general inhibitions to economic development associated with *ancien régime* political and social systems. Skills and capital were lavished upon luxury industries, such as fine cloths, silks, tapestries, porcelain, clocks, mirrors and plate glass and the like; or upon specialized military purposes. 'Spin-offs' could come from both; but cost-effectiveness featured in neither group. New technologies associated with immigrant skills and state promotion tended to become locked away from the rest of the economy in special enclaves of high cost. Inefficient administration, functional efficiency sacrificed to the dictates of patronage, great wastage of resources, characterized most of these operations. Sometimes, as in Spain, they were deliberately sited in backward regions, unsuited for commercial success. High import tariffs on raw materials and capital goods, to encourage local production and investment in these branches of enterprise, forced high costs and uncertain supply upon private entrepreneurs using these products as inputs for their own enterprises, and prejudiced their own commercial efficiency. There is, however, a partial defence in that such establishments should not be judged as commercially efficient businesses but as training grounds for the diffusion of new skills: foreign artisans as part of their contracts accepted the obligation of teaching a regular number of local people their skills.

II

Institutions and processes for diffusing formal knowledge and scientific ideas in western Europe and North America in the seventeenth and eighteenth centuries were remarkably effective. In Nassau Senior's phrase, transfers of 'mental capital' were most easily effected.[16] Communications amongst the geographically dispersed élite of interested, largely leisured, groups were very active: by visits, publications of proceedings and transactions, astonishingly assiduous correspondence amongst members of academies and their secretaries through the *linguae francae* of French, English and Latin, supported by a lively European trade in important scientific books. The correspondence of Henry Oldenburg, first Secretary of the Royal Society, exemplifies this.[17] Sometimes small local societies in England had, like the Royal Society, 'corresponding members' and secretaries to maintain links with others — precisely to ensure the international diffusion of ideas. Encyclopaedias, periodicals such as the *Monthly Magazine* and *Gentleman's Magazine* in England, translated simplified versions of ideas and experiments from the professional literature of the Academies, like the *Philosophical Transactions*, in a transmission belt to a wider educated if unprofessional public. The *Bibliothèque Britannique* (1796-1815) published in Geneva to translate, edit and summarize English publications, ran to 28,000 pages in sixty volumes for the arts and sciences (particularly medicine and 'useful' science) and eight volumes for agriculture. The republic of science was truly international at this time; possibly more so even than today, if only because of the much lesser degree of specialization in scientific subjects, institutions, and literature in the eighteenth century, with the much smaller number of persons engaged. The paradox concerning obstacles to the rapid transfer of new technology is therefore heightened, if formal scientific knowledge is considered the crucial carrier of the innovations, as a necessary and sufficient condition.

Equally, at a more empirical level, the operative means of diffusing formal knowledge of the new technology were becoming extant in 'blue-prints' (in the form of detailed engravings) and models of machines, with detailed printed specifications and plans in patents. By the beginning of the nineteenth century leading British engineers commonly registered patents in France as well as England (to prevent pirating of the specifications available for inspection in London, in the absence of any international code of protection), thus describing their projects exactly and in detail for overseas consumption. British patents were available for an international audience, if interested. Of course it was more difficult to provide formal knowledge about new processes than new devices. These patents became more important as sources of exact formal knowledge about technology during the second half of the eighteenth century. In the mid-century many patent specifications were equivocal, relating to quite unpractical devices or drawn in terms which were difficult, if not impossible, to understand. The motivations for taking out such unoperational patents lay in the wish to stake out claims over an indeterminate field which might frighten rivals away, or even to snare unfortunate competitors into the coils of legal actions based upon the uncertain formulations. But, as patent law changed and 'case-law' in patents developed, the 'professionalization' of patent registrations in the hands of specialized attorneys meant that descriptions had become much more specific by the end of the century, and needed to be if they were to stand a chance of being upheld in the courts.[18] A patent system invites more detailed discussion about its effects on the diffusion of techniques; but the relevant point here is to note that the existence of patent registrations added one more mechanism to the means of diffusing formal knowledge about new techniques.

Very extensive visiting by foreigners (scientifically literate and technologically aware visitors) took place to British workshops, mines and industrial plants, even if they were not allowed to see certain secret processes in places such as the Carron iron foundry.[19] Many such visits were officially sponsored. Technical encyclopaedias and dictionaries giving details, engravings and descriptions of machines had an international sale. Much purchasing of individual machines went on, again often officially conducted. Formal knowledge of technology was thus transferable, as formal knowledge of science, but the operational problems of diffusing the effective operation of innovations did not, it seems, lie principally at this level — that is, within the range of formally acquirable knowledge and ideas.

It is remarkable how quickly formal knowledge of 'dramatic' instances of new technology, in particular steam-engines, was diffused, and how quickly individual examples of 'best-practice' technology in 'show piece' innovations were exported. The blockage lay in the effective spread of technical change and more widely diffused average technology rather than single instances of best-practice technology in 'dramatic' well-publicized machines. To take Newcomen engines as an example: the first commercially operating Newcomen engine was erected at Dudley Castle, in Worcester, in 1712. There were reports of a Newcomen engine at Konigsberg in Hungary in 1721-2; at Passy, on the outskirts of Paris in 1726. The first were installed to pump out mines, the Passy engine for supplying Paris with water. By 1729 individual engines were in use in Belgium, France, Hungary, Austria and Sweden. In 1732, two engines were reputedly made in Hungary by Fischer Van Erlach (superintendent of the Royal Mines). An accurate engraving of a Newcomen engine dates from 1717; there were accurate designs published in a quite obscure German journal in 1727, and also in France in 1735. The first known international licensing agreement, with English down the right-hand side of the page and a German translation down the left-hand side, giving a local power of attorney in Hungary by Isaac Potter, the English erector of the engine, dates from 1730.[20] All these engines were erected and adjusted by English mechanics sent out from the workshops where they were made; and they had a very brief working life, most of them working only spasmodically during that formal existence.

Within the fields of large-scale iron working, machine construction, steam-engine manufacture, later machine tools and associated skills the story for the rest of the century was much the same: almost all such initial transfers involved English fitters and mechanics, if not English entrepreneurs. The sources already cited contain a very long list of instances which space does not allow to be elaborated here.[21] The implications of this veritably commonplace and universally acknowledged fact — that transfers of new technology initially always involved the movement of the artisans, in whom these skills were embodied, and capable entrepreneurs (also having such skills in addition to business capabilities) — have not fully been drawn in general discussions about the sources of technical change in the Industrial Revolution. The rest of this chapter seeks to investigate certain aspects of the matter. From the processes and difficulties involved we can learn much about the advance in techniques during these first phases of industrialization. From the struggles to indigenize this technology elsewhere we can gain insights into the context which favoured the development of these skills and techniques in Britain.[22] It is not to say, of course, that the skills discussed in this paper were the sole requirements for invention and innovation. But invention and successful innovation in new technology had to be translated into action through such skills, which remain a conditioning factor in their success or failure.

III

The critical technical blockage to attempted diffusion is probably not to be explained in terms of effective legal prohibitions at the British end. By the end of the eighteenth century, a battery of statutes had consolidated against the export of certain pieces of technology (particularly textile machinery) and the emigration of certain skilled artisans. Some such prohibitions had a paradoxical effect, as so often happens. For example, when the export of rolled copper was prohibited in 1779, to deny England's continental enemies the only main source of sheathing for naval vessels, this at once stimulated the export of rolling equipment, and exposed the problems of technological inter-relatedness in such specialized heavy engineering equipment that were experienced with the Newcomen engines.[23] Prohibitions on the export of capital equipment stimulated greater efforts to entice entrepreneurs and artisans abroad to establish local plants. There are, however, many reasons for doubting the effectiveness of these prohibitions.[24] In the parliamentary enquiries considering their abolition in 1824 and 1841-3 much was made, sometimes tendentiously, of their weaknesses. Artisans, in fact, emigrated very frequently, even in wartime, to enemy countries. Prohibited machines could be sent abroad as component parts without much difficulty. Prohibitions did not apply to plans or models, or to general ranges of castings which might be used eventually to make up into machinery. Smuggling was said to be easy because of the lack of expertise amongst customs inspectors. More particularly, some new inventions of the late eighteenth century, unmentioned in the general schedules of mainly textile machines, were not covered by the statutes, amongst the more important of which were the steam-engine itself and various machine tools, such as pre-set lathes, etc.

The contract for the sale of Boulton and Watt's famous first engine to France was made on 12 February 1779 at the height of the American War of Independence.[25] Boulton and Watt had been granted a fifteen-year monopoly by the Council of State in France for making and selling their improved engines in the kingdom, and they pronounced in the contract that they were 'desirous of establishing the use of their fire engines in France'. The contract involved, as was usual, not only the sale of the machine, but transfers of 'plans, sections and drawings', supplies of necessary collateral equipment, such as piping, and, in practice, fitters to assemble, adjust and maintain the engine. Significantly the brothers Perier also wanted English files and what we should now call 'special steels' — hardened steel for metal-cutting, *'principalement de celui qui réussit le mieux pour tourner les métaux'* — all these being related aspects of the new technology of large-scale, precision metal-working where the technological gap between the two countries was at its widest. No insuperable difficulty seems to have been experienced in getting the engines to France, either in obtaining the requisite documents for export and import or in making arrangements for the ship. There were bureaucratic delays, tedious technical problems about insurance, even the suggestion that they might need to organize a neutral vessel from Ostend; but in the end transporting the machines to France during the war was much speedier than getting the remittance from Paris in peacetime, five years later, with the Perier firm dependent upon official subsidies.

The whole tenor of Boulton and Watt's relations with overseas operations emphasizes the equivocal character of the legal restrictions officially governing the exports of new technology.[26] In some ways the firm sought to use the existing laws to enforce restraint in their own interests; they tried to bring what action they could against foreign entrepreneurs whom they thought might be taking pirated cylinders or other parts from John Wilkinson and others; they energetically pursued their erstwhile fitters who went abroad to a lucrative official monopoly on their patented inventions (or even just as commercial rivals). They were hypersensitive to reports of foreigners visiting Birmingham to inspect industrial establishments or to seduce artisans into emigrating. They sought to prevent such skills being exported, but only where this was against their own direct business interests, conceived in the interests of their firm, rather than industry as a whole or the national interest. More generally, as the manufacturers of capital goods, they eagerly sought export orders for themselves and were willing to adopt all necessary means to establish such an export of the new technology — entertaining potential customers at their works, taking monopolies overseas, giving long credits, lowering their terms for initial orders in the interests of the long-term advantages which the demonstration of the new devices in foreign countries might yield, sending over fitters to assemble and look after the machines and train their operators. They stood ready to supply the whole package of supporting skills and technology as required. Where Boulton and Watt led, William Wilkinson, Aaron Manby, John Cockerill and his son, and a steady trickle of other British engineers followed.

Thus, already by the end of the eighteenth century, a commercial interest had become established in the British economy developing an impetus of its own for the diffusing overseas of the crucial new technology — a 'push effect' supplementing the many officially sponsored 'pull effects' for importing such desirable new skills in other lands. When the engineering industry and the machine-makers, the capital goods suppliers, emerge as independent firms, identifying a specific commercial interest in selling capital goods to other manufacturers, and claim export markets for themselves a new impetus is added to the process of diffusing technology; and a force begins to operate against the older tradition of official restraints against letting foreigners acquire such secrets on the grounds that products made by them would undercut exports of manufactured final products.

IV

Where were the critical *technical* blockages holding back the spread of the new innovations, when so much effort was focused upon their diffusion? It seems to have been at the level of what can be called 'artisan technology' where 'learning by doing' was all important; not in such traditional skills as handicraft textiles, carpentry, mill-wright and blacksmith skills, which were wide-spread in Europe, but in a narrow range of more specialized expertise which ruled the passage into the new world of iron machinery, mineral fuel technology and power technology. It lay in engineering rather than in science. In particular, precision metal-working on the scale necessary for large machines and the metal fabricating required for this was crucial; and this involved very hard steels, for files, etc., eventually machine tools, cutting edges for shaping metals, the means of establishing plane surfaces, exact joints for pipes, valves, cylinders, pistons and bearings at the precision end of the scale, and cheap mass-produced iron for constructional uses, castings, etc. at the 'bulk' end of the scale. Skills for exact fashioning of small metal objects were traditional and widepread in Germany, France and elsewhere. Exact working of large objects in iron proved a main blockage — cylinders, crankshafts, and piping — for large-scale power technology and iron machinery. The problems of scale changed the *nature* of the operations and not just their *degree* of difficulty, quickly invoking special tools for boring, planing, turning and cutting; special materials in hard steels, with special skills, in an inter-related group. A later example showed this inter-relatedness at the frontier of technology when James Nasmyth developed the steam-hammer as a pre-condition for forging the crankshaft of the paddle-drive for the *Great Britain*, a steamship of unprecedented size.[27] These formed a crucial, if narrow, zone on the frontiers of advance of the new technology, as clearly a pre-condition for progress in the late eighteenth century as new metals or carbon fibres are for aeronautics in our own day; or solid-state physics for electronics. The blockage may be on a narrow front, but failure to overcome it can hold up innovations and development in a widening arc of activity behind it. Hewing coal was done by pick and shovel, in traditional medieval technology, but the extension of output, as mines got deeper in the main English coalfield, depended increasingly on steam pumps. This was not just a matter of factor prices — that coal was cheaper in England than elsewhere in eighteenth-century Europe — but a matter of developing skills integral with resources. The period of strategic advance, as Professor J.R. Harris and others have argued, may well have been 1660-1720, when all metals except iron swung onto mineral fuel and such industries as glass and pottery were set within the new matrix of a coal-fuel technology.

Scientific or formal knowledge at a certain abstract level, was not, it seems, the crucial mode of knowledge for these skills and their transference. Artisan technology and skills, even simple traditional skills, were not very amenable to literary descriptions or to instruction books (as anyone can discover by trying to build a stone wall or make a watertight barrel). 'Knack', 'know-how' — all that is summed up in the modern phrase 'learning by doing' — lie behind this. Professor Harris stresses this point with 'coal-fuel technology'.[28] Very subtle adjustments have to be made according to individual variations in the quality of materials, which governs all processes and the making of all objects. Different grades of raw materials and fuels demanded slightly different management or mixtures of fluxes in furnaces.[29] Even methods of stoking had to be different, as well as the design of the furnaces and chimney. Coal and iron are very far from being homogenous commodities. Before precision machine tools everything was 'one-off', save in crude castings and for some very specialized manufacturing processes such as watch components, where mini-machine tools such as pre-set lathes, screw-cutting lathes, fusee lathes, were already giving greater precision by the mid-eighteenth century. Thus all rested upon the individual skills of the artisan, given the better materials and, therefore, tools available. It is difficult to realize how scarce these specialized skills were in the late eighteenth century; how few the centres where precision metal-work in iron on a large scale could be conducted and could be learned; how limited the institutional means of acquiring such skills. The equivalent scarcities today would lie in coping with such problems as designing the operating parts of a nuclear power station or a linear accelerator or putting out a large fire at an oil well. This was a world without mechanics institutes or technical schools, without large apprenticeship schools in such businesses as railway workshops or large engineering works producing their own supply of skilled fitters. In the late eighteenth century the centres were few and small: Boulton and Watt above all, Maudslay's workshop in London, Woolwich arsenal and a few others. The only way of getting training, therefore, was to work in these very few specialized workshops for some years if they would take you on.

The profile or pyramid of skills in this eighteenth-century context had very steeply sloping sides, with sharply pointed apex. Below the very few centres of top skills, the next echelons were much inferior. This is often a characteristic of an underdeveloped country — an acute shortage of special skills in its modernized sector — whereas the pyramid of skills in an advanced economy has sides with a very shallow slope and a wide plateau at its top. For every top man, or ten men, there are ten almost as good, for each of them a hundred almost as good. Where skills are scarce, dependence on the single person, or the small group, can be extreme. Forfeit a few at the top and the whole technology embodied in their skills could be at risk. Loss of the skilled artisans was crucial to a firm or a process, as Boulton and Watt knew well when seeking to prevent their own fitters from emigrating. Conversely the only way to transfer new technology was to attract the skilled artisans overseas. Virtually all recorded instances of transfer of new equipment, the invariable mechanism of diffusion, involved the emigration of skilled artisans and fitters. It was not just a question of erecting and adjusting the machine but staying to operate, maintain and repair it. The position in France, Petersburg, Sweden, Prussia, Bohemia, Hungary, Spain, in these new skills exemplifies this sort of dependence — for machine-building, power technology, producing things like calendering machines, roller-printing machines, copper sheathing rollers and sheathing nails for ships.

Where technology was so specifically embodied in the persons of the skilled artisans many of the problems of diffusing skills centred upon the difficulties of their settlement in alien lands. Of necessity they formed very high-cost, privileged groups as a condition of their emigration. Not infrequently they were feckless people, leaving their own countries for dubious motives and succumbing to the delights of drink and other distractions in their new-found prosperity. Social acclimatization proved difficult outside major commercial centres because, as privileged aliens, they attracted local hostility, the enmity of guilds and the like. The process of settling foreign artisans generally proved much more difficult than attracting them in the first instance.[30]

V

Analogies with twentieth-century experience are legion; and much recent literature on the problems of transferring modern techno-logy at this level from advanced economies to developing countries reveals very similar diagnoses.[31] It can be argued, as Nathan Rosenberg has done, that three processes of diffusion of skills are involved. The first can be considered simply as international trade in finished products, which, in the case of consumer goods, does not invoke a very high level of skills. Next is the transfer of capital equipment for making these products, originally the subject of commodity trade. This requires skills of operating the new equip-ment, and also the surrounding administrative and commercial expertise in running the business, as well as the plant, effectively. But such skills directly involved in operating the equipment have to be supplemented with engineering skills of maintenance and repair, making spare parts and the like. This package is much bigger and involves much wider inter-relatedness. Then comes the further package of adaptive and creative skills necessary if the imported technology is to be successfully adapted to local circumstances. Building-in technological creativity, indigenizing inventiveness, carries these adaptive skills to a higher order. This sequence (or attempted sequence) is certainly observable in Europe in many instances during the eighteenth and early nineteenth centuries.

The introduction of the new devices invariably depended upon foreign entrepreneurs and artisans (foremen and steady, skilled men being as important as the entrepreneurs), and the attempts so often failed. New devices and processes were not transplanted for decades; when the single man or the small group left or died, the ventures so often collapsed. They did not progress as technology was growing in the originating country. Frequently there was an inability to maintain machines or repair them and replace them, even if local artisans had been successfully trained to operate them. Advanced capital equipment very often remained in this state of suspended animation, needing transfusions of skills from fitters sent from Soho or other British workshops, whenever it broke down. The important spare parts also had to be sent. Not accidentally, the successful cotton factory at Avila, established as a royal manufactory of Spain in 1788 by two Englishmen, had a degree of vertical integration said to be unique in Europe. The plant had workshops for making the tools to make the machinery, even making its own scissors for shearing from special high-grade steel. The whole 'package' of technology and skills had to be 'internalized' within the enterprise.[32]

These symptoms are failures to 'indigenize' innovations and new technology in circumstances where the minimum critical level of demand was absent and also where there was very little insitutionalizing of these processes and where 'artisan technology' was the crucial medium for carrying technical change. In particular the failure to import successfully a total 'package' of new technology illustrates how extensive was the 'interdependency' and 'interrelatedness' of the new technology.[33] It proved quite impossible to hope to take an attractive bit of the new technology and slot it into a matrix of older technology. The techniques which were envied, and exported, were only the visible tip of a submerged mass of relationships. So often it proved impossible to transfer the desired devices successfully without carrying over a portmanteau of new techniques, materials, practices and skills upon which they depended — much more obscure, much less advertised, not localized necessarily in the same place or within the same groups as those who produced the final products.

Interdependence was far more widely structured than was usually apparent, as the lack of success in so many of these 'transplants' quickly showed. The inter-relatedness tracked back from the final product, the machine and the skills for operating it, to the nature of its manufacture, maintenance and repair, with the skills, materials and special tools for those auxiliary and prior functions. Particular demands might be made upon its raw materials and their preparation, or the local fuels; all dependent upon different strata of skills and inputs in a context where there were very little exact controls possible beyond those learned in an empirical way. And so many of these came back to mineral fuel technology, large-scale metal technology, and power technology — the new crucial matrix of materials, devices, processes and skills, which stood behind a seemingly discrete, even simple, artifact such as an exactly shaped large cylinder or valve or forged crankshaft, or a large sheet of copper; a casting with the necessary exactness of tolerance or a chemical with a required standard of purity. More generally, such inter-relatedness reveals that the advance of technology was not just a Schumpeterian-style process, with major strides forward giving identifiable discontinuities in innovation, and entrepreneurs wrestling with the problems of making the new machines profitable by overcoming intractable workmen, organizing finance and discovering markets. At the back of this sequence lay a much less publicized, less dramatic world of a 'continuum' of piecemeal improvements meshed across a wide span of activities: in Nathan Rosenberg's words: 'a continuous stream of innumerable minor adjustments, modifications and adaptations by skilled personnel ... the technical vitality of an economy employing a machine technology is critically affected by its capacity to make these adaptations.'[34] The process of diffusion of technology thus involved, in eighteenth-century as in twentieth-century Europe, transfers between advanced and less developed economies, not just of imitative functions but of innovative functions. Adaptive, creative skills were required.

These comments raise the question of deliberate secrecy as a further constraint against the diffusion of new technology.

Contemporary literature has much to say about secrecy and what we would now term 'industrial espionage'. Industrialists certainly were hypersensitive about allowing visitors to see secret processes. Much of the delay in diffusing new techniques, such as the coke-smelting or iron, has been explained by such secrecy, and this tradition is counter-balanced by a 'heroic' view of the acquisition of secret processes from foreigners or rivals by patriotic artisans disguised as innocent visitors watching the process or smuggling out the device. The importance of much of this has to be discounted: the successful diffusion of technology was a more complex process than the individual transfers of secrets implied by these folk traditions.[35] A blend of less visible, more anonymous, undramatic reasons, which cannot be articulated so succinctly, becomes subsumed in a 'secrecy' explanation which is intellectually satisfying at a certain level of discourse, and may also have elements of the truth in it. Unprofitability is doubtless one of the most common explanations for the failure to diffuse an innovation: but there are other aspects of the secrecy issue which have relevance. The consequence of discounting the importance of formal knowledge as the main 'carrier' of innovations is to discount the 'secrecy' which was associated with formal knowledge as a constraint against diffusion: stopping visitors from seeing 'secret' devices and keeping descriptions and plans confidential. On the other hand preventing one's trained artisans, in whom these skills and 'learning by doing' had become established, from moving to another employer or setting up in business elsewhere for themselves could be critically important. Attempts to prevent this, by long-term contracts, could not be legally enforced within Britain when a man was out of his apprenticeship; and the law against the emigration of skilled artisans was scarcely effective, as we have seen. However, the law was sound in intention, if skilled artisans were the key 'carriers' of the technology which their skills embodied; and it was no accident that prohibition of emigration was associated with the prohibition of the export of machinery, and that the questions of repeal were considered jointly in 1824 and 1841-3. Slowly accumulated empirical skills were not amenable to being identified, learned and carried away in a short visit, no matter how aware or experienced the visitor. The need to adapt materials, the design of plant, and the know-how of its operation, to the tricks of local circumstances also meant that creative and adaptive skills were required, not just those of observation and imitation. Even the detailed formal knowledge laid out in a patent specification would not be amenable to this sort of cumulative expertise.

Secrecy also had an important economic aspect, apart from the technical, which is less discussed. The first mode of secrecy is that of the actual process or device (or some critical part of it) remaining private knowledge. Its economic counterpart is that the costs involved in making a new process or device, in particular the degree of profitability, remain unknown. If costs and profitability are secret (and it may well prove much easier for an entrepreneur to keep them so than the technology itself), there may well be less incentive to diffusion than if both the economic and the technical aspects are known. Knowledge of the technicalities and the costs of new techniques are both relevant when assuming that information is a critical variable or necessary condition in the process of diffusion. Of course, with experiment, costs are eventually discoverable *ex post facto*, provided the necessary technical information exists to experiment with the innovation: the point is simply that *ex ante*, in the absence of such information, there may be less incentive to experiment.

The intricate links between such rising skills and the emergence of the capital goods industries, as specialized engineering firms emerged for the first time in the Industrial Revolution, are only now being given the general importance they deserve. For too long, in fact, the history of technology has been separated from the more general analysis of economic development in the eighteenth and nineteenth centuries; pursued as the antiquarian study of actual techniques in their own right rather than viewed in relation to the dynamics of economic change as a whole.

Notes

1 See chapter 3; also P. Mathias (1971) 'Technological change on the grand scale', *History of Science*, X.
2 J.T. Fuhrmann (1972) *The Origins of Capitalism in Russia*, Chicago; W.L. Blackwell (1968) *The Beginnings of Russian Industrialization, 1800-1860*, Princeton, N.J.; P.I. Lyaschenko (1949) *History of the National Economy of Russia*, New York, pp.327-9; J.P. McKay (1970) *Pioneers for Profit*, Chicago.
3 J. Vicens Vives (1968) *An Economic History of Spain*, Princeton, N.J., pp.525-30, 538; J.C. la Force (1964) 'Royal textile factories in Spain,

pp. 525-30, 538; J.C. la Force (1964) 'Royal textile factories in Spain, 1700-1800', *Journal of Economic History*, XXIV; (1964) 'Technological diffusion in the eighteenth century: the Spanish textile industry', *Technology and Culture*, V, pp.322-43; (1965) *The Development of the Spanish Textile Industry*, 1750-1800, Berkeley, Calif.

4 See, amongst many other sources, W. Cunningham (1897) *Alien Immigrants to England*, London, chapter 6; T.C. Barker (1960) *Pilkington Brothers and the Glass Industry*, London, esp. chapters 2 and 5; D.C. Coleman (1958) *The British Paper Industry,* Oxford, chapters 2, 3, and 7; P. Thornton and N. Rothstein (1958) 'The importance of the Huguenots in the London silk industry', *Procs. of the Huguenot Society*, XX; W.C. Scoville (1960) *The Persecution of Huguenots and French Economic Development 1680-1720*, Berkeley, Calif., esp. chapter 10; (1952) 'The Huguenots and the diffusion of technology', *Journal of Political Economy*, LX; (1951) 'Minority migrations and the diffusion of technology', *Journal of Economic History*, XI; S.T. McCloy (1952) *French Inventions in the Eighteenth Century*, Lexington, Ky; A.E. Musson and E. Robinson (1969) *Science and Technology in the Industrial Revolution*, Manchester.

5 F.B. Artz (1966) *The Development of Technical Education in France, 1500-1850*, Cambridge, Mass.; R.E. Cameron (1961) *France and the Economic Development of Europe, 1800-1914*, Princeton, N.J., chapters 3 and 12; D. Landes (1969) *The Unbound Prometheus*, Cambridge.

6 There is a large bibliography on this general theme. See surveys in Landes, op. cit.; W.O. Henderson (1972) *Britain and Industrial Europe, 1750-1870*, 3rd edn., Leicester; C. Ballot (1923) *L'Introduction du machinisme dans l'industrie française*, Paris; L'Acquisition des techniques par les pays non-initiateurs [*Colloques internationaux du CNRS* No. 538, Pont a Mousson, 1970), particularly contributions by Dr M. Teich and J. Lukasiewicz. The best recent analytical study is to be found in A. Milward and S.B. Saul (1973) *The Economic Development of Continental Europe, 1780-1870*, London, esp. chapter 3 and pp.270-87.

7 W.L. Blackwell (1968) *The Beginnings of Russian Industrialization, 1800-1860*, Princeton, N.J., pp.47, 114.

8 A.P. Wadsworth and J. de L. Mann (1931) *The English Cotton Trade and Industrial Lancashire, 1600-1780*, Manchester, p.413.

9 For a theoretical exposition of some of these themes in a modern context see W.E.G. Salter (1969) *Productivity and Technical Change*, 2nd edn., Cambridge.

10 C.K. Hyde (1973) 'The adoption of coke smelting by the British iron industry, 1709-1790', *Explorations in Economic History*, X.

11 For the best survey of recent theory and applications see N. Rosenberg, (ed.) (1971) *The Economics of Technical Change*, Harmondsworth. Major individual studies are: E. Mansfield (1968) *The Economics of*

Technical Change, New York; Salter, op. cit.; J. Schmookler (1966) *Invention and Economic Growth*, Cambridge, Mass.; E.M. Rogers (1962) *The Diffusion of Innovations*, New York; R.R. Nelson (ed.) (1962) *The Rate and Direction of Inventive Activity*, Princeton, N.J.

12   S.B. Saul (1972) 'The nature and diffusion of technology', in A.J. Youngson (ed.) *Economic Development in the Long Run*, London, chapter 3.

13   See below pp.36-40.

14   As Arthur Young commented wryly on the lack of progress in completing the Canal du Charolais: '…it is a truly useful undertaking and therefore left undone; had it been for boring cannon, or coppering men of war, it would have been finished long ago.' Quoted in C. Maxwell (ed.) (1950) *Travels in France during the Years 1787, 1788 and 1789 by Arthur Young*, Cambridge, p.199.

15   See, for example: S.T. McCloy (1946) *Government Assistance in Eighteenth Century France*, Durham, N.C.; W.O. Henderson (1958) *The State and the Industrial Revolution in Prussia, 1740-1870*, Liverpool; W. Fischer (1963) 'Government activity and industrialization in Germany (1815-70)' in W.W. Rostow (ed.) *The Economics of Take-off and Sustained Growth*, London; W. Fischer (1962) *Der Staat und die Anfänge der Industrialisierung in Baden, 1800-1850*, I, Berlin.

16   N. Senior (1836) *An Outline of the Science of Political Economy*, London, pp.193-4. I owe this reference to Dr M. Berg.

17   A.R. Hall and M.B. Hall (eds) (1965-73) *The Correspondence of Henry Oldenburg*, Madison, Wisc.

18   A critical investigation into the economic and financial implications of the patent system in the eighteenth century is still awaited. See K. Boehm (1967) *The British Patent System*, I, Cambridge, chapter 2; E. Roll (1930) *An Early Experiment in Industrial Organisation*, London, app. vi; E. Robinson (1972) 'James Watt and the Law of Patents', *Technology and Culture*, XIII.

19   For example: G. Jars (1781) *Voyages Métallurgiques*, 3 vols, Paris; F. de St Fond (1797) *Voyages en Angleterre…*, Paris; W.O. Henderson (1966) *J.C. Fischer and his Diary of Industrial England, 1814-51*, London; J. Chevalier (1947-9) 'La Mission de Gabriel Jars dans les mines et les usines Britanniques en 1764', *Transactions of the Newcomen Society*, XXVI; M.W. Flinn (1957-9) 'The travel diaries of Swedish engineers of the eighteenth century as sources of technological history', *Transactions of the Newcomen Society*, XXXI; W.O. Henderson (1968) *Industrial Britain under the Regency*, London.

20   I am grateful to Dr M. Teich for this information. See M. Teich, 'Diffusion of steam, water and air power to and from Slovakia during the eighteenth century and the problem of the Industrial Revolution' in *L'Acquisition des techniques par les pays non-initiateurs* (see note 6).

21   Casual observations are scattered through many travellers' diaries,

Arthur Young offering a particularly interesting contemporary account of such immigrant enterprise in France in 1787-9. For example: (at Nantes) '...to view the establishment of Mr Wilkinson, for boring cannon.... Until that well-known English manufacturer arrived, the French knew nothing of the art of casting cannon solid, and then boring them.'; (at Louviers) 'View the cotton mill here, which is the most considerable to be found in France.... It is conducted by four Englishmen from some of Mr Arkwright's mills. Near this town also is a great fabric of copper plates, for bottoming the King's ships, the whole an English colony' (*Travels in France*, pp.117, 310; 119). See also A. Klima (1975) 'The beginning of the machine building industry in the Czech lands...', *Journal of European Economic History*, IV; F. Redlich (1944) 'Leaders of German steam engine industry...', *Journal of Economic History*, IV; Henderson *Britain and Industrial Europe*.

22 For a brief discussion see P. Mathias (1969) *The First Industrial Nation*, London, pp.134-44.

23 W.H.B. Court (1938) *The Rise of the Midland Industries*, Oxford, pp.241-3; J.R. Harris (1966) 'Copper and shipping in the eighteenth century', *Economic History Review*, XIX.

24 T.S. Ashton (1951) *Iron and Steel in the Industrial Revolution*, 2nd edn., Manchester, pp.200-5; A.E. Musson (1972) 'The Manchester School and the exportation of machinery', *Business History*, XV.

25 J. Payen (1964) *Capital et machine à vapeur au XVIIIe siècle*, Paris.

26 E. Robinson (1958) 'The international exchange of men and machines 1750-1800', *Business History*, I, reprinted in Musson and Robinson, *Science and Technology in the Industrial Revolution*, chapter 4.

27 S. Smiles (ed.) (1883) *James Nasmyth Engineer: an Autobiography*, London, chapter 13.

28 Professor J.R. Harris is extending his enquiries into this field, the first results being reported in his inaugural lecture, 'Industry and technology in the eighteenth century: Britain and France' (Birmingham, 1971).

29 Some of these intricacies can be inferred from the diary of an informed visitor: A. Raistrick (ed.) (1967) *The Hatchett Diary: a Tour through ...England and Scotland in 1796 visiting their Mines and Manufactories*, Truro, pp.35-6, 50-1, 58-9, 74-6.

30 A typical individual comment is that of Arthur Young, when visiting the Wilkinson glass factory at Montcenis, in France: 'I conversed with an Englishman who works in the glass house, in the crystal branch. He complained of the country, saying there was nothing good in it but wine and brandy; of which things I question not but he makes a sufficient use' (*Travels in France*, pp.199-200). See also la Force, 'Technological diffusion in the eighteenth century' (note 3).

31 D.L. Spencer and A. Woroniak (eds) (1969) *The Transfer of Technology to Developing Countries*, New York; W.H. Gruber and

D.H. Marquis (eds) (1969) *Factors in the Transfer of Technology,* Cambridge, Mass. Doubtless there is some connection between this neglect in contemporary development economics and policy and the fact that economic historians have largely taken developing skills for granted in their explanations of industrialization in Western Europe.

32 La Force, 'Royal textile factories in Spain' (note 3).

33 The importance of inter-relatedness (more widely considered) is stressed in M. Frankel (1955) 'Obsolescence and technical change in a maturing economy', *American Economic Review,* XXXV.

34 S.C. Gilfillan (1970) *The Sociology of Invention,* Cambridge, Mass.; N. Rosenberg (1970) 'Economic development and the transfer of technology: some historical perspectives', *Technology and Culture,* XI; (1973) 'The diffusion of technology', *Explorations in Economic History,* XX; (1969) 'The direction of technological change: inducement mechanisms and focussing devices', *Economic Development and Cultural Change,* XX; (1974) 'Science, technology and economic growth', *Economic Journal,* LXXXIV. This chapter has been much influenced by Professor Rosenberg's work.

35 For a typical example in silk and steel see: W.H. Chaloner (1963) *People and Industries,* London, pp.12-13; S. Smiles (1884) *Men of Invention and Industry,* London, pp.112-13; (1886) *Industrial Biography,* London, pp.107-9.

3

WHO UNBOUND PROMETHEUS? SCIENCE AND TECHNICAL CHANGE, 1600-1800

I

An economic historian is interested in science not for its own sake (which for an historian of science is doubtless the only academically respectable way of looking at it) but for his own utilitarian purposes. He asks the questions: how was science related to technology at this time? how far did scientific change influence the process of technological change? to what extent was the Industrial Revolution associated with scientific advance? Taking the very long view from medieval times to the present day is to see a dramatic change in these relationships. Broadly we may postulate the earlier position as a context where empirical discoveries and the development of industrial processes in such industries as metals, textiles, brewing, dyeing took place and advanced without being directly consequential upon knowledge of fundamental scientific relationships in the materials concerned. The chemistry of what happened inside a blast furnace was not known until the mid-decades of the nineteenth century. The secrets of fermentation were first revealed by Pasteur. There might be close links between science and technology in other ways, but this was none the less a world very different from our own where industrial advance becomes more directly consequential upon the advancing frontier of scientific and technological knowledge, with a developing institutional relationship between science and industry to consolidate the connection.[1]

For the pivotal period of the seventeenth and eighteenth centuries, however, which saw dramatic advances in both scientific knowledge and industrial techniques, varying answers have been offered to these questions by economic historians and scholars generalizing about the relationships from the side of science. Professor A.R. Hall summed up for the earlier period 1660-1760: 'we have not much reason to believe that in the early stages, at any rate, learning or literacy had anything to do with it [technological change]; on the contrary, it seems likely that virtually all the techniques of civilization up to a couple of hundred years ago were the work of men as uneducated as they were anonymous.[2] Sir Eric Ashby concludes for the period 1760-1860: 'There were a few "cultivators of science" (as they were called) engaged in research, but their work was not regarded as having much bearing on education and still less on technology. There was practically no exchange of ideas between the scientists and the designers of industrial processes.'[3] Professor Landes is equally firm in this opinion to as late as 1850.[4] A.P. Usher is in the same tradition.[5]

Equally forthright assertions crowd the other side of the stage. 'The stream of English scientific thought', wrote Professor Ashton, 'was one of the main tributaries of the Industrial Revolution.... The names of engineers, iron-masters, industrial chemists, and instrument makers on the list of Fellows of the Royal Society show how close were the relations between science and practice at this time.'[6] Professor Rostow, considering the whole sweep of economic change in Western Europe, gives the two essential features of post-medieval Europe as 'the discovery and re-discovery of regions beyond Western Europe, and the initially slow but then accelerating development of modern scientific knowledge and attitudes'.[7] When considering the essential propensities for economic growth (relationships that he does not specifically limit in time or place) the first two on his list are: 'the propensity to develop fundamental science and to apply science to economic ends'.[8] For the English case Musson and Robinson have recently sought to demonstrate how extensive the linkages were between innovation and science, between scientists and entrepreneurs.[9] They see this co-operation assisting England to 'retain that scientific lead over the continent upon which she established her industrial supremacy'.[10] The Lunar Society, now documented at great length, has been called: 'a pilot project or advance guard of the Industrial Revolution' on the argument that 'strong currents of scientific research underlie critical parts of this movement'.[11]

Many more such summary assertions could be deployed on either side. It seems likely that, as historians explore more systematically and in more local detail the development of different branches of the chemical industry and other industrial processes involving chemistry (following up the seminal work on the *Chemical Revolution* by A. and A.N. Clow, published in 1952); as they find out more about the various local societies of gentlemen meeting in small towns up and down the country in the eighteenth century on the lines of the Lunar Society of Birmingham, the balance will tip heavily towards the positive equation. This theme is captured in the remark 'science is the mother of invention; finance is its father'.[12]

The question, therefore, invites discussion. The arguments, however, should be prefaced with one or two comments. Without the assumption that a simple, linear, cause-and-effect relationship exists between phenomena like scientific knowledge and innovations in technique, multi-dimensional historical developments such as the Renaissance or the French Revolution or the Fall of the Roman Empire or the Industrial Revolution, cease to be analysable in terms of single-cause, single-variable phenomena. In the last analysis, quantification of contributory causes of them is impossible, given the intractable nature of the evidence and the subtlety of the inter-relationships, direct and indirect, involved. Therefore, no intellectually satisfying proof becomes possible that one answer is demonstrably 'correct' in a scientifically provable way. Quantification does not offer any obvious solution either. One might hope that, taking a defined population of innovations, it would be possible to determine the percentage which depended upon scientific knowledge, or to allocate degrees of such dependence upon some quantified scale. But establishing the criteria of such a scale would be subjective enough, while yet greater discretion would remain in allocating most innovations to the different boxes. Moreover, innovations form a most heterogeneous collection, differing very greatly in relative importance. Bringing qualitative considerations into the argument would imply further discretionary allocation of innovations into a scale of importance so that the degree of dependence of innovations upon scientific knowledge could be construed against some norm of economic significance.

Were the scientifically orientated innovations in the 'population' more, or less, important than their arithmetical proportion suggests?

The question of the *strategic* importance of innovations raises a further issue. For example, despite the percentage of total technical change subject to the linkage with science being small, a strategic blockage on a narrow front at the frontier of technical possibilities might hold up innovation in a wider span behind it. One strategic science-linked innovation could make possible a large number of empirically based innovations which were, to a degree, dependent upon that initial advance, and vice versa. Moreover, it is impossible to demonstrate the potential quantitative importance of this by being able to indicate what would have happened if an absolute blockage at the frontier had occurred without substitute arrangements bypassing the obstruction. Perhaps detailed analysis can be applied in the micro-study of particular innovations (carefully chosen), but it is difficult to see how a quantified assessment can be made for the wide sweep of innovations under discussion here. History is a depressingly inexact science as economists — let alone natural scientists — discover to their frustration.

Conclusions in this field are also much influenced by methodological or definitional problems. Controversies on such general themes characteristically sink under the weight of semantic disagreement and pleas for more systematic research. What do we include in (or exclude from) the concept 'innovation'? Were the activities of these seventeenth- and eighteenth-century people, properly speaking 'scientific'? Was it *real* science identified by some later, designated, objective norm — in the 'Baconian' mechanistic tradition — or was it bogus, mistaken, irrational — and following a magical, alchemical or Hermetical tradition?[13] How much, for example, can one claim for Jethro Tull, eagerly pursuing 'scientific' technique in agriculture on the assumption that air was the greatest of all manures and that the fertility of soil consequently varied in direct correlation with the amount of ploughing and pulverizing that it received, to the exclusion of all else. Bogus science, quasi science, mistaken science, amateur science which was so very prominent in the seventeenth and eighteenth centuries, particularly in the field of chemistry (where the direct linkage between science and industry are probably most diffused) does raise interesting issues. Does one judge these practitioners by their intentions, their motivations or by their results, however mistaken their assumptions, looked at *ex post facto* with hindsight. Also, the arguments about distinctions between 'pure' and 'applied' science relate to these controversies, for the seventeenth and eighteenth centuries no less than the nineteenth and twentieth.[14]

This paper will first explore the positive case and then consider its qualifications.[15] The key question to be answered is not what examples can be found of links between science and industry in the period but rather how important relative to other sources of impetus was scientific knowledge to industrial progress? Can it be judged 'an engine of growth' for innovation, or a pre-condition? In short, how extensive were the linkages, how strategic and how direct?

II

If economic history is written from the evidence of intention, of aspiration and endeavour, rather than the evidence of results (which is often less accessible) then these connections appear very intimate indeed. In the first place, a very large number of persons — scientists, industrialists, publicists, and government servants — said loudly in the seventeenth century and have gone on saying ever since, even more loudly, that the linkage was important and ought to be encouraged. For most of the 'professional' scientists of the Restoration the improvement of techniques in the material world, science in the service of a technological Utopia, was a subordinate quest, a relatively low priority. But, even so, many such as Robert Boyle were active on both sides of the watershed between searching for knowledge and applying knowledge to practice, and certainly acknowledged that *one* of the roles of science was to help where it could. Boyle's *Usefulness of Natural Philosophy* (1664) was a systematic survey of the methods then used in industry and of the ways in which science was improving them and would continue to do so. 'These [mechanical] arts', he wrote, 'ought to be looked upon as really belonging to the history of nature in its full and due extent.'[16] 'There is much real benefit to be learned [from mathematical or philosophical inquiries]', wrote Dr J. Wilkins in 1648, 'particularly for such gentlemen as employ their estates in those chargeable adventures of Drayning, Mines, Cole-pits, etc.... And also for such *common artificers* as are well skilled in the *practise* of the arts.'[17] Boyle was himself active particularly in investigating the techniques of mining, assaying and agriculture. In evidence of intention, if not of result, John Richardson changed the title of his book on *Philosophical Principles of the Art of Brewing*, much taken up by the largest brewers in London, to *Philosophical Principles of the Science of Brewing*.[18] R. Shannon's more empirically titled work *Practical Treatise on Brewing* was primarily a plea that brewers and distillers should profit from contact with 'men of reflection acquainted with first principles who have more methodically considered the subject'. 'Chemistry', he remarked, 'is as much the basis of arts and manufactures, as mathematics is the fundamental principle of mechanics.'[19] They were echoing a traditional sentiment which continued to reverberate until scientific discoveries with major implications for technology in the industry really were made by Pasteur and others in the mid-nineteenth century.

Two eminent Victorians out of many, may be quoted to show the canon during the nineteenth century. Charles Babbage, writing *On the Economy of Machinery and Manufactures* (1835) concluded: 'it is impossible not to perceive that the arts and manufactures of the country are intimately connected with the progress of the severer sciences; and that, as we advance in the career of improvement, every step requires, for its success, that this connexion should be rendered more intimate'.[20] Dr Lyon Playfair, the forward-looking Scot who helped to organize the Great Exhibition of 1851 wrote, with justly famous perception: 'Raw material, formerly our capital advantage over other nations, is gradually being equalized in price, and made available to all by improvements in locomotion, and Industry must in future be supported, not by a competition of local advantages, but by a competition of intellects.'[21] The assertion of the linkage has formed a continuum; and still does.

Apart from such aspirations, look also at what endeavours actually took place. The state actively sought to press scientists into utilitarian endeavour. A long list of instances can be drawn up. Typical examples are ballistics and navigation (improvements in cartography, scientific instruments, astronomy, mathematical tables, accurate time-keeping lay behind this). Much medical experimentation went on sponsored by the Admiralty, facing particular problems of maintaining efficiency in fleets, long on foreign station, from scurvy and other diseases. Standardization in production, in dockyards, of interchangeable parts, exact measurement techniques, were much encouraged. Industrial and scientific skills likely to be useful in war received particular attention. More widely, national rivalries became important in the seventeenth century for stimulating inventions in many industries where there was most technical progress — export industries, sugar refining, distilling, glass blowing, silk, tobacco, book printing, paper making and others.[22]

The Royal Society in England, of 1662, as the French *Académie* of 1666, personified such state patronage (although in England with virtually no public resources) for utilitarian ends, an intention explicitly stated in its first charter. The draft preamble of the statutes of the Royal Society ran: 'The business of the Royal Society is: to improve the knowledge of natural things, and all useful arts, Manufactures, Mechanic practices, Engynes and Inventions by experiment.'[23] Nothing could be more explicit. Its first historian stressed this need to focus the work of scientists upon technology; in the words of Thomas Sprat in 1667 its work was intended 'for use of cities and not for the retirements of schools'. [24] Pepys urged its members to 'principally aim at such experiments or observations as might prove of great and immediate use', and had the record searched for helps to navigation. The King, petitioned by 'projectors' with secret weapons to save an industry or confound the French, referred such proposals to the Society for vetting and report. Members divided themselves into special committees for this purpose. The *Philosophical Transactions* in the seventeeth century exemplify the common concern; experiments and reports intended to have practical applications, to agriculture as well as industry, had as much space or more devoted to them as any other. This, surely, is the breeding ground for innovation. The spark then jumps from the metropolitan scene of the Royal Society in its early days to the many provincial societies linking amateur scientists with gentlemen-manufacturers in the Lunar Society of Birmingham and very many others of lesser renown. Relatively obscure towns like Spalding, Northampton, Peterborough and Maidstone for example, boasted such gatherings. Almost thirty are known to have existed.[25]

William Shipley called the Northampton Philosophical Society specifically a 'Royal Society in Miniature' — 'a Society of

Gentlemen that are much addicted to all manner of natural knowledge'.[26] Most of these local societies had the specific aim of popularizing science and using scientific knowledge for practical ends in the improvement of practical skills in industry and agriculture — as with the national institutions of the Society of Arts (1754) founded by William Shipley and the Royal Institution (1799), founded by Count Rumford, both of whom were passionate advocates of the application of science.

Next look at a growing list of examples of innovations which sprang, or appeared to spring, from this fertile soil of scientific discourse and social nexus between the men of science and industry. Steam power above all; but also the adolescent chemical industry with chlorine-bleaching, sulphuric acid production, soda making, coal distillation.[27] James Watt, Dr John Roebuck, Josiah Wedgwood, Lord Dundonald, George and Charles Macintosh are the most well-known individuals who personify these connections. The *extent* of interest in 'amateur science' coupled with the extent of endeavour in relating science to industry is remarkable, and in this England is certainly unique in Europe. The important research of Musson and Robinson has placed all economic historians in their debt by revealing how extensive these interests were — almost, one might say, a 'sub-culture' of interest in science, faith in the possibilities of applying science, and enthusiastic advocacy.

In fact, mathematics may well have played a wider role in these relationships than science until the end of the eighteenth century. Navigation techniques and improvements at sea (not only sponsored by the navy), land surveying techniques for estates, accountancy for business, assaying, architectural drawing, spectacle making are examples of practical skills that gained and were seen to gain, from mathematical knowledge. The Nonconformist and Quaker groups gave a prominent place to modern studies, particularly mathematics, that had a greater presence in new educational movements than science.[28] The observations of a distinguished user of the new mathematical knowledge for practical purposes underline this truth:

We are sure of finding a Ship's place at Sea to a Degree and a half and generally to less than half a Degree [wrote Captain James Cook]. Such are the improvements Navigation has received by the Astronomers of the Age by the Valuable Table they have communicated to the Public under the direction of the Board of Longitude .... [By] these Tables the Calculations are rendered short beyond conception and easy to the meanest capacity and can never be enough recommended to the Attention of all Sea Officers ... Much credit is also due to the Mathematical Instrument Makers for the improvements and accuracy with which their instruments are made, for without good instruments the Tables would lose part of their use.[29]

The utility of such mathematical expertise, coupled with precision measurement by new instruments, for a trading, industrial, seafaring nation was sufficient for it to become institutionalized in schools on a fairly wide scale in eighteenth-century England. Rather than enlarge the catalogue of instances, however, let us now look at some of the problems — acknowledging that a long list of such individual instances exists. It is the nature of the connections between science and technical change, no less than the extent of the association between them which is in question.

III

The first complication is, perhaps, not a fundamental one within the European scene, although it raises important questions when relating science to innovation within a single country; or perhaps even more fundamentally when one compares scientific knowledge and its relation to technique (the general level of diffused technique rather than individual instances of 'best-practice' technology) in Europe and beyond — say in China. The point is, simply, that we are much concerned with differences between national performances in industrial growth and innovation, in striving to explain the fact that the British economy advanced more extensively than others in this way, and became *relatively* so much more forward in adopting new techniques and developing new industries in 1750-1850 than other economies. This is particularly true of the general level of technique, productivity and output characterizing growth industries (textiles, metal production, metal-using techniques, machine tools, machine-making, particularly power engineering, chemicals, pottery, glass).

Scientific knowledge does not show, at all, the same concentration within Britain, particularly in the case of chemistry where the linkage between scientific knowledge and industrial innovation was probably most intimate. The advance of scientific knowledge was a European phenomenon. There was, in France, much greater state patronage for science through the *Académie des Sciences*, by military sponsorship, and direct industrial sponsorship, as with the research department attached to the Sèvres porcelain factory working on glazes, enamels and paints. Provincial academies also flourished in the main regional cities.[30] In the *Description des Arts et Métiers* of Réamur, 1761, one had a more elaborate schema published than any known in Britain. On balance, more systematic work was carried out in technology by scientists in France than on this side of the Channel. Countries innocent of industrialization (but with pressing military needs) also established equivalent academies, with state patronage for the useful arts — especially arts useful for military success — supported by much private interest. Sweden, Russia, Prussia and Italy are examples.[31] A Royal Irish Academy also flourished. The 'Dublin Society for Improving Husbandry, Manufactures and other Useful Arts' was the first of the 'popularizing' associations, established in 1731.[32] The Welsh Society of Cymmrodorion followed in 1751. One of the earlier of the agricultural improvement societies was that of Brecknockshire, founded in 1753. The institutionalizing of practical science in these societies clearly was evidence of motivation; but it may well have come, in such instances, where the need was greatest, rather than where the links were closest. It should also be said that the English societies flourished with very tiny material resources indeed, being amateur and self-financing. The very small cash premiums or medals they offered as inducements to inventors cannot be seen as 'research and development' costs in the modern sense of capital investment in innovation. The fact that endeavour was stimulated by the chance of winning a medal offered by such a private society or appearing in its transactions, says much for the prestige attached to science and to the quest for 'improvement' in practical matters. But clearly these investments and endeavours could be made on a scale more extensive absolutely than England (in the case of France) and on a scale relatively greater (judged against the resources of the country) without much of a 'spin-off' giving a boost to industrial growth.

The French record of scientific growth and invention in the

eighteenth century was a formidable one.[33] Berthollet first revealed to the world the bleaching possibilities of chlorine, first isolated as a gas in 1774 by a Swedish chemist Scheele, which was followed by energetic efforts to promote its manufacture in France. A similar sequence followed with Leblanc making soda from salt and sulphuric acid.[34] Very sophisticated work was done in the production of dyestuffs in France, with varnishes, enamels and many other techniques and materials. Yet the difference in the rate of industrial growth based on these advances in chemistry between France and Britain in the period 1780-1850 was remarkable. Almost all the theoretical work on structures, stresses and the mechanics of design in civil engineering was French. This did not appear to have much relationship to the speed of development, or even innovations in these fields, as far as economic progress was concerned. The same was true of power engineering and hydro-dynamics.[35] The record of development and implementation was also significantly different from the record of invention.

The wider question, not to be pursued here, is even more interesting. The sophisticated scientific mechanical knowledge in China produced even less impetus to the general levels of industrial technique representative of that vast region, or to industrial growth. It remained more sealed up in a small enclave of scholars, civil servants, and isolated groups under noble and royal patronage than in — say — St Petersburg. By itself, therefore, it becomes difficult to argue that a flow of new scientific knowledge and applied science is a key variable; it may be a pre-condition for advance, but it does not necessarily give the operational impetus.

Secondly, the problem of time-lags between knowledge and action raises awkward problems for the 'positive' one-to-one equation in its simple form. The economic historian is more interested in innovation and the diffusion of innovations than in invention for its own sake. Putting inventions to productive uses involves all the costs and problems of translation from laboratory technique into industrial production, from the largely non-commercial context of the pursuit of knowledge to profitability as a condition of existence. One is not even very interested in isolated examples of new industrial techniques but rather in their diffusion to the point where innovations begin to affect general levels of output, costs, productivity in an industry; when their adoption is on a sufficient scale to affect the performance of the industry significantly. To mention a few of these astonishing time-lags. The screw-cutting lathe, foundation of the precision engineering skills which made an efficient machine-making industry possible, was clearly documented by Leonardo da Vinci in the *Note-Books*, laid out again in the section on watch-making tools in the *Description des Arts et Métiers* in mid-eighteenth-century France and developed, spontaneously, again by Maudslay, to become — from that innovation — the basis of a progeny of machine tools. Sir T. Lombe's silk-throwing machine, which was used for the first time in a factory in England in 1709, had been used and known in Italy since 1607 — with an accurate engraving in a book on the open shelves of the Bodleian Library by 1620.[36] The same is true of gearing and the design of gear wheels, bridge design, pumps, Archimedean screws, the 'pound' lock, mass production needle-grinding machines and a host of others (all to be found in Leonardo's work).[37] In certain respects, steam power is another example. The pound lock — being the basic technology of a dry dock — was known in Dutch shipyards in the fifteenth century, perhaps much earlier, and appeared in England in the sixteenth century. But a still-water canal system of which this is the only important piece of technology was an eighteenth-century phenomenon in Britain.[38] Equally dramatic time-lags exist in the opposite direction — between empirical improvements in technique and the beginning of scientific interest in explaining them.[39]

Bound up with this problem of time-lags between knowledge and invention, invention and adoption, adoption and diffusion are correlated phenomena such as simultaneous inventions (developed spontaneously and independently in different places at about the same time), re-inventions of lost techniques, 'alternative' inventions coming very close together in time for providing different ways of getting the same thing done.[40]

The 'profile' of technical change usually shows an evolutionary curve as well as revolutionary discontinuities. The interstices between the discrete advances made by identifiable individuals are filled by 'continuum' improvements made on the job, by countless improvements without known, or identifiable and published authorship. Collectively the latter may yield a cumulative advance in productivity greater than the identifiable discrete innovations. This has been likened to biological change, improvement and survival by the techniques most efficiently and economically adapted to their function — a kind of technological Darwinism.[41] The burden of all this is, of course, that invention waits upon economic opportunity before it can come to fruition in innovation and the diffusion of new techniques. The determinants of timing are usually set — in the long run — by non-technical criteria. These determinants may be economic criteria of different sorts — the widening of the market giving inducement for larger production and hence new methods, greater facility in the supply of capital, a change in factor prices[42] (for example, labour becoming relatively more expensive or intractable, raising the incentives to cut labour costs). Boom conditions, creating bottlenecks in supply, higher profits, and greater incentives to expand may create the operational incentives. In a dynamic sequence, when an economy is on the move with innovations flowing, a depression may equally induce further innovation by creating pressures to cut costs. The process of innovation itself creates a dis-equilibrium in various ways — that dis-equilibrium, to be resolved, creates the need for further changes, which become self-reinforcing. These may indeed be technical in nature, but they are need-creating in the way they operate. The causal arrows flow from industrial demand towards the absorption of new knowledge. The timing is set from within the industrial rhythm and the economic context, rather than given to it exogenously by new acquisitions of knowledge.[43] There are other determinants — social, political and legal — affecting the condition of risk. 'Entrepreneurship' may also prove to be greater than the sum of these other criteria.

These sorts of motivations tend to be the operational criteria in this period, I believe, determining which bits of scientific knowledge were taken up, developed, applied, and which lay unused; which inventions remained known, but sterile, and which quickly became adopted, perhaps outside the country which gave them birth. Clearly, this is the style of explanation behind the very rapid adoption of 'chemical' bleaching in the cotton industry in Britain more than in France: the enormous expansion in the output of cloth made a more rapid means of bleaching imperative. Great stress has recently been placed by historians of science on the ways in which empirical processes and skilled artisan technology in the mechanical arts stimulated scientific advance in these centuries.[44]

This does not, however, necessarily subvert the core of the 'positive' equation. It can be argued that applied science needs to build-up a capital 'stock' or a 'library' of knowledge, so to speak, which is thereupon available for industrialists to draw upon in innovation — across national frontiers, no doubt, for science now enjoyed, in printing, a very effective means of diffusing knowledge in the seventeenth century and after; and with a timing doubtless profoundly influenced by conditions and incentives within industry. But, without that capital stock produced by the advance of scientific knowledge, runs the argument, a limit would have been placed upon the range of advance.

This begs a question as to how far the impetus deriving from industry was able to produce the conditions — of innovation as well as other things — needed to sustain its own progress. To what extent was the flow of innovations produced from within the empirical world of industry and not given to it from an 'exogenous' world of science, advancing under its own complex of stimuli? That in turn begs the question as to how far industrial demand, with the needs of the 'empirical' world, was itself the stimulus for creating new scientific knowledge in this period, of what 'feedbacks' or 'feedforwards' there were?

Judging the effectiveness of the contributions of science by results, *ex post facto*, rather than by endeavour, is to greatly reduced their importance. Little of the mass of experimentation in agricultural projects of the Royal Society in its early years, for example, seems to have had much direct effect upon improving the efficiency of farming.[45] Most of the more direct links between advancing knowledge of chemistry and the expanding chemical industry came only at the end of the eighteenth century. This disconnects the timing of much of the new knowledge, particularly in chemistry, from the initial phases of industrial growth. The great advances in mechanics in the seventeenth century — then one of the most advanced of the sciences — had given birth to very sophisticated theoretical schema about ballistics, which do not appear to have significantly affected the processes of innovation in making metals or working metals, of gun-founding or of gunnery, again judging by results, until after the Crimean War. The 'science' remained almost purely abstract. Each cannon cast and bored remained slightly different from every other; each shot and each charge of powder were equally 'unique', which kept techniques of gunnery strictly empirical. A precision engineering industry to produce the guns, and a precision chemical industry to produce the propellants, were required before this theoretical knowledge could become operational.[46]

The empirical stimulus creating response within the immediate context of production accounts for a very high proportion of the advance in productivity, even in those industries most exposed to the impact of science, and a great determinant of timing and the rate of diffusion of new techniques. Great areas of advance were relatively untouched by scientific knowledge, judging by result rather than by intention or endeavour, until the nineteenth century: agriculture, canals, machine-making, the mechanization of cloth-making (as distinct from bleaching and dyeing), iron- and steel-making. Taking the occupational census of 1851, a very small percentage indeed of the labour force was engaged in trades where the linkages were — superficially at any rate — high, as in chemicals.

IV

Steam power is important enough to merit separate attention. Here was the greatest gift from science to industry, it has often been claimed, born exactly from the world of the Royal Society, of noblemen's laboratories, from an international competition amongst scientists and their leisured patrons in the seventeenth century. Watt, in his generation, carried on this precise linkage between scientific knowledge and commercial application in the series of formal experiments to analyse the properties of steam and the conductivity of metals which lay behind his own inventions of the separate condenser and steam power proper (as distinct from 'atmospheric' power). This can be called the classical example of science in alliance with practice. But other factors also conditioned the rates of advance of efficiency in steam power and the timing of stages of growth of this innovation. Thomas Newcomen and Savery were not so directly within this educated scientific tradition. And historians of science continue to push back the genealogy of the basic scientific awareness of steam power — knowledge as distinct from laboratory experiments that worked.[47] The jump to the world of Thomas Newcomen, who had no personal contacts with the leading scientists of the day,[48] fashioning an effective commercial device, meant problems of manufacture, of standards of accuracy in metal-working, that alone made effective use possible on a commercial basis. This, it can be argued, more than anything else set the limits of efficiency. And this, as a blacksmith, was Newcomen's world, not that of the Royal Society. Once again, the context within which Watt's inventions had to become operational meant that the accuracy of working metal, of fitting a piston to a cylinder throughout its length, of getting steam-proof valves and joints set the limits to the rise in the degree of efficiency which potentially resulted from the new inventions. These efficiencies came from the empirical world of John Wilkinson and Matthew Boulton, with rising standards of its own, a world increasingly working to rule, but still mainly innocent of formal scientific thought.

And, subsequent to Watt, most of the pioneering of 'high pressure steam', the adaptation of steam to traction, to small-bench engines, to ships and the continuum of improvement to the Watt-style engine itself, belonged, for the most part, to the empirical world of the obscure colliery engineers, the captains of Cornish mines, the brilliant mechanics such as Murdock. Some of them were trained in the best precision workshops of the country, such as Maudslay's, but remained nevertheless innocent of scientific fundamentals and were not seeking to create their improvements in the light of awareness of such fundamentals. Yet the cumulative total effects of 'continuum' innovation, effected on the job, at the work bench, bit-by-bit, were profound. Taking steam power efficiency again as one example, the first Newcomen engine had a duty[49] of *c.* 4.5 m., it has been calculated.[50] This had been raised to 12.5 m. by the time of Smeaton's improvements in 1770. The initial Watt separate condenser engine raised this duty to *c.* 22 m. By 1792 it had been raised by continuing improvement to over 30 m. The best recorded Watt-type engine in 1811, working in Cornwall, had a duty of 22.3 m. In 1842-3, under continuous gradual improvement, the best duty was recorded at 100 m. Average duty rates recorded on Cornish engines quadrupled between 1811 and 1859 as a result of this continuum-type improvement.

V

Although this essay is primarily concerned with sources of innovation in industrial techniques, improvements in agriculture are relevant to the issue, both because agriculture potentially stood to gain from the application of science, comparably to industry (and has gained as dramatically from its connection with science as has industry in the twentieth century), and because contemporaries certainly gave agricultural improvement at least as high a priority as industrial advance. Agricultural improvement also had a more general appeal to the upper and middle classes of English society than any other branch of production, if only because larger and more influential social groups were concerned with the land. Agricultural innovations and scientific experiments in agriculture featured in virtually all the scientific and philosophical societies mentioned above; while other societies were specifically agricultural in their terms of reference. The Georgical Committee of the Royal Society was established in 1665 (as one of eight sectoral groups). Many experiments in husbandry found a place in the *Philosophical Transactions* over the years; and eleven reports are known to have been made about agricultural practices, produced from national enquiries.[51] A 'Society of Improvers in the Knowledge of Agriculture in Scotland' was founded in 1723 (forty years before that in Brecknockshire) and many local agricultural societies followed, particularly in the 1790s.[52]

Scientists concerned themselves with agricultural experiments, advocating the experimental method and lauding the claims of science in farming no less than in industry. Francis Bacon's *Sylva Sylvarum* (1651) included a comparative study of different modes of fertilizing. In 1671, Boyle urged farmers to experiment. 'Chymical experiments ... ' he wrote, 'may probably afford useful directions to the Husbandman towards the melioration of his land, both for Corn, Trees, Grass and consequently Cattell.'[53] John Evelyn's various works contained a curious — if typical — mixture of magic and shrewd common sense, in circumstances where virtually anything organic, and much inorganic, could be thrown onto the land with advantage.[54] Hale's *Vegetable Statics* (1727) continued the line, for the first time challenging the view that plants were composed simply of water. Francis Home, both a doctor and subsequently a professor in Edinburg, also deliberately set out to apply science to agriculture to see 'how far Chymistry could go in settling the Principles of Agriculture'.[55] Lavoisier set up agricultural experiments and ran a model farm.[56]

Thus, taking the evidence of intention and endeavour, agricultural innovation shares with industry a common link with science in the seventeenth and eighteenth centuries. The problems about concluding from these aspirations and associations that applied science was the prime source of such innovation in agriculture as actually occurred are even greater, if anything, than with industry. There, at least, in the specialized sector of the chemical industry and immediately related fields there is solid evidence for the connection in a direct way (though causal links could flow in both directions). Much theorizing was plainly mistaken, based on quite irrational premises. The innovations which characterized progressive farming did not owe much, if anything, to such science; while only the very exceptional farmer or landowner was directly influenced by the scientists. Russell, as a leading present day agricultural scientist is profoundly sceptical of the relevance of chemistry to agricultural advance before the generation of Liebig, Davy's *Elements of Agricultural Chemistry* (1813) and the Rothamsted experiments of Lawes and Gilbert in the 1840s.[57]

But scepticism about the significance of the direct application of formal scientific knowledge to agrarian improvements in these two centuries does not end the story of the relevance of this evidence. To anticipate a tentative conclusion drawn below, one can certainly take this large body of data as strong evidence of *motivation* for agrarian advance. Coupled with false premises about chemical reactions were urgent pleas for experimentation, shrewd observation and recording, the comparative method, seeking alternative ways of doing things which could be measured and tested to see if they were superior to the old. This was a programme for rejecting traditional methods justifiable only because things had always been done in that way (even though such customs, hallowed by the passing of time, often did embody strict rationality, even if unselfconscious and inarticulate on the lips of their practitioners). Scientific procedures and attitudes encouraged by the scientists may have been more influential than the scientific knowledge they dispensed. 'I should not, therefore, proceed a single step', wrote Francis Home, 'without facts and experiments.'[58]

The publicity given to new methods, new crops, rotations and implements by these same groups may also have increased the pace of diffusion of innovations in agriculture. Certainly the flood of writings, at all different levels, is evidence of an intellectual world where progress was written into the assumptions of the age.

VI

The institutional development of science creates certain problems, because the patterns of development in science do not always fit sequences of innovation and development in industry. The foundation of the Royal Society and the Lunar Society are always quoted as evidence of the developing nexus between science and industry. But one must then face the issue of the decline in the utilitarian orientation towards applied science of the Royal Society after 1670, its decline during the first half of the eighteenth century and in parts of the nineteenth century, and its great weaknesses compared with the equivalent academy in France. The Lunar Society also withered into a state of collapse after the 1790s. In some fields also it seems perfectly possible — even in that most applied of sciences, medicine — for the accumulated advances of several generations, well institutionalized, not to result in any major impact upon national demographic trends in death rates or disease rates. Medicine, we are told, did not begin to have such a major impact — that is, upon a statistically significant proportion of the population — until the second half of the nineteenth century, apart, perhaps, from the effects of inoculation and vaccination on smallpox. And this was in a field where there was very great interest, considerable advances in scientific knowledge, a greater flow of money, and probably more scientifically trained persons than in all other branches of science put together.[59]

The problem of numbers is also relevant. Persons professionally trained in medicine, in chemistry, the 'scientific' members of the Royal Society (as distinct from the much larger number of 'gentlemen' innocent of professional commitment) remained the merest handful. The average number of elections to the Royal Society in the early eighteenth century was about ten. The average number elected in each year to the College of Physicians was five or six before 1700, supplemented only marginally with those with degrees from foreign universities. These numbers did rise after 1700 but remained very tiny. This may be taken as an index of the professionalization of science to the extent that this term possessed its modern connotation in the eighteenth century. Beyond this there were, of course, much larger numbers of amateurs and people in business, such as opticians and distillers, who practised empirical science in a commercial way. As Professor Hall has said:

the impact of any question of abstract science upon a human brain was exceptionally infrequent — it could only happen to, say, one individual in a hundred thousand. But, in the history of technology the situation is very different; the proportion of human beings who could have been very well acquainted with handmills and ploughs and textile- and horsegear has always been very large indeed, until the last century or so in the West. Very few of these ever effected the slightest variation in any technique; but the potentiality for effecting a variation was virtually universal. It is only when the use of relatively uncommon machines or techniques is introduced that the potentiality for innovation becomes restricted.[60]

In England no great expansion of institutions in 'professional' science developed in this period outside the Royal Society, either within the universities or outside them, apart from the amateur groups and the popularizers. Science did not become an established part of the educational system, either within the traditional institutional hierarchy or beyond it in special organizations of its own. The Mechanics' Institutes subsequently became the only widespread national movement to get institutionalized in this way in the first half of the nineteenth century, and they trained the aspiring literate artisan, not the research chemist. The greatest contrast existed between the English experience and French and German developments in the *École Polytechnique* and the *Technische Hochschule*. The School of Mines and the Royal College of Chemistry in London were the two institutions that challenged this generalization. They remained very small, isolated geographically, socially and technically from having any significant impact upon mining or industry in Britain as a whole during the first half of the nineteenth century.

VII

In conclusion: it was the same Western European society which saw both great advances in science and in technological change in the great sweep of time and region across the fifteenth to the nineteenth centuries. It would be carrying nihilism to the point of dogma to write this off as a mere accident, even though the case of China suggests that it is perfectly possible for sophisticated scientific and technological knowledge in some fields to produce a very small impetus towards lifting general levels of industrial technique. The simplest assumptions of causation flowing directly and in one direction need to be questioned: the presumption that connections between science and industry were direct, unitary, simple. Negatively it can be argued that the many other conditioning factors in technical change were collectively of much greater importance during the first century of industrialization and that, in the immediate context of manufacture, formal scientific knowledge was much less strategic in determining commercial success than some modern studies have suggested. In longer perspective we may see that the main impetus from formal applied science to innovation came after 1850 on an ever widening front, but in a context which was highly favourable for many other reasons. That this was the real pivot in the connections between science and industry was shown by default, to a large extent, in the case of Britain lagging most in exactly those fields of innovation where the connection was becoming most intimate.

But much depends upon whether we are looking at the immediate context of innovation or at the general nature of the society, and its intellectual parameters, within which industrial advances were burgeoning. 'We have to see', as Sir George Clark concluded, 'not a gradual and general mutual approach of these elements in society, but the joining of contact, first at isolated points, then at more points; finally almost everywhere.'[61] Until the end of the eighteenth century — that is, until long after systematic, cumulative change on a scale quite uncharacteristic of medieval technical change was under way — that inter-penetration was confined to fairly small areas, even if some of them were strategic.

It should also be acknowledged that scientific attitudes were much more widespread and diffused than scientific knowledge. Attitudes of challenging traditional intellectual authority, deciding lines of development by observation, testing, experimentation and adopting — indeed, actively stimulating the development of — scientific devices such as the thermometer and hydrometer, which enabled industrialists to reduce their empirical practices to rule wherever possible, were certainly being strengthened.[62] The quest for more exact measurement and research for the means to fulfil it was certainly characteristic of these linkages, even where the object was not to subvert empirical techniques, of which the chemistry remained unknown, but to standardize best practice within them. Scientific devices and techniques were thus often used to buttress empirical techniques rather than to challenge them. In this sense, the developing Baconian tradition of the experimental sciences, the tradition of research based upon systematic experimentation (as in late eighteenth-century chemistry) had closer links with the process of innovation than did advances in cosmology, mechanics or physics in the seventeenth century. And in such linkages science probably learned as much from technology as technology from science until the nineteenth century: scientists were much concerned with trying to answer questions arising from industrial techniques. 'Technological progress implied the idea of intellectual progress, just as chance discoveries implied the possibility of systematic ones.'[63]

We may conclude that together both science and technology give evidence of a society increasingly curious, increasingly questing, increasingly on the move, on the make, having a go, increasingly seeking to experiment, wanting to improve. This may be the prime significance of the new popularizers of science and technology, the encyclopaedias, the institutions like the Society of Arts, the Royal Institution, the Lunar Society and the various local philosophical and scientific societies, the new educational movements, the intriguing links between radical nonconformist scientific and business groups in the eighteenth century or between Puritans and the founders of the Royal Society in the seventeenth century. So much of the significance, that is to say, impinges at a more diffused level, affecting motivations, values, assumptions, the mode of approach to problem-solving, the intellectual milieu, rather than a direct transference of knowledge. In this sense, of course, the conclusion is banal, that the advances in science and in technical change should both be seen as characteristics of that society, not one being simply consequential upon the other.

Notes

1 For surveys see A.E. Musson (ed.) (1972) *Science, Technology and Economic Growth in the Eighteenth Century*, London; P. Mathias (ed.) (1972) *Science and Society 1600-1900*, Cambridge.
2 A.R. Hall, 'The historical relations of science and technology', (Inaugural lecture, London, 1963); J.D. Bernal (1954) *Science in History*, London, pp.345-6, 352, 354-5, 365-6, 370, argues in a similar vein.

3 Sir E. Ashby (1958) *Technology and the Academics*, London, pp.50-1.
4 D. Landes (1965) in *Cambridge Economic History of Europe*, Vol. VI, pt I, Cambridge, pp.332, 343, 550-1; also (1969) *The Unbound Prometheus*, Cambridge, pp.104, 113-14, 323.
5 A.P. Usher (1954) *A History of Mechanical Invention*, Boston, contains very little reference to the role of science in this period.
6 T.S. Ashton (1948) *The Industrial Revolution*, London, pp.15-16.
7 W.W. Rostow (1960) *The Stages of Economic Growth*, Cambridge, p.31.
8 W.W. Rostow (1952) *The Process of Economic Growth*, New York, p.23.
9 A.E. Musson and E. Robinson (1960) 'Science and industry in the late eighteenth century', *Economic History Review*, XIII, p.222-4; (1969) *Science and Technology in the Industrial Revolution*, Manchester. For a persuasive case history see N. McKendrick, 'The role of science in the Industrial Revolution: a study of Josiah Wedgwood...' in M. Teich and R. Young (eds) (1973) *Changing Perspectives in the History of Science*, London.
10 E. Robinson (1957) 'The Lunar Society and the improvement of scientific instruments II', *Annals of Science*, XIII.
11 R.E. Schofield (1963) *The Lunar Society of Birmingham*, Oxford, pp.410, 437. The argument is summed up on pp.436-40. See also the special issue of the *University of Birmingham Historical Journal*, XI, no. 1 (1967), devoted to the Lunar Society, particularly the articles by E. Robinson, M.J. Wise and R.E. Schofield; E. Robinson (1962-3) 'The Lunar Society: its membership and organization', *Transactions of the Newcomen Society*, XXXV.
12 T.H. Marshall (1925) *James Watt*, London, p.84.
13 P. Rattansi (1925) 'The social interpretation of science in the seventeenth century' in Mathias (ed.) (1972) *Science and Society 1600-1900*, Cambridge, pp.1-32.
14 R.K. Merton (1938) 'Science, technology and society in seventeenth century England'. *Osiris*, IV; A.R. Hall (1963) 'Merton revisited: science and society in the seventeenth century', *History of Science*, III; C.C. Gillespie (1957) 'The natural history of industry', *Isis*, XLVIII.
15 An equivalent, and connected debate, which will not be considered here, is in progress over these relationships, and that of religion in the seventeenth century. See J.F. Kearney (1964) *Origins of the Scientific Revolution*, London; C. Hill (1965) *The Intellectual Origins of the English Revolution*, Oxford; C. Hill, H.F. Kearney and T.K. Rabb in *Past and Present*, XXVIII, 81; XXIX, 88; XXXI, 104, 111; XXXII, 110. The thesis was formulated by R.K. Merton (1938) 'Science, society and technology in seventeenth-century England', *Osiris*, IV. See also S.F. Mason (1953) 'The scientific revolution and the Protestant revolution', *Annals of Science*, IX; D.S. Kemsley (1968) 'Religious influences in the rise of modern science', *Annals of Science*, XXIV. This, in turn,

is an extension of the much older debate about the links between Protestantism and capitalism, from Max Weber.

16 Cf. A.R. Hall (1952) *Ballistics in the Seventeenth Century*, Cambridge, p.3; also G.N. Clark (1937) *Science and Social Welfare in the Age of Newton*, Oxford, p.14.

17 J. Wilkins (1649) *Mathematical Magick ...*, London, p.vi.

18 J. Richardson (1788) *Philosophical Principles of the Art of Brewing*, Hull; (1798) *Philosophical Principles of the Science of Brewing*, Hull.

19 R. Shannon (1804) *Practical Treatise on Brewing*, London, p.48-9.

20 C. Babbage (1835) *On the Economy of Machinery and Manufactures*, London, p.379, para.453.

21 Lyon Playfair (1852) *Lectures on the Results of the Great Exhibition of 1851*, London. Royal Commissions joined the chorus in 1864 with the publication of the Taunton Commission report on technical and scientific education. Mark Pattison made the same plea in *Suggestions on Academical Organization ...*, Edinburgh, 1868.

22 G. Clark (1937) *Science and Social Welfare in the Age of Newton*, Oxford, pp.51ff.

23 See also M. Ornstein (1928) *The Role of Scientific Societies in the Seventeenth Century*, Chicago, pp.108-9. For details of the utilitarian aims of the French *Académie des Sciences*, chapter 5.

24 T. Sprat (1667) *History of the Royal Society*, London. See also J.G. Crowther (1967) *The Social Relations of Science*, London, pp.274-87; C.R. Weld (1848) *A History of the Royal Society ...*, Vol. 1, London, pp.146ff; Vol. IV, section V; M. Purver (1967) *The Royal Society: Concept and Creation*, London.

25 D. McKie 'Scientific societies to the end of the eighteenth century' in A. Ferguson (ed.) (1948) *Natural Philosophy Through the Eighteenth Century*, London; E. Robinson (1953) 'The Derby Philosophical Society', *Annals of Science*, IX; R.E. Schofield (1963) *The Lunar Society*, Oxford; D. Hudson and K.W. Luckhurst (1954) *The Royal Society of Arts*, London.

26 D.G.C. Allan (1968) *William Shipley*, London, p.169.

27 A long bibliography is contained in Musson and Robinson, *Science and Technology in the Industrial Revolution* (note 9).

28 S. Pollard (1965) *The Genesis of Modern Management*, ch. 4; J.D. Bernal (1954) *Science in History*, London, p.346; N. Hans (1951) *New Trends in Education in the Eighteenth Century*, London. A Mathematical Society was established in Spitalfields in 1717, and another at Manchester in 1718 (T. Kelly (1957) *G. Birkbeck — Pioneer of Adult Education*, Liverpool, p.66).

29 *Journals of Capt. James Cook (1768-1779)* ed. A. Grenfell Price, New York, pp.112-13 (for 14 January 1773).

30 F.A. Yates (1947) *The French Academies of the 16th Century*, London; H. Brown (1934) *Scientific Organisations in 17th Century France*, New York.

31 R. Hahn (1963) 'The application of science to society: the societies of arts', *Studies on Voltaire and the Eighteenth Century*, xxiv-xxvii, 829-36. This article lists a dozen such societies in different countries.

32 H.F. Berry (1915) *A History of the Royal Dublin Society*, London, Allan, *William Shipley*, p.61.

33 See, in illustration, S.T. McCloy (1952) *French Inventions of the Eighteenth Century*, Lexington, Ky, and (1946) *Government Assistance in Eighteenth Century France*, Durham, N.C.

34 C.C. Gillespie (1957) 'The discovery of the Leblanc process', *Isis*, XLVIII.

35 D.S.L. Cardwell (1965) 'Power technologies and the advancement of science 1700-1825', *Technology and Culture*, VI; (1966-7) 'Some factors in the early development of the concept of power, work and energy', *Brit. J. History of Science*, III; R. Hahn (1965) *L'hydrodynamique au XVIIIe siècle* Paris; D. Landes (1965) *Cambridge Economic History of Europe* Vol. VI, Cambridge, p.333.

36 Quoted Clark, *Science and Social Welfare in the Age of Newton*.

37 I.B. Hart (1961) *The World of Leonardo da Vinci*, London.

38 Surveying techniques were certainly advanced enough in the late sixteenth century to facilitate canal cutting. The New River project bringing water from Hertfordshire to north London involved very sophisticated routing and exactness in calculating levels.

39 A.R. Hall and T.S. Kuhn in M. Clagett (1959) *Critical Problems in the History of Science*, Madison, Wisc., pp.16-17.

40 R.K. Merton (1961) 'Singletons and multiples in scientific discovery', *Proceedings of the American Philosophical Society*, CV; W.R. Maclaurin (1953) 'The sequence from invention to innovation...', *Quarterly Journal of Economics*, LXVII.

41 S.C. Gilfillan (1935) *The Sociology of Invention*, Chicago; (1945) 'Invention as a factor in economic history', *Journal of Economic History*, Supplement.

42 'Every price change, by creating cost difficultie. in certain fields and opportunities for profit making in others, provides a double stimulus to invention.' (A. Plant in *Economica* (1934), p.38, quoted Clark, *Science and Social Welfare*.)

43 J. Schmookler (1966) *Invention and Economic Growth* Cambridge, Mass; (1962) 'Economic sources of inventive activity', *Journal of Economic History*, XXII; W.F. Osburn and D. Thomas (1922) 'Are inventions inevitable?', *Political Science Quarterly*, XXXVII; R.C. Epstein (1926) 'Industrial inventions: heroic or systematic?' *Quarterly Journal of Economics*, XL; R.K. Merton (1934-5) 'Fluctuations in the rate of industrial invention', *Quarterly Journal of Economics*, XLIX. The very large literature about technical change and innovation now developing is seeking to establish criteria for measuring and evaluating this phenomenon in economic theory. Almost all of it relates to twentieth-century examples and assumptions, particularly that concerned

with research costs and applied science. Conclusions are therefore not *ipso facto* applicable to innovation as a phenomenon in the seventeenth and eighteenth centuries.

44 E.g. P. Rossi (1968) *Francis Bacon*, London, p.9; E.J. Dijksterhuis (1961) *The Mechanisation of the World Picture*, Oxford, pp.243-4; T.S. Kuhn 'Energy Conservation ... ' in Clagett (1963) *Critical Problems in the History of Science*; A.R. Hall (1963) *From Galileo to Newton 1630-1720*, London, pp.329-42; A.R. Hall (1962) *The Scientific Revolution*, London, pp.221, 225, 236; J.D. Bernal (1954) *Science in History*, London, pp.345-6, 371. At its extreme this case becomes the doctrinaire Marxist position that advances in scientific knowledge were determined purely by the bourgeoisie's commercial and industrial needs. See B. Hessen (1932) *Science at the Cross-Roads*, London, and the debate given in condensed form in G. Basalla (1968) (ed.) *The Rise of Modern Science*, Boston.

45 See below, pp.60-2.

46 A.R. Hall (1952) *Ballistics in the Seventeenth Century*, Cambridge. Geology is another example of such paradoxes. See R. Porter (1977) *The Making of Geology*, Cambridge.

47 A.R. Hall has gone so far as to state: 'No scientific revolution was needed to bring the steam engine into existence. What Newcomen did could have been done by Hero of Alexandria seventeen hundred years before, who understood all the essential principles' (*From Galileo to Newton, 1630-1720*, London, 1963, p.333).

48 D.S.L. Cardwell (1963) *Steampower in the Eighteenth Century*, London, p.18.

49 The number of pounds of water raised one foot by the consumption of one bushel of coal.

50 D.B. Barton (1966) *The Cornish Beam Engine*, Truro, pp.28, 32, 58. These figures are suspect, but there is no reason to suppose that the degree of suspicion advanced with time — rather the reverse. Other factors went into these duty counts as well as the intrinsic technical potentiality of the engines.

51 R.L. Lennard (1932) 'Agriculture under Charles II', *Economic History Review*; G.E. Fussell (1969) 'Science and practice in eighteenth-century British agriculture', *Agricultural History*, XLIII.

52 These include the Canterbury Agricultural Society, Odiham Society, London Veterinary College, Bath and West and Southern Counties, Norfolk Agricultural Society.

53 R. Boyle (1671) *Some Considerations Touching the Usefulness of ... Natural Philosophy*, Oxford.

54 J. Evelyn (1644) *Sylva*, London; (1664) *Kalendarium Hortense*, London; (1676) *A Philosophical discourse of earth ...* , London.

55 F. Home (1757) *Principles of Agriculture and Vegetation*, Edinburgh.

56 E.J. Russell (1966) *A History of Agricultural Science in Great Britain, 1620-1954*, London, p.53.

57 E.J. Russell, *A History of Agricultural Science*, pp.25, 37, 46. See also G.E. Fussell (1969) 'Science and practice in eighteenth-century British agriculture', *Agricultural History*, XLIII. But see the comments of D.J. Brandenburg.

58 F. Home (1757) *Principles of Agriculture and Vegetation*, Edinburgh. He urged the Edinburgh Society to raise 'a spirit of experimental farming over the country'.

59 This conclusion may need to be modified in the light of research undertaken by Dr E. Sigsworth of York. See Mathias (ed.) *Science and Society 1600-1900*, pp.97-110.

60 A.R. Hall (1963) *The Historical Relations of Science and Technology*, London.

61 Clark, *Science and Social Welfare*, p.22.

62 The brewing and distilling industries, with the excise authorities anxious to have more precise calculations in gauging for taxation, offer a good example of such a sequence. See P. Mathias (1959) *The Brewing Industry in England, 1700-1830* Cambridge, pp.63-78; E. Robinson (1957) 'The Lunar Society and the improvement of scientific instruments', *Annals of Science*, XIII.

63 A.R. Hall (1962) *The Scientific Revolution*, London, p.369.

SCIENCE AND TECHNOLOGY
DURING THE
INDUSTRIAL REVOLUTION:
SOME GENERAL PROBLEMS

I

The general relationship between science and technology is difficult to subject to satisfying testing techniques — methodologically as well as practically. We cannot assume that just simple or direct links govern the relationships between diffuse and complex phenomena like scientific knowledge and technical innovations. So many variables potentially come into the equation, with complex and subtle inter-relationships, direct and indirect, involved. The sprawl of data is enormous. Many individual instances can be assembled to support directly opposing generalizations. In many ways a quantitative answer to the question would prove the most intellectually satisfying — as for so many unresolved debates in economic history — in order to test the degree of representativeness of individual instances and piecemeal evidence. Following a statistical imperative, could we not take a defined 'population' of innovations (if not the total flow of innovations over a period) and seek to determine the percentage governed by the advance of scientific knowledge or dependent in different degrees upon scientific linkages? But there are grave problems. Apart from the numbers of possible variables, all subject to mutual cross-influences, and some unquantifiable; what do we include in (or exclude from) the concept 'innovation'? This has important consequences. The wider the specification is — including, say, advances in financial or legal techniques — then the lower the 'scientific' percentage is likely to be. And in a golden age of amateurs, cranks, quacks, and crazy theorizing, what do we specify as 'science' or 'scientific'? How can we measure on a quantitative scale 'degrees of commitment' to applied science, apart from some arbitary classification according to the discretionary judgement of the classifier, which is likely to give a misleading sense of measurement to rather spurious quantifying. Adopting such a procedure is to re-admit all the fallible, subjective criteria, disguised by numbers, into the property through the back door when the main purpose of the exercise was to push them out by the front door.

Correlation, of itself, does not explain causation which can go in different directions: the advance of technology, from stimuli other than accepting the gifts of new knowledge offered by the advance of science, itself promoted new scientific enquiry. Discretionary judgements may also have to be made, therefore, about the proportional division of causation between the variables. Each can be cause, effect, or mutual response to other 'prior' influences in differing proportions. Inter-relationships *ex ante*, when asking about the strategic importance of innovations, may be significantly different from the measurement of their contributions *ex post facto* — though this is a challengeable assumption. Many restrictive assumptions lie behind such exercises, and their validity has been strongly criticized. I do not believe that such an approach is very meaningful in the analysis of the contribution of science to technical change in the eighteenth century — quite apart from the practical impossibility of putting the numbers into equations.

It is impossible to treat a 'population' of inventions as a collection of discrete, atomized, instances, each of equal significance in the correlation of variables. Some innovations are more strategic, with greater spread effects, than others. Despite the percentage of total technical change subject to a causal link to science, established in this way, proving to be small, a strategic blockage on a narrow front at the frontier of technical possibilities might be holding up a wide span of innovations in the empirical tradition, and that blockage, if resolved by the application of science, might allow very wide 'spread effects' indeed through the process of empirical change. For example, let us assume that steam power was, in fact, purely the gift of scientific knowledge to industrial innovation — or at least that new scientific knowledge was a necessary condition for the attainment of effective steam power, as that evolved between 1700 and 1800. In the iron, textile and coalmining industry — let us also suppose — the stream of innovations other than steam power was purely in the empirical tradition, not dependent upon the acquisitions of new scientific knowledge. In a statistical analysis of a given population of innovations in this sector, scientifically orientated innovations would emerge as a very small percentage of the whole. Yet, clearly, the continuing stream of empirical innovations was increasingly dependent upon steam power, because increments to coal output and the immediately associated empirical innovations in mining were increasingly dependent upon steam-operated pumps. The same was true in textiles. Considering the stream of innovations as, in some measure, an organic development exposes the intricacies of these interdependencies, which preclude much significance, in my view, from a purely quantitative analysis. Measuring the total change *ex post facto* and allocating it to science or non-science would not necessarily reflect at all the dynamic importance of the scientifically related innovations in relation to the sequence as a whole. And also *vice versa*. Statistical correlation or identification, the historian needs always to remind himself, is not *per se* evidence of a causal relationship, if established, any more than guilt by association is accepted in law. We can hope that a series of intensive micro-studies will allow a 'typology' to be built up; but this sort of historical significance is of a different methodological order to 'scientific proof' about a general relationship, statistically established.

It is also very difficult to isolate a developed innovation as a discrete entity. That which seems so in the textbooks, one or two cases of 'high' technology apart, such as the separate condenser, tends upon close analysis of primary sources, to dissolve into a stream of attempted inventions, innovations and improvements, a jumble of advances in formal knowledge, creative individual contributions, improvements made on-the-job in a 'learning-by-doing' process by nameless artisans and machine-makers which form a 'continuum process'. The leading edge of change is seen to derive from many different sources so that a medley of different influences impact upon the sequence of development — the stages of growth — of any innovation. The analysis then becomes more that of organic growth, a largely anonymous, or at least collective, technological Darwinism in a Gilfillan-style analysis.[1] One conclusion from this multi-dimensional analysis of the process of innovation does have important implications for the role of scientific knowledge, or 'formal' knowledge of any kind. The more that advances in technique, or improvements in the efficiency of machines, can be seen to depend upon continuum-style improvements, on-the-job 'learning-by-doing', skills then the more the role of formal knowledge in the process becomes downgraded. But one has to be careful in these assumptions. There is a tendency, when analysing innovations in one technology — say, innovations in the cotton industry — to put down advances in the productivity of machines employing the same basic technology, such as mule-spinning between 1840 and 1870, to 'learning-by-doing' efficiencies and the continuum-style improvement within that technology. However, they may derive also, if unacknowledged, from and depend upon advances in neighbouring technologies which are more closely dependent upon new knowledge and 'formal' innovations in their own right — not just improvement. The progressive speed of machines, for example, was a function of new-style bearings and new-style lubricants, improved metals tolerant of higher stresses, finer tolerances in the machining of metals which came from new tools. That which may be assumed as a residual from 'learning-by-doing' improvements in one technology may actually prove to be the unacknowledged gift of formal innovation in another. The indirect effects of all these interdependencies, which make the process of innovation in any one sector a product (or a dependency) of very wide inter-relatedness in others, complicate the analysis of causation. As we all know, indirectly everything influenced everything else.

II

Throughout the discussion we have to acknowledge the implications that, for the United Kingdom and most of Western Europe, military technology apart, most innovation took place within a commercial context. Profitability was a condition of an innovation remaining in use, if not a pre-condition of it coming into existence. Thus a 'commercial Darwinism' interacted with a 'technological Darwinism', evidence for which is abundant — from the high proportion of 'stillborn' inventions, the small proportion of patents ever put to use, the very large number of instances where formal knowledge of a device or a process had been known for a long time, sometimes for centuries, but where the commercial (and also often the supporting technological) context did not provide conditions of viability. Leonardo's notebooks are full of such instances, part of an accumulating capital fund of formal knowledge but where cheques cannot be drawn on it. Only where and when changes in the commercial and technical context underwrite such innovations can they be drawn from stock and used. This is not just a matter of changing factor prices of capital, resources and labour, although this was very often the case, but also of falling transaction costs from improved transport, scale economies valorized by improvements in demand and the like. We also need to acknowledge that the relaxation of technological constraints can be as influential as the relaxation of economic constraints in valorizing items from the capital stock. Higher strength/weight ratios in materials; better power/weight ratios in machinery; fuel input/ energy output ratios in prime movers all allow devices and processes long known about in formal terms to become operational. There is a flourishing minor industry of combing old patent files looking for such possibilities.

The debate has also often assumed that the advance in knowledge and science was completely autonomous to the world of innovation and technical change. For example, Sir John Hicks has just said of this early phase of industrialization 'at that stage ideas were growing wild, like wild plants ...' and were only subsequently 'cultivated' by investing large resources in research and development. 'Science,' he wrote, 'at that stage was a luxury; it was pursued as an amusement, or as a cultural activity in which some gifted people were privileged to pass their time. Like other luxuries it was income-elastic... thus it was an expanding activity and the stream of ideas that flowed from it expanded with it.' But this process was essentially autonomous with fortuitous links to the productive world; 'At the stage when ideas "dropped from Heaven",' he continued, 'the appearance of economically productive ideas must have been almost random.'[2]

Of course the eighteenth-century world was very different from that in our own day where the greater part of spending on applied science by governments and business organizations is deployed precisely with a view to its productive effect. But the assumption that the stream of scientific ideas flowed at a pace and in directions quite uninfluenced by the productive world of innovations in the eighteenth century can be challenged just as much as the opposite assumption that the whole stream of innovations flowed at a pace and in directions essentially uninfluenced by the advance of scientific knowledge. There is a lot of evidence about the motivations of science for utilitarian endeavour, particularly in Great Britain; and British science was criticized by academic scientists in German universities in the early nineteenth century for exactly this vulgar concern with its application. Amateur science in the eighteenth century, as the Royal Society in its early years, was enthused by this cult of utility. Many scientists did involve themselves with productive processes; the advance of much scientific knowledge in chemistry and thermodynamics was stimulated by the intellectual problems raised by new technical advances. From the side of the history of science, no less than economic history, it seems inadequate to assume that the world of science and the world of innovations were growing independently, quite uninfluenced by each other, mutually unknown, save for the occasional casual, random collision of two ships in a fog.

Those who have stressed the links between science and innovation during the Industrial Revolution have tended to follow certain paths.[3] They produce a long list of individual instances, which is getting longer year by year, where there was an association between science or scientists and productive processes. The nature of the association, particularly the nature of the causal connection, is usually not very critically investigated or assessed, and what is meant by 'science' has usually not been specified very distinctly. Such a list of instances, though getting more impressive as it lengthens, is without formal statistical significance. Quite a lot of reliance is placed upon evidence of intention and aspiration; upon evidence of scientific experimentation. The assumption behind the enquiry is usually that the interconnections between science and technology were those of transfers of formal scientific knowledge *from* science *to* industry in a one-to-one, direct, linear process — that, in its most extreme form, innovation was the gift of science to the Industrial Revolution. Another strand in the debate argued that, at an earlier stage, the scientific revolution was at the heart of those special differences which set Western Europe apart from the rest of the world in an intellectual sense and which then paid off in practical terms.

The opposing thesis concentrates upon other evidence, but has also accepted similar terms for the debate over the nexus between science and innovation — that the links from science to industry was a one-to-one, direct connection through transfers of formal knowledge. Commentators stress the economic and commercial criteria required for successful innovation and diffusion. They tended to focus interest upon sustained innovation and diffusion of new techniques rather than inventions. By concentrating on the evidence of results rather than of experimentation they showed that much of this scientific endeavour was unsuccessful — the results *ex post facto* proving less sanguine than the expectations *ex ante* (for example, comparing the actual course of improvements in agriculture with contemporary reports of scientific experiments). They saw that the evidence for close association between science, scientists and innovation was principally concentrated in narrow, specialized sectors of productive industry: the chemical industry in rare metals, bleaching, dyestuffs and sulphuric acid; steam power. Connections were complex, shifting over time and not always with a progressive advance towards the dependence of technology upon science: with steam power, for example, the two generations after Watt saw a widening gap between advances in theory and practice. They identified large areas of innovation seemingly innocent of any significant direct links with scientific knowledge. They stressed that 'learning-by-doing', artisan skills, or those of the brilliant amateur were the essential basis of innovations in fibre-spinning and cloth-making or iron production.

Some historians viewing the process of innovation as essentially independent of science, then took the offensive in seeing this empirically based world of technical change, advancing under its own complex of stimuli, giving momentum to the advance of scientific knowledge, as scientists strove to hang on to the coat-tails of the innovating artisans.

It has proved possible to combine both theses. David Landes, for example, in *The Unbound Prometheus*, maintains in his introductory chapter that the scientific and intellectual revolutions of the seventeenth century were one of Europe's principal secret weapons for economic growth.[4] Science, he writes, 'not only upset specific articles of religious faith but implicitly discredited all traditional wisdom and authority ... it made possible a more effective response to or manipulation of the natural and human environment.'

Science produced 'rationality in means and activist, as against quietist, ends' as the intellectual trends in no other civilization did.[5] But when we reach his more detailed investigation of the British lead-in to industrialization science does not feature in the list of local advantages or the means of achieving technical advance. Before 1850, Landes concludes, instances of the connection between science and technology were 'exceptional and often adventitious'; the two activities preserved 'essential independence' from each other during the Industrial Revolution and ' ... such stimulus and inspiration as did cross the gap went from technology towards science rather than the other way ... '. Technology was 'essentially empirical and on the job training'; the innovators were a 'line of tinkerers that had made the Industrial Revolution'. An intellectual bridge can be thrown across the gap between the two positions even if Prof. Landes does not explicitly do so in his text. Main trends in the historiography of science reinforced this dichotomy amongst economic historians. Historians of science (like historians of technology) concentrated principally upon the progressive advance in scientific discoveries, the expanding knowledge of science as a branch of knowledge, through the work of individual scientists and specific scientific subjects. The 'idealist' tradition, exemplified in the work of Koyré, saw the advances of science as a search for truth through the disinterested pursuit of knowledge, autonomous and universal. Marxist historians of science, on the contrary, assumed in general argument that the growth of science was a dependent variable evolving in response to demands from the state or the bourgeoisie or industrial capitalists. In the 'idealist' case there was no direct structural connection with industrialization, even though industry may have picked up some useful tips from science; in the Marxist case the Industrial Revolution produced the advance of science.[6]

More recently, as work in the history of science and technology has expanded so it has diversified and much research effort is now going into the exploration of the relationships between scientific knowledge and its context; being concerned with science not just as an evolving corpus of knowledge and ideas but as an activity — the 'prosopography' of scientific institutions and societies, the resources devoted to science, with the nature and sources of such support; its growing professionalization and changing institutionalization, the status, remuneration and 'job opportunities' for scientists. As the whole institutional basis of science is being explored, with the social and cultural status of science identified, it seems clear that the pace and direction of growth of scientific activity has been much influenced by these roles and the 'image' of science held in different contexts. This tradition of research is rapidly opening up new horizons of joint concern with economic historians.

III

For historians of technology in earlier years, the history of techno-logy was principally an antiquarian pursuit in following out similar sequences in the advance of theoretical knowledge in mechanical devices or the evolution of 'best-practice' technology in individual instances of applied invention, if not just the record of inventions, without innovation. Historians of technology are now looking outward from the record, or catalogue, of the advance in technical knowledge and the history of inventions, to relating their field of enquiry to the evolution of scientific knowledge — with all the complexities that these inter-relationships involve. They are now concerned also to relate inventions and technical advances to the economic and business contexts from which they sprang, and to which they responded. Economic historians, on their part, are also moving beyond the rather sterile antagonism of opposing view-points which characterized views on the relationships between science and industrialization up to very recent years.

A long academic tradition, particularly in England, argued against the importance of the connections between science and industry before the mid-nineteenth century. Generations assured of the superiority of the 'practical man' over the professionally trained expert, which became an important general cultural norm of late Victorian society, looked to 'uneducated empiricism' as the secret of innovation in eighteenth-century industry. The 'inspired artisan', the 'dedicated amateur', were part of an interpretation of innovation which emphasized the 'heroic' efforts of individual inventors and businessmen, the self-educated artisan made good. This was in support of a contemporary tradition hostile to an integrated public educational system, funded on a very large scale by the state, or a state-financed official hierarchy of science and research. Much support came to this tradition through business history. It also cast a long shadow back over the Industrial Revolution — which was seen as innocent of state initiative, state funds, or state science; devoid of significant research costs; independent of public educational systems and formal knowledge. To this interpretation 'idealist' and Marxist traditions in the history of science then gave weight, from their very different points of view. It should be noticed that such a burden of ideology did not characterize France, Germany or other continental countries in the late nineteenth century, and individualist historiographical traditions did not characterize business history there so strongly. An effective national public educational system had long been seen as an important national advantage; science had official stakes in the academies and in state agencies; the state had long taken a much greater role in initiating economic growth; business quickly consolidated its links with higher education through consultancies and research departments while a special tier of university-level *Technische Hochschule*, based on the earlier *École Polytechnique* in France, had quickly institutionalized the application of science to technology from the mid-decades of the nineteenth century. More generally, with the powerful corporate influence of the investment banks, cartels and the state, supported by the economic philosophy of List and Schmoller, individualism and the passive state had never been endowed with the powers of an accepted national myth, or shibboleth, as in Britain.

The very great expansion in the institutionalizing of science, and the rise of a 'sub-culture' of interest in science, in all the countries of Western Europe in the late eighteenth century has a great indirect influence in this sort of way. The growth of societies in most of the important cities of Western Europe, and some quite small towns, which brought together those interested in science and often published transactions was the most spontaneous evidence of this movement.[7] In England it was the science and values of Manchester — a rising provincial, professional and business élite — more than that of the public schools, 'Oxbridge' and London. Interest in science gave a channel for cultural accredition to a rising class of manufacturers in these centres. It was also no accident that Scottish universities, such as Edinburgh, where professors received their remuneration almost completely from students' fees, and were often appointed by shrewd town councils, should have had a much greater commitment to 'practical' science, particularly medicine, than Oxford and Cambridge, where professorships were sinecures.[8] In continental countries, where universities and academies of science were promoted directly from state funds, scientists had utilitarian commitments, although 'pure science' had much higher status there.

A study of the Royal Institution of London, designed to popularize science, shows how this grew out of societies to promote progressive agriculture and provide employment for the poor — under aristocratic, landed patronage.[9] This 'ideology' of science, its association with particular values and objectives, and particular patronage, is very significant. The direct commitment of industrialists to science, or scientists to industry, through published papers or patents, in Manchester societies seems to have been slight. Professor Thackray has argued that the direct technological utility of science was slight. 'To search for such a connection in the period 1780-1840', he writes, 'is to miss the deeper cultural meaning of the spectacular growth of science during the British Industrial Revolution'.[10]

This was not so true of specialist fields of research or the production of certain specialist materials arising from them. Professor W.J. Braun's work on phosphorus, Prussian blue, platinum, cobalt, blacklead crucibles and techniques for preparing iron for tinning show a common world of 'academic' chemists and entrepreneurs, with rapid international responsiveness to need.[11] Markets were very specialized: cobalt and Prussian blue for dyeing; phosphorous for dramatic chemical tricks and then for matches after 1781; platinum for unmeltable crucibles, sulphuric acid containers and jewellery; black-lead crucibles for assaying. Chemists in Germany, France and England were all working on these problems; very complex 'pulls and pushes' existed between empirical skills and scientific knowledge in explaining the progress in these fields. State incentives were important, and also the international responses to initiatives by the Royal Society and the Society of Arts. This is a similar pattern of interconnections known in other specialized fields, such as military technology in arsenals and dockyards (such as cannon casting and copper sheeting), new chemical bleaching methods, dyestuffs and the like. The international efforts in chemical research and manufacture of aniline dyes in the nineteenth century are in the same long tradition.

Steam power provides a special well-documented case of the

complex relationships, changing over time, between scientific theory and practice in the evolution of a major innovation.[12] A successful device was innovated by Thomas Newcomen without significant benefit of formal scientific knowledge. Although Watt's knowledge of the formal properties of steam and expansion was much greater he devised the separate condenser, double-acting engine without formulating a conceptual link between heat and energy. A 'tug of war' then continued between advances in theory and practice. Between 1800-50 little major advance in techniques occurred (except in Cornwall, largely unaware of advancing theory) while theoretical knowledge leapt ahead of practice with the work of Carnot in the 1820s, Joule and then Clausius and Kelvin after 1840. Cornish miners gained extra efficiency from increasing steam pressures, which could not be explained satisfactorily by existing theoretical knowledge. Carnot's work on heat-engine theory was partly inspired by reports of these high-pressure engines. Devices developed to measure pressures and temperatures inside the cylinder then provided data — and questions — for theorists and engineers. Initially Carnot's ideas were ignored by the most influential practical engineers, such as Brunel and Stephenson, but eventually scientific knowledge, with the theory of heat, posed vital questions to engineers by demonstrating the very great extent of the inefficiencies of all actual steam engines. Science and practice were reconciled in the 1860s with engineers moving forward in the awareness that the steam engine was essentially a heat engine and not a pressure engine.

IV

Research is revealing that the patterns of connection between science and industry are much more complex than earlier debates had assumed, with great differences between one field of enterprise and another. Many more instances of association between science and industry have now been demonstrated. This still leaves the question of the representativeness of these cases open to debate. The causal nature of the associations varied between one field of innovation and another, and changed very much over time. The evidence of intention and endeavour in the application of science is much stronger than the evidence of successful results. Many other variables affected the nature and pace of invention: the diffusion of *known* inventions and innovations was principally governed by different criteria than the advance of formal scientific knowledge. Inter-relationships between advances in empirical practice and scientific knowledge were subtle and certainly not confined to one direction. The indirect roles of science in intellectual, social and cultural relationships were important. The different ways and the different degree to which science was institutionalized in a country profoundly affected its impact upon the economy — and depended heavily upon its accepted social and cultural roles.

The demands of the state for deploying scientific technology for military or official purposes did sponsor institutions which became focal points for developing new skills and educational program-mes: The Corps des Ponts et Chaussées, École Militaire, and École des Mines in France, the *Seehandlung* in Prussia, national admiral-ties, dockyards, arsenals and hospitals are examples relevant for new technologies in such fields as exploration and map making; civil engineering; preventive medicine; shop design; precision operations in metal-technology; development of machine tools and the like. Although not representative of the general processes of innovation in the first phases of industrialization, in the longer term these focal-points, at some points on the frontiers of advance of the new technology, had possibly a more strategic influence for processes of innovation in later times.[13]

V

The wider perspectives of research now modify the alternatives, both for explanations of the advance of science and its relations with innovation. It is acknowledged, for example, that aspects of the growth of science other than transfers of formal knowledge, may well have been of great importance, particularly *scientific method* as distinct from formal *scientific knowledge*. Science was not simply the harbinger, or the instrument, of bringing the rationality of the experimental method into technology. Seven-teeth- and eighteenth-century scientists were often infused with wild, imaginative and most uncritical, optimism about the possibi-lities of invention and their potential command over natural forces — as the long-standing interest in perpetual motion machines suggests. Historians of science are currently much concerned with studying these other motivations in the growth of early science, from medieval roots in alchemy, astrology, Hermeticism and other 'magical' traditions.[14] The drive of boundless imagination and the possibilities of change, of wringing the secrets out of nature, is also a contribution of science, but it was given a cutting edge when intellectually disciplined by a scientific method which emphasized rationality in a new mode through the experimental tradition.

Naval medicine affords an example of the application of scientific method, as distinct from intrinsic scientific knowledge.[15] The doctors transforming the standard of preventive medicine in the navy at the end of the eighteenth century had a sustained articulate belief in scientific method, by which they meant, essentially, the experimental tradition.

Paradoxically the advocacy of preventive measures in hygiene did not spring from any exact awareness of the intrinsic nature of the main infectious diseases involved (save scurvy). None of these bacilli or viruses were identified before 1850. The essence of the matter was sustained application of scientific method in noting correlations between infection and environmental conditions, a procedure of systematic observation and experiment, in the Baconian tradition, rather than formal scientific knowledge. It was much more effective in explaining the association between disease and habitat, by which to determine preventive action, than in promising cures once a disease had been caught. The experimental methods, however, presupposed and embodied a motivational structure, a mentality which encouraged activism in the search for new knowledge and new measures. The assumption was that the secrets of nature *would* yield to the efforts to understand them and that enhanced control over nature would follow. When disease was accepted as the consequence of divine providence, then less activism was induced. Doubtless this was more a response to medical ignorance than its cause, as the responses to plague had been five centuries earlier, but such a response reinforced the intellectual structures of which that scientific ignorance was a part.

The more systematic employment of measuring devices during the eighteenth century is an embodiment of the intellectual acceptances of the experimental method — systematic observation with scientific 'controls' and decision-making in the search for improved efficiency in the light of the conclusions from such observations. The intellectual authority of traditional 'rules of thumb' expressing the hallowed 'mysteries' of a technology, were increasingly put to this new test. Thermometers and hydrometers, for example, became routine instruments for monitoring processes in the brewing and distilling industries. Data was recorded for each 'guile' brewed in larger establishments and these observations, which exact technologies of measurement made possible, over the temperature, strength and timing of operations, were the means of producing greater technical and economic efficiency. Wedgwood's 'pyrometer' and devices to measure temperatures and pressures inside steam-engine cylinders and the increasing tendency to reduce empirical processes to rule through systematic observation and measurement over a wide range of productive processes signify a similar trend. Magic was being driven out of technology.

Although much neglected in the debate, a further symptom of this process, because it was so often the means of attaining the same end, is the increasing deployment of mathematics for such purposes during the Industrial Revolution. Indeed, the application of mathematics is probably more significant than the application of science, if only because it can be more widespread. It, too, is the embodiment of scientific *method*; as much as the means of deploying scientific knowledge. Watch- and clock-making, scientific-instrument-making, and optical equipment, navigation, designing gear-wheels and other aspects of mill-wright's work, measuring the efficiency of engines, are amongst the processes where the application of mathematics was influencing practice. The very large number of textbooks of mathematics printed in eighteenth-century England and the establishment of several 'mathematical' schools in principal ports to give boys the mathematics necessary for navigation and book-keeping, are indicators of the rising demand for such expertise.[16]

Notes

1 S.C. Gilfillan (1970) *The Sociology of Invention*, Cambridge, Mass.; J. Schmookler (1966) *Invention and Economic Growth*, Cambridge, Mass. See above, chapter 2 and pp.56-7.
2 Sir John Hicks (1974) 'The future of industrialism', *International Affairs*, April.
3 See authorities cited in chapter 3.
4 D. Landes (1969) *The Unbound Prometheus*, Cambridge, pp.25-32, 61, 108-14, 151, 258-9, 323-4; P. Mathias (1971) 'Technological change on the grand scale', *History of Science*, X, pp.113-17.

5 See also J.U. Nef (1952) 'The genesis of industrialism and of modern science', in N. Downs (1953) (ed.) *Essays in Honour of Conyers Read*, Chicago.

6 J.D. Bernal (1939) *Social Functions of Science*, London; B. Hessen (1932) *Science at the Crossroads*, International Congress of the History of Science and Technology, London; G.N. Clark (1937) *Science and Social Welfare in the Age of Newton*, Oxford; J.U. Nef (1952) op. cit.

7 Chapter 3. R. Hahn (1971) *The Anatomy of a Scientific Institution: The Paris Academy of Science 1666-1803*, Berkeley, Calif.; (1963) 'The application of science to society: the societies of arts', in *Studies on Voltaire* XXIV-XXVII, Geneva; H. Brown (1937) *Scientific Organisations in Seventeenth Century France*, New York; M. Ornstein (1928) *The Role of Scientific Societies in the Seventeenth Century*, Chicago; S. Shapin (1972) 'The pottery philosophical society ...', *Science Studies*, II.

8 J.P. Morrell (1970) 'The University of Edinburgh in the late eighteenth century', *Isis*, LXII.

9 M. Berman (1972) 'The early years of the Royal Institution', *Science Studies*, II.

10 A. Thackray (1975) 'Natural knowledge in its cultural context', *American Historical Review*; (1970) 'Science and technology in the industrial revolution', *History of Science*, IX.

11 See papers by W.J. Braun, H. Pohl and R. Schaumann in K. Glamann and H. van der Wee (eds) (1978) *Proceedings of the Sixth International Economic History Congress*, Theme 4, Copenhagen; H.J. Braun (1971) 'Germanic Association of the Society of Arts in the eighteenth century', *J. of Royal Society of Arts*, LXIX.

12 D.S.L. Cardwell (1963) *Steam Power in the Eighteenth Century*, London; (1971) *From Watt to Clausius...*, London.

13 See F.B. Artz (1966) *The Development of Technical Education in France 1500-1850*, Cambridge, Mass.

14 P.M. Rattansi (1972) in P. Mathias (ed.) *Science and Society 1600-1900*, Cambridge; A.-J. Festugiere (1950) *La Révélations d'Hermes Trismegiste*, Paris; F.A. Yates (1971) *Giordano Bruno and the Hermetic Tradition*, London; H.F. Kearney (1971) *Science and Change 1500-1700*, London. See also the controversy between C. Hill, H. Kearney and T.K. Rabb in *Past and Present*, XXVIII-XXXII.

15 See chapter 14.

16 N. Hans (1951) *New Trends in Education in the Eighteenth Century*, London.

5

CAPITAL, CREDIT AND ENTERPRISE IN THE INDUSTRIAL REVOLUTION

Introduction[1]

Considerable revaluation has recently occurred in assessing the role of capital in the Industrial Revolution in late eighteenth-century Britain. Although much of the present article is concerned with micro-economic relationships, in the firm or the locality and region, these reassessments have also applied to more aggregate judgements about capital in the economy. Expressed very crudely, much of this revision stems from the implications of two contrasting features of the eighteenth-century economy, which the flow of research has been revealing: the extent of savings being produced in the economy, both prior to industrialization and during its initial phases, and the modest capital demands made by the new technology for investment. A long intellectual tradition emphasized that capital was the critical factor of production and that shortage of savings, and hence capital, was a critical constraint upon the growth of an economy. This certainly was the main emphasis of classical economists, led by Adam Smith, who emphasized that expansion was limited by the powers of 'accumulation'; and that capital was created by 'parsimony' — sparing resources from consumption. The possible limits upon growth brought by the failure of effective demand to rise, although not completely absent from the debate, was given very much less prominence, and was denied by definition in the main stream of classical economics.

The Marxist tradition of scholarship then elaborated this emphasis on capital constraints in parallel to its elaboration of the labour theory of value, also taken over from classical economic thought. Particular emphasis was then focused on the primary accumulation of capital in the pre-industrial economy (or non-industrial sectors in the industrializing economy) from which the extra resources demanded for investment could be extracted; and also upon the pressure exerted upon levels of consumption. It was assumed to be inevitable that the greatly increased rate of capital investment involved in industrialization would be largely found at the expense of current consumption — in short that the masses of the nation would be supplying these capital requirements through one transfer mechanism or another, via taxes or inflation, by a fall in the standard of living.

In turn, much stress in the modern literature of development economics, concerned with the problems of generating economic growth in the underdeveloped countries, was laid upon the absolute shortage of savings and the incremental demands made upon rates of investment to sustain even a modest rate of growth. The simple quantification proposed by W.A. Lewis received wide currency: that to increase the rate of growth of an economy from below 1 per cent per annum to above 2 per cent required a more than doubling of the rate of capital investment from 5 per cent of G.N.P. or below, to above 10 per cent.[2] When this was adapted by W.W. Rostow in *The Stages of Economic Growth* and applied specifically to the British economy in the late eighteenth century, it became the dominant interpretation. When Miss Phyllis Deane made initial detailed investigations to quantify increments to capital, however, she discovered that rates of capital investment rose only slowly, taking a century to rise from 5 per cent to 10 per cent of G.N.P. and reached over 10 per cent only with the unprecedented laying down of fixed capital in the railway construction boom of the 1840s.[3] The alternative estimates of Professor Pollard, revising upwards some of these calculations (but for *gross*, rather than net, investment rates), do not significantly alter this conclusion. Professor Feinstein has recently calculated investment rates increasing, as follows, as a percentage of gross domestic product: gross domestic fixed capital formation 7 per cent (1761-70) to 11 per cent (1791-1800) and total domestic investment from 8 to 13 per cent over the same thirty years. Professor Feinstein thinks these rates were not exceeded in the decades after 1800. This research brought into new perspective the extraordinarily percipient comments of Professor M.M. Postan in 1935, when he asserted that no shortage of aggregate savings for productive investment afflicted the British economy in the eighteenth century.[4]

Capital shortages resulting from inadequate internal savings relative to the great demands made for productive investment may indeed be a profound constraint upon industrialization in very poor countries in the twentieth century — where technology is now massive in a wide range of industries; where massive demands on social overhead capital are made for urbanization, transport, public utilities, national health and education programmes; and where governments demand very high rates of growth to catch up with the neglect of centuries. But none of these characteristics was true of the British economy in the eighteenth century; nor of the processes of growth in England during the Industrial Revolution. England was a rich country, with a fertile, commercialized agriculture and extensive internal and foreign commerce. To the extent that such comparisons over great differences in context and time mean anything at all, per capita wealth at the end of the eighteenth century was probably two or three times greater than post-1945 Nigeria, itself one of the richer of the African states.[5] Rates of growth were slow, moving up gradually from 1 per cent per annum to 3 per cent per annum over fifty years. Britain, we can say with some historical assurance in the 1970s, has always been a slow-growing economy, growing more slowly at some times than others. Technology was simple, social overhead capital expanding at a modest rate, and the demands of productive investment, given all these conditions, very modest in relation to the savings already being generated in the economy. This is the background to the modest rates of growth in investment actually charted by Miss Deane.

Productive investment probably absorbed less than a quarter of total investment, which was dominated by domestic building. The evidence for the assertion that there was no aggregate shortage of savings for the requirements of productive investment in eighteenth-century England are manifold. The extraordinary efflorescence of new building, whether in the countryside or the towns, showed the prosperity of those groups in whose pockets much of the nation's savings were accumulating — landowners and prosperous tenant farmers, merchants, professional groups. Unprecedented sums flowed into the permanent National Debt during the eighteenth century and were expended for war purposes — with only modest repercussions in inflation and slower rates of growth. The very rapid rebuilding of London after the great fire in 1666 and speculative manias, such as the South Sea Bubble, showed the plentifulness of money on offer at these times. The steady fall in the rate of interest on government stock from 6 per cent in 1700 to 3.5 per cent in the 1750s, indicating changes in the general structure of interest rates, evidenced the progressive availability of savings in relation to investment opportunities, on the assumption that conditions of risk and institutional arrangements did not counter this in the sector where increased productive investment was required. The usury laws prohibited commercial borrowing at above 5 per cent per annum between 1714 and 1832, which seemed to have been the standard conventional rate for private lending. The scale of military expenditure during the French Revolutionary and Napoleonic wars is particularly significant. It cost £1000 m. in direct costs of the armed forces alone to beat France between 1793 and 1815, with £500 m. added to the permanent National Debt in those years. Yet the total accumulated capital in the entire canal system of the country in 1815, one of the 'lumpiest' pieces of productive investment required for industrialization in this period, spread out over a much longer time-span since the 1750s, reached only c.£20 m. The economy was able to absorb and adjust to the imposition of these vast military costs with only a very modest effect upon rates of growth, and (judged by twentieth-century wartime examples) only modest rates of inflation, most of which was occasioned by rising food prices which were not directly a result of financing the war. Rapidly growing industries like cotton and iron, with technical innovations making high demands on capital for investment in fixed assets and stock, were concentrated in a small enclave in the economy until the closing years of the century.

All these considerations do not mean that there were no problems, difficulties or constraints about capital accumulation for productive enterprise and the supply of credit to business during the Industrial Revolution; just that such problems did not stem from an aggregate shortage of savings in the economy. Many gaps had to be spanned between those groups receiving most of the savings and those requiring most of the credit. There was no national capital market in eighteenth-century England, in the sense of a coherent, nationally organized entity with flows responding quickly throughout the economy to changes in the supply and demand for funds. The nearest that conditions approached to this was in the capital market for government securities, which did call on a national (indeed international) catchment area, with adequate information and accepted security, apart from isolated years of crisis. A national market with correspondingly narrow differentials in interest rates, was also approached in mortgages on the first-class security of freehold land and buildings. The law governing such transactions was clear and effective, for both creditor and debtor. London acted as a clearing house for larger mortgage deals, within what approached a national market, but local mortgage markets flourished. Equally with short-term credit for business based on the bill of exchange. This was an effective legal instrument, giving creditors unambiguous and rapid recourse in law. Much traffic in bills of exchange flowed through London (see p.99), superimposed upon the equation of supply and demand in countless local commercial centres across the country. Sensitive movements in the 'bill rate', over time and between different centres, also suggest the operation of an effective market, even though subject to many interruptions.

With long-term credit requirements the situation was different. Being family-owned, except for a few insurance and mining companies, business did not seek equity capital through a public capital market; but took long-term credit in the form of personal borrowings, raising mortgages, or accepting such creditors as partners, with full legal responsibilities for the debts of the concern. Here, even more than with the supply of short-term credit, many institutional rigidities and imperfections operated in the capital market. These rigidities were such that one cannot speak of them simply in terms of 'transaction costs' adding to the price of obtaining accommodation: they were more rigid in price and less certain in supply, with the usury laws putting a ceiling of 5 per cent upon commercial interest rates after 1714. With local pools of savings being accumulated and local accumulations of demand for credit, many conduits and intermediaries had to be evolved to link demand and supply. In the institutionalization of such conduits between savings and those demanding credit lay the resolution of the main restraints on economic growth occasioned by capital in eighteenth-century England. The gaps were manifold. There was a geographical gap involving inter-regional transfers (particularly between the industrializing regions of Lancashire, the West Riding of Yorkshire, industrializing counties in the Midlands, and the agricultural regions of the east, south and west of England). There was a gap in time which had to be spanned, with seasonal unbalance or where credit demands were out of phase with offers of credit, and where long-term needs conflicted with short-term offers (raising a 'funding' problem). Above all there was a sociological gap between landed, commercial and professional wealth and entrepreneurs in humble stations in life without face-to-face contact. The spending habits and attitudes of those groups receiving surpluses also become crucial for the disposition of available savings in relation to the demand for capital and credit by productive enterprise. All these gaps eventually required mechanisms, intermediaries, progressively specialized financial middle-men and firms to resolve. This gives the institutional development of the financial structure of eighteenth-century England, as new intermediaries specialized out, a new significance. They institutionalized the means by which gaps between savers and borrowers became linked, drawing the threads of the capital market together. The line runs from goldsmiths and scriveners, to local attorneys, London bankers, jobbers and brokers of different styles in the London capital market and the Stock Exchange, country bankers, bill brokers by 1800 and even the incipient provincial 'offices' which canal companies opened to sell shares.

Almost all decisions governing investment in productive enterprise in the eighteenth-century economy were taken by private individuals, families and firms. It was also the 'private sector', the collectivity of the same individual enterprises, which generated most demands for short-term credit. With so much of this enterprise conducted at a local level, with its catchment areas for capital and credit local, or at the most regional rather than national, the consideration of these financial problems at the macro-economic level of national aggregates must lead into their analysis in the micro-economic context. It is also at this level that most research is being done, and from which, in recent years, much re-assessment has come. The present essay seeks to evaluate some of these re-assessments, and to report recent research, more than to provide a general coverage of the rôle of capital in the Industrial Revolution. For the latter, readers are urged to turn to Professor Crouzet's publication.

Asset structure and credit needs[6]

Several lines of research have converged to reveal several new facets about the credit requirements of eighteenth-century British business and their relationship to available credit supplies, as well as to confirm some traditional assumptions. The capital structure of eighteenth-century firms is now being studied in detail from business archives; a steadily growing number of business histories is adding more primary data about the sources of credit; research into banking history is bringing more data from the side of suppliers of credit; regional investigations are showing the intricate local patterns of credit flows and the mobilization of capital.

One of the most important conclusions of the analyses of capital structure of firms is to show how small a proportion of their total assets, even for the most capital-intensive business such as a large iron-works or a London porter brewery, lay in fixed assets.[7] The more that production processes used handicraft methods and took place as 'outwork' in the private dwellings of workmen the less fixed capital was owned by the entrepreneur. Indeed, the merchant employer might well only own a warehouse as the total fixed capital in his business; although stocking frames were often owned and rented to workers, unlike looms. The assets requiring short-term credit were usually at least four or five times greater — sometimes much more than this — than the fixed assets in large-plant industry.

These short-term credit needs mainly covered the purchasing of raw materials, the financing of stocks in course of manufacture and the provision of the customary credit period to customers for goods in course of being sold. The relative slowness of the distribution system in the eighteenth century meant that a very high level of stocks had to be financed relative to turnover. Historians have had a tendency to overemphasize the importance of fixed capital, fascinated (as contemporary commentators were) by the physical presence of dramatic new machines and large buildings. A salutary truth has been reinforced by the study of the account books of firms in re-emphasizing the dominance of 'circulating' capital in the financing of business.

Short-term credit supplies

Various implications arise from this structure of assets. Even if the banks did not usually provide regular long-term credit for industry in England (a generalization which is subject to growing qualification — see p.104) through supplying short-term credit, particularly by discounting bills of exchange, they were supporting by far the largest credit demands of industry. In turn, by supplying short-term credit to merchants selling materials to industry, they were also supporting the credit requirements of industry in a very important indirect way — because of the credit period enjoyed by industrialists with their purchases of raw materials meant that often they did not have to pay cash for these inputs until they had been made up into final products and sent off for sale several months later. Once a contract for sale had been struck, equally, the industrialist could hope to avoid bearing the capital requirements involved in the credit period he had to grant to his customers by discounting the bills of exchange with his banker for cash and maintaining liquidity. The importance of mercantile credit for the industrialist, or 'ledger credit', provided with his purchases of materials is very sharply enhanced.

The smallness of the actual cash requirements of eighteenth-century business is also remarkable, given the web of credit supporting business in its normal day-to-day functioning. Ready cash was needed mainly to pay wages; and many devices were available by which businessmen economized in the use of cash in wage payments — payment could be made only at long intervals; payment might consist in giving claims on others (truck payment, tickets or vouchers to authorize purchasing from shops, etc., the provision of private notes and tokens). The relative unimportance of access to ready cash in normal circumstances (i.e. in the absence of a general liquidity crisis in the monetary system or a particular liquidity crisis facing a firm when rumours were circulating about its soundness or liquidity) above this minimum, explains the ability of the economy to tolerate complete confusion and inefficiency in the supply of regal silver and copper coin from the Mint during the eighteenth century — particularly during the second half of the century when the pace of industrial and commercial growth was increasing. Chapter 10 explores this theme.

Economies in fixed assets

The modesty of the demands made on capital for fixed assets, particularly when a firm was setting up for the first time in industry, was also remarkable. Coupled with the wide availability of modest amounts of capital for long-term lending (see p.100) this had major implications for the strength of competitive forces operating in eighteenth-century industries in Britain, even the most capital-intensive, and for the recruitment of new entrants. They did not need great personal wealth (implying high social status and large family resources) provided that they had a good enough local reputation to command credit and access to a modicum of long-term capital.

Various features of eighteenth-century enterprise explain why the capital demands for fixed assets were so small. Technology was simple and individual productive units could be small until the end of the century — even for the largest indivisible 'lumps' of capital embodied in a piece of technology such as for a blast furnace. A large multi-storey cotton spinning mill of the 'Arkwright' type cost perhaps £5,000 in the 1790s but it was possible to become a principal in the trade in a very much smaller establishment. Between 1780 and 1800 £2,000 was the average insurance valuation for the larger cotton mills. Of course, £2,000 in buildings and plant was still a large sum to collect for a man without savings of his own, or access to savings. However efficient the institutional means of acquiring capital, even in the most sophisticated industrial economies of the twentieth century, the initial requirements pose a problem for the would-be new entrant to an industry. The multi-millionaire can acknowledge that his only real problem lay in making his first million.

Local investigations are demonstrating how extensive were the capital-economizing techniques employed by new entrants to industry. It was very unusual to set up in business for the first time in a large new mill full of machinery. Buildings, particularly existing water mills, could be bought and then adapted for a new function in a very makeshift way; often buildings were rented or leased, with the owners offering to make the necessary alterations from their own capital. Even power and machinery could be leased, or the fixed plant in a water-powered mill (with the necessary embankment works and reservoirs) rented with the building. It was standard practice to sub-lease just a floor of a building with machinery and power. In many rising commercial localities a flourishing local property market existed for renting industrial buildings, which enabled aspiring industrialists to reserve their savings for working capital. Some of these procedures allowing the industrialist to economize on the amount of capital he had locked up in long-term fixed assets are reminiscent of modern techniques of 'gearing' a company, with a high ratio of debt to equity capital, or using 'sale and lease-back' devices to achieve similar objectives.

The large splendid prestige mill tended to be built out of accumulated profits after some years, once a business had become well-established; and mills were usually filled with machinery only gradually. Machinery was often built — and rebuilt — with direct labour to save the high and 'lumpy' capital costs of purchasing machinery. A flourishing market in second-hand machinery also quickly came into existence for capital-starved entrepreneurs.

In all these ways the need for initial capital was minimized and the reliance on short-term credit needs maximized. The current account of the business could thus shoulder by very much the greater part of the financial obligations pressing upon the firm, relieving what we would now see as the capital account from major responsibilities.

The growth of provincial wealth and savings

This asset structure of eighteenth-century business, which implied a particularly structure of credit requirements, has to be related to the sources of capital and credit available, with the developing institutions and intermediaries through which savings were being mobilized and the means of credit created.

Given the extent of aggregate savings and the dominance of short-term credit needs governing the expansion of eighteenth-century commerce and industry, the most important single development lay in the progressive efficiency, and the expansion of conduits and institutions serving the short-term end of the money markets. Much more research is needed here to complement the detailed study of Dr P.G.M. Dickson on public credit. The expansion of financial facilities, more particularly in London, which made sugar bills and tobacco bills as freely negotiable at equivalently fine margins as government securities meant that short-term credit became the most efficient and the most mobile factor of production in the eighteenth century. During the first half of the century London dominated these financial flows, supported by satellite centres at the older provincial bases of foreign trade, such as Bristol. During the second half of the century the London money market maintained its dominance, but increasingly on the basis of the great creation and mobilization of provincial wealth which was an important feature of economic development in eighteenth-century England, rather than just on the expansion of London-based savings. Rising provincial wealth came partly from the diversification of foreign trade, with west coast ports such as Glasgow, Whitehaven, Liverpool and Bristol becoming main centres of long-distance trade; and partly from the great development of agricultural wealth, industry and commerce in provincial England. Banking specialized out primarily to serve foreign trade in Bristol and Glasgow after 1750, in Liverpool after 1770.

The financial revolution which spread country banks over the face of the land after 1770 was no less important for the credit flows available to industry. Savings created from agriculture were mobilized for short-term commercial credit via bankers and merchants, both within localities and regions, and then with inter-regional flows. Long-term capital was also involved with the mobilization of much fast-growing provincial wealth. Generalizations have tended to be drawn too much from London, and from the major financial institutions. The growth of industry was primarily provincial and local, from the very small-scale beginnings with equally local, small-scale financial resources sustaining it. Long-term credits were created through wide networks of personal lending on bond (long antedating the emergence of specialized bankers) with local attorneys and scriveners as the main inter-mediaries. This was as important for the long-term credits required in the transatlantic trades (particularly for sugar and tobacco) as it was for industrial finance. Dr J.R. Ward has documented the strategic importance of provincial urban wealth in the shareholding of canal companies after 1760 (conspicuously absent from the financing of river improvement schemes in earlier generations, which was dominated by London capital). The dominance of London-based investors in the National Debt in the mid-century conceals the importance of the provincial savings then being generated. This also needs documentation.

Short-term credit flows

For short-term credit transfers the provincial 'bill on London' became a dominant financial instrument; the country bankers institutionalizing this flow as they emerged, with the bill brokers becoming specialized intermediaries in this national market after 1800.

The direction taken by these cross-national flows of short-term credit from this time is well known — from the agricultural areas of east, south, and west, flush with cash after the harvest, to the industrial and commercial districts of the Midlands and the north-west with credit requirements greater than locally available supplies. At what point in the eighteenth century do they become significant? The season flows of short-term credit also need documenting by further research. In the months before the harvest the tide of credit swung towards the farmers, running short of cash, needing to buy stock and seed and facing their heaviest wage bills in hay-time and harvest. Because the products of the harvest made up the largest single sector of commercial transactions in the economy during the eighteenth century — one-third of the national income deriving from agriculture in 1800 — the credit flows responding to the harvest and its processing probably dominated the seasonal swings. As farmers received money in the early autumn from their sales of crops (usually for cash), and this credit reached their country bankers during the winter months, so those next in line purchasing the crops for cash would go to their bankers for accommodation — the grain merchants and factors, the malt factors and maltsters, the millers, mealmen and bakers, who were having to lay in stock at this time of year for the bulk of their year's work, and to pass on credit to their own customers over the next months. The brewers bought on two or three months' credit from malt and hops merchants and factors in October, by December they were facing their peak demands for credit, to cover these bills, their heaviest annual outlays. Sales were spread over the year, but production expenses were concentrated between October and May and purchasing expenses peaked in the autumn and winter. Equivalent credit tides swung to and fro following the sales of beasts and the chains of transactions in the leather and wool markets in subsequent months. In the sugar trade the planters would be drawing on merchants in advance of the sale of crops in the spring and the merchants be looking to their bankers. Between May and September most sugar cargoes were being landed and sold in Britain, so that the demands for credit from merchants and refiners were at their maximum. The seasonality of shipping, which was not active during the winter months from November to March, as well as that of the harvest, concentrated these demands for credit within certain months of the year. In the main transatlantic trades, such as tobacco and sugar, the heaviest pressures came in the autumn, as with the credit needs arising from the domestic harvest. An equivalent seasonal fluctuation followed the Newcastle to London coal trade, where very few shipments took place over the winter months until the last decade of the century. More research would doubtless produce a much more detailed time-table of these seasonal tides of short-term credit flowing across the face of the economy. Undoubtedly the autumn saw the peak demand for credit — more particularly in years when agricultural prices were high — and the greatest financial pressures. Balance of payments crises, like internal commercial and financial stringencies, commonly fell at this time of the year.

Long-term credit supplies

The long-term credit available for enterprise also appears surprisingly responsive to demand, and from very diverse sources, despite constraints upon the legal forms of enterprise which might be thought, at first sight, to have severely restricted the supply of long-term risk capital in England. Because of the modest size of initial requirements, the absence of formal, institutional mechanisms for mobilizing capital was not inhibiting. Indeed, contemporaries were correct in assuming that these constraints prevented waste, by reducing the opportunities for fraud and speculation, more than they denied capital to viable enterprise.

Short-term capital supplied by banks and merchants for the main credit requirements released the accumulating surplus of the enterprise for the creation of fixed assets. Personal borrowing on bond (or even note of hand) was also a most important means of acquiring modest amounts of money — counted in amounts of a few hundred pounds — at a modest rate of interest. Five per cent per annum seems to have been the near universal cost of such personal borrowing throughout the century and after: borrowed in pounds, repaid in guineas. Where the lender took security for the loan this was usually in the form of freehold property, so that a flourishing local mortgage market developed around the supply of capital for industrial and commercial purposes. The legal instruments covering mortgages, like those covering bills of exchange, were well established, effective and cheap, developed upon land and urban property transactions in the seventeenth century more than for business purposes, but this made the mortgage market in the eighteenth century one of the most efficient and widely used instruments of business borrowing. The rate of interest on first-class security here usually lay between that on government stocks (3-4 per cent in peace time) and the 5 per cent legal maximum — surprisingly modest.

Regional studies are showing how extensive were the local networks of such borrowing on bond, passing outside the banks, and how central the local attorney was as the intermediary between borrower and lender. It was advisable for the lender to have the details of the loan drawn up in a legal document, and his attorney was therefore the natural professional to act as intermediary. In addition much money often lay with the attorney as trustee or executor for an estate, or of a minor. The lender had as great an interest in a secure, remunerative transaction as the borrower — and such loans on bond, if secured, were not subject to the hazards of changing capital values, which investments in government stock involved.

From the borrower's point of view, this flourishing informal local capital market made the crucial demand — as did the request for credit from merchants — that he be trusted, that his local 'credit' was good, that he be a respected member of the local community. Eighteenth-century business in Britain operated in as uninstitutionalized a way as eighteenth-century politics. It was a 'face-to-face' society of personal, family and kinship links. In no set of business relationship were the implications of this more important than in the search for credit.

Kinship links

The 'personal' world of the entrepreneur — his immediate family and friends — could also provide critical 'external' sources for long-term borrowing, given the modest initial requirements for such capital. The dowry brought by a wife; the property of one's wife, be it never so modest (in the days before Married Women's Property Acts); access to the savings of a cousin, a father-in-law, the family solicitor or banker who had become a personal friend, or the local gentleman who had accepted an informal patron-client responsibility might all prove strategic. This 'personal' kinship world was usually the first resort for cash, whether to establish a firm in the first place, or to save it from a crisis. Such borrowing was usually upon the security of property, where the entrepreneur had any title which might be pledged.

Eighteenth-century business operated in a context of high managerial risks; and the higher the risks the greater the premium on kinship links in business. Quite apart from the requirements of the law, which forbade joint-stock enterprise in manufacturing and commercial functions, great pressures existed to identify ownership with management — and also to consolidate these connections with a kinship tie. Where a woman had inherited (or would foreseeably inherit) a business, if she wanted to maintain the ownership of it, she had a great incentive to marry its would-be new manager, and he her, if he wanted to enjoy the profits. The traditional success story of the industrious clerk or apprentice who married his master's daughter (or sometimes — even more strategically — his master's widow) is, more properly considered, the traditional tragedy of a family firm without a male heir.

Undoubtedly the first rule for a successful entrepreneur in the eighteenth century, as today, was to choose his parents wisely — or at least the rest of his family. His initial capital usually came from prior family savings. The diversity of eighteenth-century business was often associated with the kinship ramifications of families. Recruitment to enterprise so often came as nephew was sent to learn a trade with uncle, cousin with cousin, or the cadets of one family joined with the businesses of their wives' families. Often entry into a new, but related, trade would come as the generations changed. A brewer would put a younger son into malting or grain merchanting, and *vice versa*. This diversification was very natural; one son would take on the family business, which might be too small to absorb his brothers, if the catchment area was a small town, or the unit of enterprise kept small for other reasons. Where other sons were put into related trades the family had some capital to start them off; but also knowledge of these trades and friends as principals in them, customers and suppliers, who might take in a son as junior partner. So much of eighteenth-century business was multiple enterprise on a small scale, which provided the base for growing diversity and specialisation. A person might be a manufacturer on a small scale; he might trade in the raw materials he purchased, do a little financial business on the side when he had spare funds or was involved in tranfering money to London; he might invest in land and become involved in farming. Such diversity easily accommodated new entrants when sons, or sons-in-law, or cousins needed to set up in a trade. It is therefore no accident that much capital for establishing new entrants in an industry came from neighbouring trades or branches of the same trade: merchants established manufacturing capacity from a stake in the 'putting-out' system; stationers moved back into paper-making; brewers into malting; iron masters had often moved back from being manufacturers of final products in the iron industry.

Partnerships

For the new entrant to business looking for the minimum amount of capital to get himself launched there were other possibilities apart from borrowing within the 'face-to-face' circle of family and friends.

Despite a law more hostile in England than in France or some other European countries, to sleeping partnerships (*sociétés en commandite*) business histories reveal very wide diversity of practical arrangements which flourished within the strict laws governing partnership whereby each partner became personally liable in his private estate for the debts of any concern from which he received a share of the profits, (i.e. as distinct from making a loan to the principals of a firm at a fixed rate of interest as a separate transaction). Examples abound of young men, without much capital, taking wealthier men as partners who remained relatively inactive — to the point of sleeping — and collecting further capital by being personally backed by other creditors. As they became wealthy over the years from accumulated profits so they would build up their proportion of the partnership capital and, not uncommonly, terminate the partnership at an appropriate moment when a set of articles terminated (partnership agreements commonly ran for seven years). They could then go it alone until the time when their own sons would wish to come in or other arrangements had to be made to provide a succession to higher management.

Where very large capitals were required, demanding multi-partnered enterprise, these operated formally under the standard partnership law, but they sometimes had very elaborate sets of articles indeed, creating contractual arrangements between the parties, which provided for a detailed institutional division of responsibility between those contributing capital and those 'managing partners' bearing managerial responsibility. Provision for detailed accounts, independent auditing, and elections of managing partners by annual meetings of the entire partnership brought an approximation to the *de facto* operating conditions of incorporated enterprise, splitting off the supply of equity capital from the provision of managerial skills, even though, *de lege*, all partners were on an equal footing towards creditors of the firm. Enterprise requiring such vast capitals as to have induced such a pattern were quite exceptional in manufacturing and commercial business in the eighteenth century, approximately more closely to the style of financing mines, the incorporated trading companies, canal and dock companies and the few insurance companies.

Long-term capital and bank lending

The role of the banks in supplying long-term capital to business needs separate consideration. The older generalization that English banks lent 'short' rather than 'long' — that they financed trade rather than supplied the long-term capital for financing the fixed assets of industry — misleads as much as it illumines. It is true that by far the greatest source of finance for capital investment in industry was retained profit, or 'plough back'. On a quantitative basis, at any one time, or as the main trend over the years, the overwhelming source of industrial capital investment lay in firms pulling themselves up by their own bootstraps in this way. Indeed, the stream of profits provided much more than capital accumulation by *autofinancement*. After the early days of privation and restraint on personal spending to allow the enterprise to grow as fast as possible, its owners usually drew out enough profits to live according to their station when a firm was well established, and this usually involved buying enough landed property to satisfy the demands of gentility. Richard Arkwright paid £240,000 for a landed estate in 1811 which, as Dr E.L. Jones has pointed out, was the equivalent of 60 per cent of the annual fixed investment in the entire cotton industry at the time. (This could act as security, in its turn, if the business required external funds which had to be raised by borrowing). Very often, too, profits in excess of the requirements of investment in expansion would be invested in government securities, transport stock or other non-industrial assets.

The fact that retained profits (the term 'plough back' gives the wrong impression because the profits were not taken out of the business in the first place) provided the main source of long-term funds for established businesses does not mean that external sources were not important at certain times strategic for business success — when a business was being established for the first time; when cash and longer term credits were needed to enable it to survive a depression; when a major step forward was required in expansion which was beyond the scope of current profits or accumulated reserves.

Short-term lending, whether from banks or elsewhere, as we have seen above (p.95) provided the major credit requirements and released internally generated funds for creating fixed assets. Few, if any, eighteenth-century businesses seem to have distinguished their current spending from what we would now identify as their 'capital' account; and accounting methods in use were not sophisticated enough to distinguish these categories conceptually or operationally.

Longer-term bank lending occurred, at these strategic times for expansion or survival of a business, often enough for the generalization that English bankers 'never lent long' and 'always knew a bill from a mortgage' to be challenged. Much evidence, and explanation for this has accumulated from the side of the banks and their customers. Over 50 individual instances are quoted in the documentation of this section — from recent publications alone. It is still difficult to draw any firm conclusion from such a long list of individual cases, which is not endowed with statistical significance in any formal sense.

English country banks were very unstable: in severe depression years, such as 1816, 1825, 1847, there were many bankruptcies. Although a banker can be forced into liquidation for a wide variety of mistakes this suggests that banks were lending long — by default, if not by design — much more than they professed to do. Many rural banks went down in the depression of 1815-16, with the collapse of war-time agricultural prices. Loans to farmers which could not be recalled quickly — which had been used for long-term rather than seasonal credit — played their part in these bankruptcies. Mining banks in Cornwall were notoriously unstable for similar reasons.

Banks, and the partnerships of banks, throughout the country showed a very intimate connection with wealth made in trade and industry. Rich industrialists not uncommonly became partners in banks. Two quite opposite explanations can account for this — and both were true at different times. Wealth made in an industrial or commercial enterprise could become the basis for setting up as a banker, or buying a partnership in a bank. But, on occasions thereafter (if not more continuously) the working capital, or the deposits, of the bank — or its distributed profits — might sustain the other business with longer term credit. Where a merchant or an industrialist or a mine-owner was a partner in a bank he felt he had special claims for accommodation. This has been widely documented (see p.113). Brewing enterprise became associated with banking enterprise in over 50 cases.

Where bankers became wealthy men on the profits of banking they were highly desirable candidates for partnerships, or as creditors of businessmen — and in so far as they supplied capital from their private resources, and not from the funds of the bank, this lending (which in aggregate economic terms would be designated from the banking sector) would not be identifiable in the account books of the bank.

Bankers could also be involved indirectly in longer term lending to industry, without the name of the banker appearing in the books of the firm as creditor, or the name of the industrial borrower in the books of the bank. Where merchant credit was propping up a business — and borrowing which had originated in the normal credit period of a commercial transaction had been 'funded' into a longer term loan bearing interest — then banking credit could be standing behind the merchant creditor. Similarly, personal borrowing on bond from individuals who can be identified in the books of the firm as independent men of wealth — be they members of the professions or landowners — may conceivably be themselves indebted to bankers, or have mortgages outstanding on their estates. Acknowledging the indirect, as distinct from the direct, one-to-one links between bank lending and long-term business borrowing is to recognize a very complex interrelated 'circle of credit' indeed.

A special case of bank lending lies with the financing of turnpike trusts and canals. The treasurers of these undertakings were usually bankers, and the attraction lay in the financial business which would pass through the banker's hands — apart from a credit balance in the account which he might enjoy. But when a canal company or turnpike trust needed to borrow, as they so often did when costs ran ahead of estimates, the treasurer was usually seen as the natural — perhaps the inevitable — source of accommodation. And if the enterprise was essentially sound (he was in the best position to know) the banker could find it an attractive home for his surplus money.

As the number of business histories accumulate so grows the list of entrepreneurs who received long-term credit from their bankers at certain times. With the Carron Company this indebtedness ran on for forty years or more, to no pleasure of a succession of bankers in Scotland and London. This increasing number of known instances of banks lending long cannot be given a statistical significance — individual business histories present a biased, and very tiny, sample of the total population of businesses and flows of credit. But the list is extensive enough to cast doubt on the generalization about banks not lending long, which was based mainly on affirmations made by bankers. The explanation is partly that such lending came by default rather than by design; that it was made in terms of short-term lending by the banker (and identifiable as such in his balance sheets) but received, in the result, as long-term borrowing by the business man.

The short-term loan by the banker could be conceived by both parties as the initiation of a longer term, 'rolling plan', commitment, provided that both parties had no objections. This was, in result, not dissimilar from the granting of overdraft facilities, which was a regular feature of Scottish bank lending. The banker had regular opportunities of recalling his money as the loans came up for renewal every few months; the entrepreneur might rely on their continuance if his banker was not faced with stringency. Only a long run of surviving ledgers in the bank or the borrowing firms can identify these short-term credit instruments as the means of long-term borrowing. The example of Barclay Perkins' brewery borrowing regularly in this way from their Quaker banker cousins is surely a representative example of such transactions.[8]

Such long-term borrowing could happen by default rather than by design. If, when the banker tried to recall his short-term loan, or the merchant sought payment after the customary credit period, the borrower found that he could not pay, then what were the alternatives facing the creditor? He could take the case to law and seek to recover his money through the courts. If a firm was forced into declaring bankruptcy, with the case falling into the hands of the Court of Chancery, the creditor might well find that the remedy was more disadvantageous to him than the original difficulty. Such cases involved inordinate delays, with the lawyers and the court making first claims upon the assets of the business for their fees and expenses. The legal costs falling upon the creditor alone might make the process unprofitable, if the case was protracted. Moreover, the capital value of a business as a going concern (based upon its earning capacity as well as its tangible assets) could be several times greater than the amount of money which could be realized by selling up the concern and auctioning off its assets — the probable result of going into liquidation, if no alternative buyer came forward. In such an eventuality the creditors could look forward to receiving only a few shillings in the pound of their loan, unless there were undervalued assets in property revealed by the liquidation (but these would almost certainly have been identified and mortgaged to raise money by a firm *in extremis*).

Thus, provided the business was essentially sound, it was in the interests of the creditor to 'fund' his short-term loan into a longer credit (at 5 per cent interest) and hang on for better times. The bigger the amount then the more certainly a demand for instant repayment, at the term of the initial short period for which the loan had been granted, would cause the bankruptcy of the borrower — and the greater hesitation the creditor would therefore have about foreclosing. Where the safety of his own business might be threatened by such a loss (and bankers needed to be sensitive to public reactions to such knowledge, if it got about) the banker would be even more reluctant to demand his rights by invoking the law. Besides, provided the banker could survive the pressures for liquidity on himself and presume on the recovery of profitability by his debtor, such lending could be profitable business.

Where the lender was a merchant supplier rather than a banker then such a long-term credit tie had a further advantage. While it existed the customer was not free to drive an independent bargain in buying raw materials or services elsewhere at keener prices. The merchant might hope to look for some return on his loan from the more advantageous terms upon which he would conduct his normal commercial business with this client.

Conclusions

The assertion that English banks did not lend long came more from the bankers than their customers, and have been accepted at their face value by many later historians. What was a general rule, governing normal lending to most customers, has masked the existence of unrepresentative long-term lending, even though this could be very strategic for the commercial customers who received it on the occasions when it was vital. What was affirmed as a guiding principle which should govern practice was accepted as a statement of results — of what banking practice, in fact, was. When bankers explained the rules which should govern their lending policy to parliamentary committees, or wrote books about banking, these conservative principles were affirmed. A natural bias conditioned this selection of evidence: the successful, well-established, conservative bankers tended to be called as witnesses, put forward as spokesmen for the profession, or believed most widely as authors.

The London city banking community was more conservative and cautious in lending than many country bankers (or even the West End private bankers who became involved with longer term lending to private clients on mortgage). Generalizations appropriate to the activities of the City bankers have been taken to characterize English banking as a whole. There has been a shortage of certain kinds of evidence, particularly long runs of balance sheets, which would have identified short-term lending which became the instrument of long-term credit. In the second half of the nineteenth century, as the country banks were swept up into the network of branches of the national joint stock banks, more conservative lending policies were generalized within their organizations. Generalizations based upon the development at this time, and later, have been read back into earlier times without so much justification.

Notes

1 The most important new evidence on this topic is to be found in the major research of the following scholars: L.S. Pressnell (1956) *Country Banking in the Industrial Revolution*, Oxford, pp.289-365 and F. Crouzet (ed.) (1972) *Capital Formation in the Industrial Revolution* London, which reprints various recent contributions, including F. Crouzet, 'La formation du capital en Grande Bretagne pendant la révolution industrielle', 2nd International Economic History Conference, (1962), The Hague, 1965; S. Pollard (1963) 'Capital accounting in the Industrial Revolution', *Yorkshire Bulletin of Economic and Social Research*, XV; and S. Pollard (1964) 'Fixed capital in the Industrial Revolution in England', *Journal of Economic History*, XXIV. Individual citations from these sources are too numerous to be mentioned separately below. See also, P. Mathias (1969) *The First Industrial Nation*, London, chapter 5, pp.144-51, 165-78 and R.E. Cameron (1967) *Banking in the Early Stages of Industrialization*, London, chapters 2 and 3.

2 W.A. Lewis (1955) *The Theory of Economic Growth*, London, pp.201-83, especially pp.201-4, 207-8, 225-6.

3 See references cited below for section IV, *The growth of provincial wealth and savings*.

4 M.M. Postan (1935) 'Recent trends in the accumulation of capital', *Economic History Review*, VI; reprinted in Crouzet, op. cit.

5 P. Deane (1965) *The First Industrial Revolution*, Cambridge, pp.6-7.

6 The reference and authorities for the following sections of this paper are grouped in the documentation below.

7 Although the absolute value of fixed assets rose as technology at the single plant became more massive, increasing productivity and the intensity of use of plant meant that capital costs *per unit of output* could fall; and raw materials as a percentage of total costs of the final product increase. This certainly happened in the London brewing industry. The steam engine, in this sense, was capital saving as well as increasing productivity through lowering working costs from inputs of raw materials and wages relative to output. The capital costs of horses, stables etc. as well as the costs of maintaining horses were both higher than the capital costs and current costs of a steam engine.

8 See chapters 11 and 12.

Authorities for sections

Asset structure and credit needs
S.D. Chapman (1971) 'Fixed capital formation in the British cotton manufacturing industry', in J.P.P. Higgins and S. Pollard (eds) *Aspects*

of Capital Investment in Great Britain, 1750-1850, London, pp.64-71, 78;
P. Mathias (1959) *The Brewing Industry in England 1700-1830*, Cambridge, pp.253-4, 557-8; M.M. Edwards (1967) *The Growth of the British Cotton Trade, 1780-1815*, Manchester, pp.182-233, 255-9; S.D. Chapman (1967) *The Early Factory Masters*, Newton Abbot, pp.125-44; R. Boyson (1970) *The Ashworth Cotton Enterprise*, Oxford, pp.10-11; R.H. Campbell (1958) 'The financing of Carron Company', *Business History*, I; E. Sigsworth (1958) *Black Dyke Mills*, Liverpool, pp.174, 223-4, 228-9; W.B. Crump (ed.) (1931) *The Leeds Woollen Industry, 1780-1820*, Leeds, p.257; S. Shapiro (1967) *Capital and the Cotton Industry in the Industrial Revolution*, Ithaca, p.79. The fixed capital of Oldknow, Cowpe and Co. at Pleasley Mill (Chapman, op. cit.) was most unusually high, ranging from 34 per cent to 90 per cent of total assets between 1786 and 1799, compared with the many different firms quoted by M.M. Edwards, which range between 0.75 per cent, 15 per cent, 20 per cent and 35 per cent. Other figures quoted by Dr Chapman suggest that fixed assets in other firms were generally a lower percentage. Fixed assets in the Ashworth's New Eagley Mill in 1802 (Boyson, op. cit.) were less than 30 per cent of total assets (£3,100 out of £9,800). At Black Dyke Mills (Sigsworth, op. cit.) machinery and buildings ranged between 20 and 40 per cent of total assets between 1834 and 1854, but then declined to between 7 and 4 per cent in 1859-67, as stocks and investments outside the business built up. The buildings were credited to the private account of John Foster after 1859; and machinery may have been undervalued. At Bean Ing, Benjamin Gott's assets (Crump, op. cit.) were £23,000 in buildings and machinery and £43,600 in stock in 1801.

All these proportions are much dependent upon the actual valuations of the assets (particularly land and buildings, which may well not have been revalued regularly), depreciation practices and the 'gearing' of capital, through economizing techniques of renting and leasing fixed assets.

Short-term credit supplies

R. Boyson, op. cit., pp.19, 21, 33; W.W. Edwards, op. cit., pp.225-9; P. Mathias, op. cit., pp.458-9; E. Sigsworth, op. cit., pp.221-2; W.B. Crump, op. cit., p.225; B.W. Clapp (1965) *John Owens, Manchester Merchant*, Manchester, pp.14-15, 26; T. Balston (1954) *William Balston, Paper Maker 1759-1849*, London, pp. 54ff.; D.C. Coleman (1958) *The British Paper Industry, 1495-1860*, Oxford, pp.252-3; A.P. Wadsworth and J. de L. Mann (1931) *The Cotton Trade and Industrial Lancashire, 1600-1780*, Manchester, pp.235-97; A. Raistrick (1953) *Dynasty of Ironfounders*, London, pp. 6, 13, 277; A.H. John (1950) *The Industrial Development of South Wales*, Cardiff, pp.24-7, 31-4, 46; J.P. Addis (1957) *The Crawshay Dynasty*, Cardiff, pp.2-5, 158-9; B.L. Anderson

(1970) 'Money and the structure of credit in the eighteenth century', *Business History*, XII; W.E. Minchinton (1957) *The British Tinplate Industry*, Oxford, pp.97-9; R.S. Fitton and A.P. Wadsworth (1958) *The Strutts and the Arkwrights*, Manchester, pp.25-54; S. Shapiro, op. cit., pp.57-63.

Economies in fixed assets
C.H. Lee (1972) *A Cotton Enterprise, 1795-1840*, Manchester, pp.101-5; W.W. Edwards, op. cit., pp.186-94, 202-4, 211-12; E. Sigsworth, op. cit., pp.155, 168-9.

The growth of provincial wealth and savings
M.M. Postan (1935) 'Recent trends in the accumulation of capital', *Economic History Review*, VI (1st Series); P. Deane (1961) 'Capital formation in Britain before the railway age', *Economic Development and Cultural Change*, IX; H. Heaton (1937) 'Financing the industrial revolution', *Bulletin of the Business History Society*, XI; L.S. Pressnell (1960) 'The rate of interest in the eighteenth century', in L.S. Pressnell (ed.) *Studies in the Industrial Revolution*, London; P. Deane and H.J. Habakkuk (1963) 'The take-off in Britain', in W.W. Rostow (ed.) *The Economics of Take-off into Sustained Growth*, London; A.K. Cairncross (1962) *Factors in Economic Development*, London, p.140; P. Deane and W.A. Cole (1967) *British Economic Growth 1688-1959*, Cambridge, pp.260-4, 304-5, 308-9; P. Deane (1965) *First Industrial Revolution*, Cambridge, pp.153-8; S. Pollard (1968) 'The growth and distribution of capital in Great Britain 1770-1870', Third International Conference of Economic History, 1965, The Hague, pp.335-65; S. Pollard and D.W. Crossley (1968) *The Wealth of Britain, 1985-1966*, London pp.196-7; J.P.P. Higgins and S. Pollard op. cit.; C.H. Feinstein in P. Mathias and M.M. Postan (eds) (1978) *The Cambridge Economic History of Europe*, VII, 1, Cambridge, pp.28-96; P.G.M. Dickson (1967) *The Financial Revolution*, London; J.M. Price (1971) 'Capital and credit in the British Chesapeake trade, 1750-1775', in V.B. Platt and D.C. Skaggs (eds) *Of Mother Country and Plantations*, Bowling Green, Ohio; J.R. Ward (1974) *The Finance of Canal Building in Eighteenth-Century England*, London; B.L. Anderson (1969) 'The attorney and the early capital market in Lancashire', in J.R. Harris (ed.) *Liverpool and Merseyside*, Liverpool; B.L. Anderson (1970) 'Money and the structure of credit in the eighteenth century', *Business History*, XII; S. Shapiro, op. cit., chapter 2.

Short-term credit flows
P.T. Saunders (1928) *Stuckey's Bank*, Taunton, p.8 (quoting Select Committee on Resumption of Cash Payments, 1819); Select Committee on Banks of Issue, *Parl. Papers 1840*, QQ. 485, 498-9, 616-70, 659-60; J.M. Price (1961) 'The Tobacco adventure to Russia', *Trans. Am. Philosophical Society*, LI; R. Pares (1950) *A West India Fortune*, London, p.194;

Select Committee on the Coal Trade, *Parl. Papers 1800*, p.553; T.S. Ashton (1959) *Economic Fluctuations in England, 1700-1800*, Oxford, pp.4, 31; S. Shapiro, op. cit., pp.93-102.

Long-term credit supplies; kinship links
T. Balston, op. cit., pp.70-88, and *passim* to p.131; R. Boyson, op. cit., p.33; D.C. Coleman, op. cit., pp.245-51; A.H. John, op. cit., pp.40-9 and *passim*, 158-9; A. Raistrick, op. cit., p.6; P. Mathias, op. cit., pp.265-322, 458-9, 528-9; M.W. Flinn (1962) *Men of Iron*, Edinburgh, pp.171-5; R.S. Fitton and A.P. Wadsworth, op. cit.; T.S. Ashton (1951 edn) *Iron and Steel in the Industrial Revolution*, Manchester, p.214-18; G. Unwin *et al.* (1924) *Samuel Oldknow and the Arkwrights*, Manchester, pp.149, 154-5; W.G. Rimmer (1960) *Marshalls of Leeds, Flax Spinners, 1788-1886*, Cambridge, pp.36-7, 40. For attorneys and long-term credit see B.L. Anderson, op. cit.; A.P. Wadsworth and J. de L. Mann, op. cit., pp.249-50; A.H. John, op. cit., p.45; R.J. Harris (1964) *The Copper King*, Liverpool, p.31 and *passim*; R. Robson (1959) *The Attorney in Eighteenth-Century England*, Cambridge, pp.111-18, 120; J.P. Addis, op. cit., p.13.

Partnerships
W.B. Crump, op. cit., pp.172-3; M.M. Edwards, op. cit., pp.194-9; P. Mathias, op. cit., pp.243-51, 261-4, 300-18; R. Owen (1857) *Life of Robert Owen*, London, pp.53-8; A. Raistrick, op. cit., pp.6-7, 13; G. Unwin, op. cit., pp.152-5; T.C. Barker (1960) *Pilkington Brothers and the Glass Industry*, London, pp.58-9; S. Shapiro, op. cit., chapter 5; E.L. Jones (1967) 'Industrial capital and landed investment...', in E.L. Jones and G.E. Mingay (eds) *Land, Labour and Population in the Industrial Revolution*, London.

Long-term capital and bank lending
The following entrepreneurs and firms are reported as receiving long-term credit from banks: Boulton and Watt (engineers); Peter Stubs (file-maker); Richard Arkwright (cotton); John Marshall (flax); J. Foster (worsted); Robert Peel (cotton); McConnel and Kennedy (cotton); John Ashworth (cotton); John Dumbell (cotton); Daniel Bell (cloth trade); John Owens (cloth trade); Barclay Perkins (brewers); Whitbreads (brewers); Truman, Hanbury, Buxton (brewers); Red Lion Brewery; various other London brewers; R. Austin (brewer); Carron Co. (iron); John Wilkinson (iron); Samuel Fereday (iron); Walker brothers (iron); Homfrays (iron); Guests (iron); Clydach and Plymouth Ironworks; Gibbons (iron); Tunshill Ironworks; other S. Wales ironworks; Kirkstall Forge; Parys Mines Co. (copper); Llanelly Copper Co.; Cwmavon copper works; Molesworth and Praed (Cornish copper mines and works); Jenkyns, Willyams and Co. (copper); Bristol Copper Co.; Rose Copper Co.; Cornish Mines; Hawkesbury Colliery; various other coal mines; Greenall-Pilkington (glass); St.

Helens Crown Glass Works; W. Balston (paper); Quirk and Son (boat-builders); Union Mill Co. (rope works); Roskills (watchmakers); Melin Crythan (chemicals); various alum works, oil and steel manufacturies.

Authorities mentioning long-term bank lending — by design or default — include: L.S. Pressnell, op. cit., pp.294-343; F. Crouzet in F. Crouzet (ed.) op. cit., pp.180-2, 192-4; S. Pollard in *ibid.*, pp.154-6; P. Mathias, op. cit., chapter 9 *passim* and pp.267-81, 458-9, 528-9; B.W. Clapp, op. cit., pp.15-16; R. Boyson, op. cit., pp.33-4; S.D. Chapman, op. cit., pp.23, 138-43; R.H. Campbell, op. cit., in *Business History*, I; W. Balston, op. cit., pp.53-131; E. Sigsworth, op. cit., pp.222-3; M.M. Edwards, op. cit., pp.198-9, 217-18; T.S. Ashton (1939) *An Eighteenth-Century Industrialist*, Manchester, p.116; T.S. Ashton (1952 edn) *Iron and Steel in the Industrial Revolution*, Manchester, p.227-32; A.P. Wadsworth and J. de L. Mann, op. cit., p.483; G. Unwin, op. cit., p.156; A.H. John, op. cit., pp.43-9; R. Cameron (1967) *Banking in the Early Stages of Industrialisation*, London, pp.52-7; T.C. Barker, op. cit., p.63; R.S. Fitton and A.P. Wadsworth, op. cit., p.63; S. Shapiro, op. cit., chapter. 3.

For the extent of links developing between industrialists and bankers in different industries see, for brewing, Mathias, op. cit., pp.322-30; for iron, Ashton, op. cit., pp.227-32; for cotton, Shapiro, op. cit. pp.107-12.

Conclusions

Rules of banking set out by Martins in 1746 included 'not to lend any money without application from the borrower and upon alienable security that may be easily disposed of, and a probability of punctual payment.... All loans to be repaid when due and yet rotation not to exceed six months. ... This prudence and advantage of a Goldsmith, that depend upon Credit, to endeavour as near as possible upon the yearly settling of accounts, to have the Investiture of that money in Effects that are easy to convert into money' (J.B. Martin, *The Grasshopper in Lombard St* (1892), p.46; quoted in D.M. Joslin, 'London bankers in war time, 1739-84' in L.S. Pressnell (ed.), (1960) *Studies in the Industrial Revolution*, London). J.W. Gilbart (1866) *History and Principles of Banking* identified three basic theses for bank lending policy: that it was not the business of banks to supply their customers with capital to carry on their trade; that it was contrary to all sound principles of banking for a banker to advance money in the form of permanent loans on dead securities such as collieries, mills and manufactories, and that it was bad policy for a bank to make a very large permanent advance to any one customer. These were seen as still the 'bed rock' principles of British banking in 1931 (S.E. Thomas (1931) *British Banks and the Finance of Industry* London, pp.113-14). See also *Letters on the Internal Management of a Country Bank* (1850), Letters IX-XII (quoted Pressnell, op. cit., p.295); L. Lloyd, to Select Committee on Manufactures, Trade and Commerce, *Parl. Papers 1833*, Q.453; S. Gurney to Select Committee on Usury Laws (1819), *Parl. Papers 1845*,

XII, Q.241; G. Rae (1885 edn) *The Country Banker*, Letters XXIX, XXX. Rae acknowledges (as most bankers did) the advantage of long-term lending as long as it absorbed only a small proportion of the banker assets, preferably being covered by partner deposits: '...these permanent overdrafts are your most lucrative form of account; and they will always be the last which you will seek to disturb, so long as they continue within their appointed limit ...' (p.222).

6

TAXATION AND INDUSTRIALIZATION IN BRITAIN, 1700-1870

I

It is surprising, given the scale of the transfer payments involved, and the excellence of the documentation (in comparison with so much of the potentially quantifiable record in the eighteenth and early nineteenth centuries), that so little attention has been paid by historians to the economic effects of taxation and its *alter ego*, government spending.[1] As Charles Wilson remarked in another context it is, indeed, an 'unfashionable theme'.[2]

Of course the significance of the sums involved is not to be appreciated in absolute terms, but relative to price changes over time and, above all, relative to the changing size and structure of the national economy which sustained the flows, and the changing numbers and wealth of the population who had to pay. The calculations behind the conclusions of this paper thus draw heavily upon the national income accounts recently reconstructed by Dr Deane, Professor Cole and Professor Feinstein. One would certainly not wish to have greater faith in these estimates than do their authors.[3] However parents, and their friends, always need to place some faith in their offspring, at least until it is shown to be demonstrably misplaced, and we are looking only for rough-hewn truths about the trends in population and national income to provide the essential context against which to form assessments about the levels and trends of taxation.

Of the importance of the scale of transfers by taxation there is no doubt. According to Professor Feinstein's most recent estimates, for example, as a share of the national income, sums raised by the central government in the 1760s were twice as high as total gross domestic fixed capital formation, and half as high again as total investment.[4] During the Napoleonic Wars tax transfers were double the level of investment and remained higher than gross domestic fixed capital formation and total domestic investment until after 1860. Only the great export of capital in the decades after 1851 brings Professor Feinstein's figures for total investment above the yields of taxes. And tax revenues in the later eighteenth century remained *five* times higher than the modest outlays required to sustain all productive investment in industry, commerce and transport put together. Given the sustained debate about the strains which the requirements of productive investment placed upon an industrializing economy, and the supposed consequent depression of consumption levels, it is remarkable that taxation has not featured more prominently in the historiography of economic and social change in this pivotal era in British history. This is even more the case when we translate the distorting effects of such transfers by taxation against the further distortions created by the pattern of public spending.

With the principal data and conclusions of this paper being expressed by figures in the accompanying tables, much of the text is condemned to be a technical commentary, prefaced by a long list of disclaimers. The data in the tables are limited to taxes raised by central government. The omission of local government levies is not without significance. In the mid-eighteenth century local taxes totalled about 10 per cent of central government levies, rising to 14-15 per cent on trend between the 1770s and the 1830s.[5] In the 1770s central government taxes totalled £11m with local taxation at £1.7m and in 1830 central government taxes were £55m. and local over £8m. The percentage of local to central taxation then fell for a short period before rising steeply in the last third of the century to about 30 per cent. Moreover, before the mid-nineteenth century, three-quarters or more of *local* taxes were expended in poor relief. Unlike the direction of central government transfer payments, therefore, local transfers through taxation mitigated the social regressiveness of taxation in Britain, being received, for the most part, by the very poor and paid by way of assessments on property by the not-so-poor.

Table 6.1   Taxation, population and national income (G.B.) 1700-1812

Year	Pop.[1] m.	Cost of living index[2]	National income (G.B. £m) current prices[3]	Tax revenue (G.B. £m) current prices[4]	National income (G.B. £m) constant prices 1698/1702 (4) ÷ (3)	(Index) 1700 = 100	Tax revenue (G.B. £m) constant prices (5) ÷ (3)	(Index) 1700 = 100	National income per capita £m constant prices (6)÷(2)	(Index) 1700 = 100	Tax revenue per capita £ constant prices (7) ÷ (2)	(Index) 1700 = 100	Taxes as share of national income % (5) ÷ (4)	(Index) 1700 = 100
(1)	(2)	(3)	(4)	(5)	(6)		(7)		(8)		(9)		(10)	
1700	6.87	108.0	49.8	4.54	46.1	(100)	4.20	(100)	6.7	(100)	0.61	(100)	9.1	(100)
1710	7.06	120.0	59.8	5.32	53.8	(117)	4.79	(114)	7.6	(113)	0.68	(111)	8.9	(98)
1720	7.14	95.4	47.5	6.11	53.8	(117)	6.92	(165)	7.5	(112)	0.97	(159)	12.9	(142)
1730	7.08	94.4	47.9	6.23	54.8	(119)	7.13	(170)	7.7	(115)	1.01	(166)	13.0	(143)
1740	7.00	104.0	55.2	5.93	57.3	(124)	6.16	(147)	8.2	(122)	0.88	(144)	10.7	(118)
1750	7.39	97.7	56.3	7.25	62.2	(135)	8.01	(191)	8.4	(125)	1.09	(179)	12.9	(142)
1760	7.82	102.4	69.4	8.67	73.2	(159)	9.14	(218)	9.4	(140)	1.17	(192)	12.5	(137)
1770	8.39	120.2	79.8	10.42	71.7	(156)	9.36	(223)	8.5	(127)	1.12	(184)	13.1	(144)
1780	8.96	126.8	97.7	12.57	83.2	(180)	10.71	(255)	9.3	(139)	1.20	(197)	12.9	(142)
1790	9.70	133.0	116.5	17.51	94.6	(205)	14.22	(339)	9.8	(146)	1.47	(241)	15.1	(166)
1800	10.69	200.4	232.0	31.03	125.0	(271)	16.72	(398)	11.7	(175)	1.56	(256)	13.4	(147)
1803	11.61	222.0	266.5	54.70	129.6	(281)	26.61	(634)	11.2	(167)	2.29	(375)	20.5	(225)

[1] Taken from P. Deane and W. A. Cole, *British Economic Growth, 1688-1939* (1962), p. 6.

[2] From E. W. Gilboy, *Review of Economic Statistics*, XVIII 3 1936. 1700 = 100, index numbers are five-year averages centring on year cited.

[3] Calculated from 1801 estimate, using index of real growth rates to give series in constant prices of 1801 (Deane and Cole, op. cit. pp. 78, 166) then converted to current prices by Gilboy index (col. 3).

[4] Taken from B. R. Mitchell and P. Deane, *Abstract of British Historical Statistics* (1962), pp. 386-8, five-year averages centring on year cited.

Table 6.2 Taxation, population and national income (GB/UK) 1801-71

Year	Pop.[1] (GB. m)	Price index (Rousseaux) 1865/85 = 100[2]	National income (GB. £m) current prices[1]	Tax revenue (UK. £m) current prices[2]	National income (GB. £m) constant prices (4) ÷ (3)	(Index) 1801 = 100	Tax revenue (UK. £m) constant prices (5) ÷ (3)	(Index) 1801 = 100	National income per capita £ constant prices (6) ÷ (2)	(Index) 1801 = 100	Tax revenue per capita £ constant prices (7) ÷ (2)	(Index) 1801 = 100	Taxes as share of national income % (5) ÷ (4)	(Index) 1801 = 100
(1)	(2)	(3)	(4)	(5)	(6)		(7)		(8)		(9)		(10)	
1801	10.7	188	232	39.1	123.4	(100)	20.8	(100)	11.5	(100)	1.9	(100)	16.9	(100)
1811	12.1	178	301	73.0	169.1	(137)	41.0	(197)	14.0	(122)	3.4	(179)	24.3	(144)
1821	14.2	121	291	59.9	240.5	(195)	49.5	(238)	16.9	(147)	3.5	(184)	20.6	(122)
1831	16.4	112	340	54.5	303.6	(246)	48.7	(234)	18.5	(161)	2.9	(153)	16.0	(95)
1841	18.6	121	452	51.6	373.7	(303)	42.6	(205)	20.1	(175)	2.3	(121)	11.4	(67)
1851	20.9	91	523	57.1	574.7	(466)	62.7	(301)	27.5	(239)	3.0	(158)	10.9	(64)
1861	23.2	115	668	69.7	580.9	(471)	60.6	(291)	25.0	(217)	2.6	(137)	10.4	(62)
1871	26.2	115	917	68.2	799.4	(648)	59.3	(285)	30.5	(265)	2.3	(121)	7.4	(44)

[1] P. Deane and W. Cole, *British Economic Growth 1688-1959* (1962), p. 8, 166.

[2] B. R. Mitchell and P. Deane, *Abstract of British Historical Statistics* (1962), pp. 392-3, 471. It is difficult to identify tax yields of Ireland. Equating United Kingdom tax yields with Great Britain national income estimates is to maximize the incidence of taxation. However, judging by the years 1801-18 Irish taxes yielded less than 7 per cent of Great Britain taxes, on a falling trend, so that the distortion is not significant.

Other observations concern the manipulations performed on the data within the tables. The national income estimates for the eighteenth century represent a triumph of hope over experience; and do not, in any case, attempt to relate to the short-term conditions influencing the specific decennial years cited. Partly for that reason five-year averages centring upon the decennial years in question have been used for the tax data and the index numbers of the Gilboy cost of living series, used as a deflator when converting to constant prices to discount the effect of price changes for purposes of comparisons over time. The Gilboy index itself, based upon sample budgets of the poor at the end of the eighteenth century, is heavily weighted towards cereals and, by not including industrial products, maximizes short-run price fluctuations from the harvest.[6] It is not comparable with the Rousseaux price index used in the nineteenth-century table, which is an unweighted average of agricultural and industrial products. Comprehensive suitable price indexes do not yet exist for the eighteenth century and beyond, which has the salutary effect of removing the temptation to make dangerous comparisons with homogeneous indexes over even longer runs than in these separate tables.

Tax revenue data for the eighteenth century represent *net* yields to the Exchequer for Great Britain, shorn of costs of collection, drawbacks, bounties and other miscellanea. Arguments about the implications of taxation usually imply drawing conclusions from what was paid over in the first place — i.e. the *gross* incidence. The gap between *gross* and *net* revenue is not known before 1788 but thereafter the margin was not more than 10 per cent.[7] However, this does minimize the implications of tax transfers to this extent. On the other hand a further discrepancy between the two tables is that the nineteenth-century data is based on gross yields of taxation in the United Kingdom (rather than net yields for Great Britain).[8] When correlated with national income and population data for Great Britain this will thus slightly inflate the incidence of taxation on both counts. However the difference is not marked because of the very small contribution made by Ireland to the United Kingdom national exchequer after 1801. Using *United Kingdom gross* tax data for the comparable calculation in the ten-year period 1803-12 (i.e. the final line of the eighteenth-century table which is for *net Great Britain data*) is to make the share of national income represented by taxes 22.3 per cent instead of 20.5 per cent. Finally, for the nineteenth-century table tax revenues and the price-index figures are taken only for the individual years cited, rather than for the five-year average centring on the years cited (as in the eighteenth-century table). Spot checks do not suggest that this short-cut produces significant distortion of the trend.

II

Having cast so many hostages to fortune, what conclusions can yet be drawn from the tables, remembering always the most important qualifications of all — that the economic and social significance of taxation can only be finally assessed in relation to government expenditures and government borrowing?

First the aggregate incidence. Table 6.1, covering the eighteenth century, suggests that, by whatever measure, the incidence of taxation increased in the course of the century, and very dramatically during the great wars against France at its end. Deflating to identify real trends, beyond monetary movements, shows tax revenue growing consistently faster than the national income; and this cumulative impact of taxation not being offset by the rise of population. By 1790, whereas the national income had supposedly doubled, tax revenue had more than trebled; and tax revenue per capita increased more than two-and-a-half times. The share of taxes in the national income had risen from 9.1 per cent to 15 per cent, the rise being principally sustained from the aftermath of the Marlborough Wars.

This rising level of taxation essentially reveals the long-term 'ratchet effects' which the mode of paying for eighteenth-century wars had upon British public finances. More than four-fifths of the 'extra' [9] cost of military expenditure in wars fought by Great Britain in the eighteenth century was met by borrowing; through one of the great British inventions of the period — the permanent, funded National Debt. As the Debt rose cumulatively, despite sinking funds, so rose inexorably the level of tax income, and the proportions of tax revenue, needed to service it. Neither the growth of national wealth nor the rise in population after 1740 were sufficient to mitigate these effects; while the financial impact of the wars between 1793 and 1815, being on an unprecedented scale both in terms of current levels of taxation and the extent of borrowing, cast a long shadow over the peace-time generation after Waterloo. Not until the 1830s did peace, continued economic expansion and demographic growth bring the share of taxation in the national income once again below the levels of the 1790s and finally overcome the cumulative financial burden which eighteenth-century wars had placed upon the British economy.

Contrary to what is often assumed Dr O'Brien and I found that general levels of taxation in Britain were high, relative to France, throughout the eighteenth century, and rising to almost three times the French level at the height of the Napoleonic Wars.[10]

The extraordinary fiscal impact of the Napoleonic Wars is apparent: tax revenue in Britain, in real terms, in these years was rising twice as fast as national income, and the share of taxes in the national income rose from 15 per cent to no less than 24 per cent.

There is no space here to explore very deeply the implications of these figures. The obvious conclusions, however, remain the most important. The main trends in the economy as industrialization was gathering pace after 1780 — the rising rate of growth of population (compounded by the changing distribution and density of population); faster rates of growth in the economy; increasing levels of investment and increasing rates of investment (relative to G.D.P.) at least until 1800; an increasing pace of urbanization; structural change — were all, in their different ways, making greater demands on the financial resources of the economy. These trends — the Industrial Revolution in short — were taking place in a context where the state was making sharply increased claims on these financial resources (and where the spending of the state was doing little of significance to sustain those trends). The borrowing of the state, on as unprecedented a scale as its fiscal demands, imposed economic costs of its own.

The progressive relaxation of these fiscal constraints upon the economy after 1815 is charted in Table 6.2. The peak of intensity in tax revenue per capita and taxes as a share of the national income occurs in 1811-21. It is noticeable that the ratio of taxes as a share of the national income falls away to a much greater extent than the ratio of tax revenue per capita. Indeed the level of tax revenue in constant prices continued to increase on trend with the expansion of the economy and population: it is just the national income which expands at so much faster a pace. Professor Feinstein's calculations indicate that rates of investment had reached their maximum, as a percentage of gross domestic product by the decade 1791-1800 (save for a contraction in total investment in the war-time decade 1801-10). However, changes in the structure of investment saw a sharp increase in the share and extent of transport investment in the decade of the great railway boom of the mid-1840s — from £9.29m. per annum to £21.07m. per annum; in current prices, and from 23 per cent to 40 per cent of domestic fixed capital formation. The relaxation of the tax burden, and the fact that the state had moved out of the loan market, making virtually no further demands on mobilized savings, eased the nation's passage into the railway age and the age of urban man.

III

It is now time to turn briefly to considering the structure of taxation and the disaggregation of the totals which dominate the two tables. However, all discussion about the incidence of taxation must be prefaced by another important caveat. Tax data concerns the *legal* incidence of taxes — the pockets from which cash was transferred to the Exchequer — from which we seek to make inferences about their *economic* and *social* incidence. The question 'who really paid' is most complicated and cannot be given a provably correct answer. In the abstract, the economic theory of taxation can say relatively little, if anything. For example, if an import tax is raised and the importer seeks to pass on the tax through an increase in the prices he charges to his customers, that might reduce demand enough to force him to limit the price rise to an amount less than the extent of the tax — and that might happen right down the chain of distribution to the retailer. A landlord might, or might not, pass on the increments in the land tax, via changes in rent levels when leases were renegotiated with his tenant farmers. In other words, some of the increments in tax (or all of it) might be paid out of landlords' income, or manufacturers' and distributors' profits and margins. It all depends on the elasticities of demand involved, and possible substitute products. If the subsistence theory of wages is to be believed then an increment in the price of the necessities of life, occasioned by an increase in customs or excise levy, would induce an increase in wages, so that the employer, rather than the consumer, would, in effect, be paying the tax.

Elasticities, in all these respects, are important and doubtless modify the impact of taxation (now, as then). But their existence need not, in my view, entirely subvert any conclusions which can be drawn. In the following discussion I shall assume, as Dr O'Brien and I assumed in another place, that the burden of indirect taxes was shifted forward to consumers and that direct taxes, whether in property or income, were 'paid' by those upon whom they were levied.[11] Are these two assumptions realistic — not in any absolute sense but sufficiently so to enable something of significance to be said about the economic incidence of taxation? The same theoretical inhibitions do not seem to deter generalizations about the economic effects of contemporary taxation — least of all by academics. We are not, of course, concerned with problems of tax evasion — the only data available, and the only consequences to consider, are those of taxes which have been paid.

Changes in rent levels do not coincide with changes in the land tax and it was usual to make specific allowances in rent levels where tenant farmers accepted liability for the land tax — an implication that the landlord accepted some actual, as well as full legal responsibility for paying it. With indirect taxes producing so much higher a percentage of total tax revenue than direct taxes in Britain, the onus of defending the second assumption (that taxes on consumption were passed forward to consumers) is the more important. Governments in the eighteenth century were under no illusions about the possibilities of tax-shifting and contemporary commentators argued out the issue in quite sophisticated terms — at least, for the greatest of all revenue-raisers: taxes on alcoholic drinks. The major commodities producing large yields had, by definition, to be those in mass consumption. Where great sums had to be obtained, as Lord North, Pitt and Fox regularly acknowledged 'the burden must lie upon the bulk of the people' — precisely in the taxation of commodities in mass demand, where elasticity of demand was limited and where substitution for untaxed articles was difficult. We would add the extra qualification and condition, I suppose, that broadly, and in general terms, such commodities should be, and were, produced under competitive conditions. The industries producing the major excises — malt, beer, gin, salt, glass, bricks, and the like, seem to qualify.

Taking malting and brewing as a critical case, it is difficult, not to say impossible, to identify all movements of elasticities, costs, profits and prices (even in retrospect), and specify what caused what changes in all the variables. But prices went up regularly when the duty went up, and the government got more money in consequence. During the Napoleonic Wars excises accounted for more than 40 per cent of the retail price of beer in London — and although doubtless profits and prices of inputs were affected by the changes in elasticities produced by tax increases the fact is that excises were greater than all the brewers' manufacturing costs and profits put together, so that the scope for absorbing extra costs imposed through taxation was extremely limited. Beer and gin remained products in mass demand at ale houses because there were no significant trends in substitution (and governments considered very carefully the limits to elasticities in demand); while tea, spreading down the social scale as a domestic drink, was also heavily taxed. In short, those who drank beer and gin paid. It is still, alas, true with increases in duty upon alcoholic drinks at the present time.

Finally, on the subsistence theory of wages. Although the tax content of the prices of articles subject to customs and excise taxation across the land was identical, wages varied markedly regionally, by occupation and over time, according to the dynamics of the labour market; they moved independently of tax and price changes and virtually never (as far as I can discover) identically with tax and price changes, so that the subsistence theory of wages — in its simpler forms at least — which would also challenge the assumptions made about the economic incidence of taxation, did not apply.

IV

Within these assumptions, what of the results? The overwhelming conclusion was the absence of the levies falling upon wealth and accumulated capital.[12] The proportion of total tax revenues produced by property taxation, the assessed taxes and income taxes (for the brief periods within the chronological limits covered here that the latter were levied) was small — and the trend a declining one apart from interludes of war, which produced an increase in the land tax and an income tax during the Napoleonic wars. From providing 32-9 per cent of total tax revenue in the early eighteenth century, direct taxation fell away to 17-18 per cent in peace-time years between 1770 and 1790; rose to 27-8 per cent in 1800-10; but then declined to a mere 8 per cent in the early 1840s. After Peel had re-established the income tax in 1841-2 the percentage settled down to 18-20 per cent. Three-quarters of this revenue falling upon property or wealth for most of the period came from the land tax alone, while other forms of accumulation were free of levies (particularly property in the form of productive assets and mobilized savings other than agricultural land). The atrophy of land tax valuations, and the consequent attrition of land tax receipts relative to the expansion of real assets in land (quite apart from the real expansion of assets other than land) thus benefited processes of accumulation. Direct taxation fell, as a percentage of the national income, from 3-3.5 per cent during the Marlborough Wars, to 2.3 per cent in the 1770s. It then rose to almost 7 per cent in 1810, under the impact of the new income tax, but afterwards fell away in peace to less than 1 per cent of the national income in the early 1840s, and remained less than 2 per cent even with the new income tax.

This should be considered against the size of the flows from government to holders of the national debt; which represents transfers to the holders of accumulated wealth. The last year in which servicing the National Debt cost less than the yield of land and assessed taxes was 1706. The gap steadily widened apart, again, from war-time years. By 1790 annual debt charges were three times the yield of the direct taxes, and were absorbing more than half (55.8 per cent) of total net public expenditure by central government. Even during the Napoleonic War interlude of high direct taxation, yields never equalled the costs of servicing the debt, which spiralled higher because of vast loans at higher interest rates, and in 1840 payments to fund holders were running at over seven times the yield of direct taxes, almost £30m. per annum against under £4 m.[13] Here, again, is a statistic which we need to bear in mind when considering the processes of accumulation lying behind the increases in investment flows required to finance industrialization and urbanization. It seems to be particularly strategic with 'lumpy' railway investment in the 1830s and 1840s, when the government was also right out of the loan market. Indeed, there were links between brokers and bankers in the capital market, channelling the bi-annual interest payments on government funds into other stocks for those seeking other outlets for their surpluses. We should also bear such transfers by taxation in mind more than has been the case in past debates when considering trends in the distribution of income and the standard of living; quite apart from issues of incentives and motivations of entrepreneurs, which feature so largely in present-day debates on the levels of direct taxation.

The conclusions to be drawn about the economic and social incidence of indirect taxation are largely the inverse of those concerning the direct taxes. Indirect taxes varied in their social regressiveness, of course — wine, silk and printed fabrics being amongst the taxed commodities — but, on Lord North's principles, most indirect taxes had to be paid by the bulk of the population, and customs and excise revenues (that is, not including indirect taxes such as the stamp duties and revenues from the post office) produced over 70 per cent of the public revenue in years of peace during the eighteenth century and the first half of the nineteenth century. The lowest percentage of total taxes formed by customs and excise receipts were 55 per cent in 1710 and 58 per cent in 1810. Not all the great revenue producers were classed as necessities of life, even by contemporaries. Adam Smith, for example, declined to see beer and ale as necessities in the same way as salt, leather, soap and candles (all excised) 'and, perhaps', he added, 'green glass'.[14] We should therefore distinguish between absolute and conventional necessities in the eighteenth-century context; or between necessities and other products in mass demand. In the course of this century, after all, products such as sugar, tobacco and tea, worked their passage down the social scale, hotly denounced by middle-class moralizers, in that traditional historical transmutation whereby the luxuries of the rich become, in time, the necessities of the poor. A word is merited about the increasing importance of the stamp duties as raisers of revenue after 1770, mentioned above. By the end of the eighteenth century the stamp duties were yielding almost 8 per cent of total income from taxes (over 11 per cent of revenue from indirect taxes), by 1840 almost 14 per cent of total tax revenue and over 15 per cent of revenue from indirect taxes. Being extracted by way of all legal documents, insurance certificates, receipts, bills of exchange, newspapers and other media they were considered by contemporaries to fall upon the rich rather than the poor, and must modify the social regressiveness of the principal yielders of revenue from indirect taxes.

Of the general social regressiveness of the customs and excise revenues there is no doubt, in my view. Until 1830 the excise yielded much greater sums than customs; for most of the eighteenth century up to twice as much and almost three times as much in the later years. One of the interesting features of the structure of indirect taxation is this change in the relative importance of excise and customs revenue after 1820, when various excises such as the salt and beer duties were abolished. The sharply increased relative importance of the customs revenue in the 1830s was significant fiscally in the reluctance of governments to accept free trade. The main excises came from drink (usually between half and two-thirds of total revenues from all the excises), followed by salt, soap and printed calicoes and paper.[15] The tribute from imported commodities was led (by the end of the eighteenth century) by sugar, tea, tobacco, wines and spirits; after 1815 joined by timber and corn in occasional years of heavy imports. Deducting wine from this list, the remainder account for over four-fifths of yields — and these were essentially commodities whose consumption was characterized by modest sales being spread over the great bulk of the population — or, in some cases, more particularly the bulk of the adult male population — rather than being confined to the purchasing of the wealthy. It should also be borne in mind that 'home brewing', which meant more the household production of farms and larger houses than home brewing by humble families (although this continued in the Midlands), escaped the beer tax, but not the tax on malt and hops.

The main economic incidence of taxation in Britain fell upon consumption levels, upon the level of effective demand in the mass market. Save in time of war, when quite a high proportion of military expenditure went towards the payment of troops and sailors, also sustaining employment in the industries supplying the army, navy and ordnance, the spending of the public revenues of central government did very little to offset these transfers away from the poorer multitude. The 'social wage' was far into the future.

Had indirect taxes been lower the majority of the nation, paying tribute through customs and excise, would doubtless have consumed more of these articles, or other goods and services, rather than have increased their savings, unless they chose to increase their leisure.[16] Given prevailing income levels, traditional habits of expenditure and the lack of institutional means of mobilizing petty savings until well into the nineteenth century, the low-income masses of the nation could not have been important sources of savings for the economy. The fiscal burdens of the state in Britain during these early phases of industrialization and urbanization are thus to be assessed according to one's judgement about the relative constraints being imposed upon the economy from problems of accumulation and investment on the one side, or from limitations in effective demand in the mass market on the other. If shortages of savings or problems of mobilizing savings were the critical blockage, as most contemporaries and many later commentators have supposed, then the social hardships imposed by the incidence and structure of taxation in Britain at least produced a major economic benefit. But if the significance of effective demand is given greater prominence, as has been the trend in recent years, then taxation has to be assessed in the light of this perspective.[14] To conclude one argument without trespassing upon another, we may assert that the scale of transfer payments by taxation are so large that their significance cannot be ignored by either party in the latter debate.

Notes

1 See, however, A.T. Peacock and J. Wiseman (1961) *The Growth of Public Expenditure in the United Kingdom*, Princeton and London, esp. ch.3 and Table 1 (this does not deal directly with taxation); P. Deane (1968) 'New estimates of gross national product for the United Kingdom, 1830-1914', *Review of Income and Wealth*, XIV. The late Professor T.S. Ashton also took the economic effects of public finance very seriously in *Economic Fluctuations in England 1700-1800*, (1959), Oxford. There is a section on taxation, and a simple summary of the data in current prices in P. Mathias (1969) *The First Industrial Nation*, London, pp.39-43.

2 C.H. Wilson (1969) 'Taxation and the decline of empires', *Economic History and the Historian*, London.

3 Unless otherwise stated data for taxation (in current prices) are taken from B.R. Mitchell and P. Deane (1962) *British Historical Statistics*, Cambridge, ch. 14; P. Deane and W.A. Cole (1962) *British Economic Growth, 1658-1939*, pp.78, 166; C.H. Feinstein (1978) in P. Mathias and M.M. Postan (eds) *Cambridge Economic History of Europe*, Vol. VII, Cambridge, Part I, ch. 2.

4 Feinstein, op. cit., Vol. VII, I, pp.40-1, 91, 93.

5 G.R. Porter (1847) *The Progress of the Nation*, London, Table of County and Parochial Expenditure, 1748-1844, p.527; Mitchell and Deane, op. cit., pp.410-14.

6 This is a further reason for using five-year averages.

7 For a more detailed description of yields see Peter Mathias and Patrick O'Brien (1976) 'Taxation in Britain and France 1715-1810 ...' *Journal of European Economic History*, V, pp.641-2.

8 I hope in the future to rework all the figures on a net yield G.B. basis, but this is not easy.

9 I.e. beyond the 'normal' level of military expenditure calculated for adjacent years of peace.

10 Mathias and O'Brien, op. cit., Table 8, p.620.

11 Mathias and O'Brien, op. cit. See the subsequent exchange with Professor McLoskey in *J. European Ec. Hist.*, VII (1978). The following remarks are drawn from our reply.

12 Mathias and O'Brien, op. cit.; P. Mathias (1969) *The First Industrial Nation*, London, pp.39-50.

13 It can be argued, in strict terms, that interest payments are conceptually different from taxation in relation to the redistribution of income via taxation. However, more generally considered, they represent a mechanism, through the processes of public finance, whereby redistribution occurred.

14 A. Smith (1776) *Wealth of Nations* Edinburgh, Book V, ch. 2.

15 The figures for the years 1804-31 are printed conveniently in J. Marshall (1833) *A Digest of All the Accounts* ..., Section 'The Proceeds and charges of collection of each of the five great branches of revenue' (not continuously paginated).

16 See chapter 8.

17 See chapter 5.

7

ADAM'S BURDEN:
HISTORICAL DIAGNOSES
OF POVERTY

I

There are two debates about poverty, one very old, the other comparatively new, invoking very similar presuppositions and employing a virtually identical conceptual scheme, which are not often brought face-to-face for comparison. The first is the long debate about the causes of poverty — the explanations offered for the burdens which press upon Adam's race — in the historical tradition of Western Europe since medieval times; the second lies within the rapidly growing recent contemporary literature of economic development and the 'Third World' — the causes of present poverty amongst nations. For an economic historian, caught between faculties as an economist amongst historians and a historian amongst economists, the juxtaposition of these debates makes their comparison less easy to avoid than it appears to be for scholars within the citadels of either discipline.

Of course, poverty has always been a subjective concept as much as an objective 'value neutral' condition, bedevilling all attempts to examine, or explain, it in exclusively objective or quantitative ways. Like beauty, to a degree it lies in the eye of the beholder, as well as being integral with the value-system, priorities, cultural patterns and life-style (not *just* the material or economic aspects of the life-style) of those experiencing the condition. Standard of living debates in history — and now in cross-cultural comparisons —

founder upon the comparability and meaning of national income statistics, or the reality of comparing real-wage indexes and costs of living in contexts widely separated in societies or in time.

For comparative history no less than comparative economics the 'index number problem', as economists call it, precludes any scientifically provable conclusion. Not all the constituents of a standard of living can be measured or priced: a smell of drains, a warm climate, a preference for leisure, do not find their way into the indexes, even though the indexes have significance only in the light of such contextual matters. The social security administration's official poverty line (in 1972) of an income of $3,800 for a family of four in the United States, has validity for that context, and for that context alone — not just in the dollar purchasing power of that sum, but also because of the levels of expectations established in American society. Attempts to measure an objective 'poverty line' differ according to different societies and also over time. The identification of a condition of poverty varies with expectations — the cultural determinants of a society — as well as through the level of productivity available in its economy, the degree of rapaciousness of landlords or the extent of the exactions imposed by grasping states. As Adam Smith acknowledged long ago, when both material standards and levels of expectation were so different: 'By necessities I understand not only the commodities which are indispensably necessary for the support of life; but whatever the custom of the country renders it indecent for creditable people, even of the lowest order, to be without.[1]

Even with United Nations investigations into the adequacy of diets in poverty, which are potentially analysable in 'real' quantified terms of calories, proteins, vitamins, without the complications of money calculations, the search for a universal norm of minimum adequacy founders upon the rock of relativism. Are we speaking of the minimum diets required by small brown people in hot climates, or large pinko-grey people in cold climates; and doing what work, living in what houses and wearing what clothes? Diets have a profound cultural overlay to them, being specific to social context as well as to purchasing power. An analysis of vitamin deficiency in the Puerto Rican community of New York revealed the truth of this, when a traditional diet was displaced to an urban environment with less sun. Least of all do such quantifications of inputs — whether of income, calories or any other measurable items of consumption — give any direct indication of the relative outputs in terms of satisfaction or happiness. Happiness and satisfactions spring from expectations, anticipations, comparisons as well as results; from relatives as much as absolutes. Events are filtered through a cultural and family matrix, which conditions the consciousness and meaning of those events.

Comparisons are not made according to objective facts but the subjective consciousness of those facts — or of myths given the status of subjective facts to serve the purpose of such comparisons. Present unhappiness and dissatisfactions, for example, have so often been validated, legitimized, given greater credence, by comparison with a Golden Age in the past. At a more everyday level, optimism or pessimism are strongly influenced by very short-run comparisons (objective or subjective); satisfactions can depend on relative comparisons with immediately past experience or immediately adjacent social groups as much as on absolute quantities. Hostilities to the status quo may be greater when a trend of improvement (which has become incorporated into the pattern of expectations of the social groups enjoying it) is checked; or when past gains become threatened, than when absolute standards deteriorate.

Changing levels of expectations as well as changing levels of consumption, affect satisfactions. When cultural trends lead to the assessment of status and satisfactions by consumption 'tests', and encourage competitiveness, then relative poverty may produce greater dissatisfactions. Certainly it seems easier to be happy if one is poor in a poor country, with a culture of poverty (in the sense, at least, that the attainment of pleasures does not depend upon purchasing), than poor in a rich country, where social values emphasize levels of spending. A similar set of explanations may be valid for arguing that it is easier to be happy when poor in a rural society than in an urban society. However, all such assessments contain inbuilt assumptions: two of the most long-standing features of the debate about poverty is the condescension of those writing from a 'culture of wealth' about the poor and their satisfactions; and the mythologizing of the rural social scene by those enjoying the choice of not having to live there; or living there on advantageous terms if they do. One way to increase satisfactions, in terms of a materialistic, acquisitive culture, the high road along which the industrialized nations have passed, and where others have set foot, is that of increasing levels of consumption and ownership. But there is a Zen way to satisfaction, a 'low road' to happiness, by way of minimizing wants. Poverty is a social status.

All such relativism in the significance of measurement against quantitative norms does not, of course, deny the reality of the devastating gap between rich and poor, whether within a society or in the community of nations. With the growth of wealth, it seems clear, both these gaps are growing wider, and the tolerance of dissatisfactions occasioned by them diminishing. A journey through the core of any great city to its suburbs will testify to that; the comparison between standards in a rural farming community in North America or India; the contrast between Calcutta and New York, Manila and Stockholm. Equally, the vicarious experience of the historian in understanding the reality of poverty in times past, survives the obfuscation of figures. Life for most people was poor, nasty, brutish and short — if scarcely solitary in societies crowding fertile land.

II

This essay is not about the facts of poverty, or a search for its actual causes, objectively determined, but a discussion of how those causes have been conceptualized in different social and economic *milieus* — a study in opinion. The debates about the causes of poverty, even more than comparisons over its incidence, have been suffused with similar subjective assumptions. Indeed, explanations of poverty have derived much more as logical consequences of general social philosophies than they have emerged from attempted scientific investigations of the facts of the matter. The nineteenth-century faith that a systematic study of the facts would provide the basis for explanation, the diagnosis upon which correct remedies might be grounded, was seen as a radical philosophy, potentially subversive of the true principles, by those traditionally called upon to govern. An equal dogmatism invades the discussion of the causes of poverty among nations at the present time in a search for a universal explanation, a residual hypothesis in the absence of detailed analysis in real terms. Proposals for legislation tend to be much influenced by such *a priori* speculation which gives meaning to the assumption about causation. Practical men, the legislators and administrators of the world, as Keynes reminded us, validate their actions more than they acknowledge or even realize, upon the academic scribblings of obscure commentators. And of this theme, that great social critic and most humane of men R.H. Tawney once remarked '...there is no touchstone, except the treatment of childhood, which reveals the true character of a social philosophy more clearly than the spirit in which it regards the misfortunes of those of its members who fall by the way.'[2]

Before the sixteenth century, more as a result of religious thought with attendant social values than of any deep-seated changes in the material standards produced by the economic system, poverty was accepted as inevitable, the elemental condition of man, save for his rulers, born into the world to labour for minimum reward. It was certainly not a problem requiring special explanation or possible elimination by social policy. Indeed, beggars, as the embodiment of destitution, symbiotically invoked almsgiving as the embodiment of charity, in a half-mystical union of squalor and glamour, which was seen as Christ-like for medieval Europe. In that guise came Christ among men. This was not such a characteristic Old Testament view (where the dependence created by poverty was seen as shameful), while from both Testaments, characteristically, may be drawn many conflicting quotations about attitudes to poverty. In very poor countries today personal almsgiving to the beggar often remains a symbolic acknowledgement of the moral responsibility of wealth, without changing the distribution of income or touching the structural problems of indigence. Indeed, with poverty universal and inescapable in an economy whose bounds were set by the meagre surplus produced by traditional agriculture, it was destitution and pauperism, more particularly the social and political consequences of the poor growing distracted to the point of importunity or insurrection, that invited social action, not poverty itself (as we would now designate it). This distinction between poverty and pauperism characterized social legislation until the end of the nineteenth century in England. It is also an inescapable distinction in social policy in very poor countries today.

III

In a medieval world where land was the only main source of wealth, and the direct sustainer of life for most people in society, it is little wonder that a continuing theme should be the explanation of destitution by the rape of the land from the people; and its restoration as the sovereign remedy. As John Baker pleaded to Henry VIII in 1538: 'If ... every man might have in towns and villages but one little home or cottage to inhabit and but a little garden ground withal, they would so order it with their labour that they would earn their living.'[3] 'The land now is to return into the joint hands of those who have conquered, that is the commoners', demanded Winstanley, for the Diggers, in 1650.[4] This canon against dispossession and enclosure, consolidation of estates and the destruction of commons lasted well into the heyday of nineteenth-century industrial society, with reverberations still heard in our own day with rural hippie communes and a demand for macrobiotic foods. One reaction against the squalors of industrialism was the quest for a rural utopia, where historical phantasies of a green and pleasant idyll sustained present and future dreams, equally mythical, of a new prosperity where a nineteenth-century peasantry, resettled from the tread-mill towns, would once more prosper by spade-husbandry. This recessive death wish for a society without poverty, without extremes of wealth, free from stock jobbers, paper money, cotton mills, taxes, an oppressive monarchy and aristocracy was given credence so often by invoking a rural utopia. 'I will make a paradise of England in less than five years', claimed Feargus O'Connor the Chartist leader, with £112,000 hard-won pennies supporting his Land Plan. How regressive these dreams were, in a crowded island, increasingly dependant on food-imports, which industrialism was beginning to lift to unprecedented standards of material reward, only the toiling peasant masses of Ireland, Eastern Europe and Asia knew. Only a nation without a subsistence peasantry, such as England then was, could give credence to such dreams. They were not without influence upon the inheritance legislation taxing the accumulation of great estates at the end of the century. T.H. Green spoke for many progressive commentators when he saw the parents of the 'impoverished and reckless proletariat' of great towns as 'landless countrymen, whose ancestors were serfs', driven from the soil.[5]

IV

From being accepted as inevitable in medieval Europe a later tradition, coming in the wake of a Puritan, Calvinist ethic, defended poverty, at least for the poor, as a necessity. This 'Utility of Poverty' doctrine translated an ethic of work against an assumed characteristic of human nature. Only if labour was cheap and wages low could exports flourish and the poor be induced to exertion.[6] High wages encouraged idleness, extravagance and debauchery, both diminishing production and raising prices. The level of wants was fixed, ran the argument, unresponsive to any ambition of widening the range of consumption or improving living standards. Leisure and drink, or those extravagances which perverted motivations against work, sobriety and thrift, monopolized the interests of the poor when that elemental level of consumption had been met. If they were not kept poor they would never be industrious. Fatalism about the inevitability of poverty thus grew a moral carapace of necessity and justification. 'It seems to be a law of nature,' wrote a commentator in 1786, 'that the poor should be to a certain degree improvident, that there may always be some to fulfill the most servile, the most wretched and the most ignoble offices in the community ... when hunger is either felt or feared the desire of obtaining bread will quickly dispose the mind to undergo the greatest hardships and will sweeten the severest labours.'[7] Where the spur of poverty was dulled by alms or poor relief, these imperatives of human nature would merely ensure further idleness and debauchery, from which point came the conclusion that the poor law itself tended to cause the condition it was ostensibly designed to cure. Hence that transcendent duty for all dispensers of alms and public gratuities, enjoined by statute and private exhortation in chorus from the sixteenth to the twentieth century, to discriminate between the deserving and the undeserving poor. The sword of justice, no less than charity itself, should cleave these asunder. For the able-bodied varlets, the rogues and vagabonds and sturdy beggars who would not work, was reserved the hostility of law, stripes, badging and obloquy. But there was discrimination. He that *will* not work let him not eat, ran the injunction, not he that *cannot* work. The 1572 statute argued ' ... charity would that poor, aged and impotent persons should as necessarily be provided for, as the said Rogues, Vagabonds and Sturdy Beggars be repressed.' In 1582 a list of those categories of paupers maintaining a moral claim upon the community included: 'fatherless children, sore and sick persons, poore men overburdened with their children, aged persons, decayed householders.'[8] This is not very different from a list of the main causes of poverty in later nineteenth-century Britain drawn up by a historian (in 1972) which ran: 'Inadequate, irregular earnings (particularly from casual labour); large families, sickness, accident or death of the breadwinner, widowhood, with dependent children, and old age'.[9] Provision of work for the able-bodied deserving poor was the third response of the state, with charity for the impotent and retribution on the able-bodied, undeserving.

Such objective categories of poverty were often transmuted into a subtle dialectic of cause and effect. Indigence became explained by idleness, and idleness by moral failings rather than prevailing circumstances. The truest charity could then be claimed to lie not in enervating the poor by relief by in so reforming their characters that relief would not be necessary.[10] Severity changed from sin to duty. As Tawney wrote tartly: 'The demonstration that distress is a proof of demerit, though a singular commentary on the lives of Christian saints and sages, has always been popular with the prosperous.'[11]

As Professor Jordan has demonstrated for private charity, and the actual measures of local public relief showed at the time, up to 1834, when the new poor law was castigated for imposing the harshness consequential upon the social philosophy emphasized by Tawney from its birth in the sixteenth and seventeenth centuries, the actual dispensation of relief did not accord with this bleak diagnosis of the causes of poverty. It was acknowledged, without benefit of philosophy, that idleness was often a consequence of circumstances, that environment often determined attitudes, that poverty produced vice and not vice alone poverty. In the eighteenth century, Christian obligations, sometimes secularized into a theory of moral sentiments or a principle of sympathy, if not of the inherent social nature of the human animal prior to the contract of the state, sustained an obligation of charity; while fear of the consequences of the poor growing importunate, in civil commotions with flaming hayricks in the countryside and food riots in towns, put salutary practical limits upon the restraints upon relief which the Puritan philosophy — never in any case the official philosophy of the ruling élite save for one brief interlude — could justify. Collective bargaining by riot, in Professor Hobsbawm's lapidary phrase, had a long history. And here poor relief was the ransom paid by the rich to keep their windows, as well as their consciences, intact.

V

The temperance movement in Victorian England exemplified this diagnosis of poverty, in caricature form at its most extreme manifestation.[12] It emerged during the 1830s in a generation much exercised by the problems of housing, feeding and disciplining the unprecedentedly growing numbers of a society increasingly committed to life and labour in industrial towns. Pessimists, interpreting Malthus via Ricardo to make the worst of all possible worlds, might proclaim economic misery to be the inevitable lot of the labouring poor. Radicals diagnosed the problem as institutional. Replace the old economic and political institutions of the nation, they claimed, and the problems will depart with them. The pessimistic conclusion was alien to the confidence of many Victorians who remained optimistic that the age was witnessing a progressive triumph of intelligence and morality over brute nature; while the revolutionary (if not reformist) conclusion also implied a wrong diagnosis for the law-abiding, the property-owning, the polite and respectable. A more general hope of these groups was that charity — private, personal endeavour — would sufficiently mitigate the hardships of society, when harnessed to produce the bourgeois virtues among the working classes, to avoid the necessity of challenging the traditional organization of society. They sought a solution without compulsory redistribution of property by taxation, and the consequent bureaucratic apparatus of state intervention and public administration.

For them, at the most naive level, the diagnosis of poverty became couched in terms of individual moral failing and of individual responsibility. There was no deep-seated institutional evil to be eradicated. Weakness of character made resort to the demon drink a substitute for facing the realities of the world. The vocabulary was that of sin and temptation. The soul could be saved for the bourgeois virtues of work and thrift, which would solve the problems of poverty by a moral crusade, casting out the devils of drink or sloth. Secularized evangelicalism characterized the style of so many of these local movements for social redemption in Victorian England; spontaneously adopted by working-class movements themselves as well as being thrust upon their heads by middle-class reformers.

VI

The parallels of this syndrome with the historical and current debate amongst the rich nations about the causes of poverty in the rest of the world are uncanny; and also have a long history. With Irish, Spaniards and Italians, Indians and Africans condemned by Northern Protestant nations for being poor because they were idle there is a long literature, from the casual observations of travellers' tales to the elaborated consequences of their religion and social philosophies. Some examples of comments in this tradition are given in the next chapter, where 'leisure preference' is explored in more detail. The canon of most contemporary comment, however, is very similar to that in the historical debate, with a strong tendency to relate immediately observed facts of absenteeism from wage employment to national, cultural, religious or class personal characteristics and motivations without much attempt to explore its rationality within the total context of work. This was often a complex pattern of part-time commitment to agriculture with seasonal work for a money wage in mine, plantation or factory.[13]

In one of the recent volumes analysing the constraints against development in the Third World there is a list of the 'differences in economic qualities' which establish the motivational structure of advanced societies compared with the poor nations: interest in material progress, industry, thrift, self-reliance, readiness to perceive and exploit economic opportunity, a questioning turn of mind and an experimental outlook. These face: a high leisure-preference, tradition, the greater prestige of a life of contemplation, resignation in the face of poverty, the recognized status of beggary, the lack of stigma in the acceptance of charity and even — without self-conscious historical irony — 'opposition to women's work outside the household.'[14] The inference then becomes that these attitudes largely cause underdevelopment or at least prevent its disappearance.

All the obloquy which castigated indiscriminate almsgiving to individuals in sixteenth- to nineteenth-century Western countries has now been applied to the foreign aid given to developing nations — particularly untied aid in the form of gifts. These 'doles'[15] (*sic!*) will encourage reckless extravagance in spendthrift governments. Aid is neither a necessary nor a sufficient condition for development, runs the argument. Indeed it is counter-productive, encouraging the insidious beliefs that the prime prerequisites of development can be had for nothing, that progress depends on external forces, reducing incentives by subverting self-reliance and initiative, and diverting attention from the basic causes of poverty. While not ascetic to the point of condemning the use of all external capital, this tradition favours the discipline of the market imposed through supplying loans, rather than gifts, or at least having aid tied, administered and financially disciplined by donor governments or the international agencies. Reverberations of the Charity Organisation Society (created to prevent the dissipation of alms in indiscriminate giving) in Victorian England echo still down the corridors of the World Bank.

But, just as the theories of Christian obligation, moral sentiment and sympathy survived alongside the Puritan ethic in pre-twentieth-century Western nations, so the international agencies, Oxfam and other 'Third World' charities, particularly for disaster relief, show in practice the survival of moral imperatives at the international level. Different views have not been lacking, whether expressed by present or past commentators. In the literature of development economics the main assumption has been — to the limited extent that motivations towards work and consumption have been singled out for analysis by economists — that appetites expand with the opportunity of consumption, with short time-lags, and that leisure-preference reflects a lack of opportunity rather than any deeply structured anti-work ethic. 'Money is no incentive,' wrote W.E. Moore, 'if there is nothing within the effective range of demand that money will buy'.[16] This reflects the views of Adam Smith and Petty, mentioned below.[17]

Blackmailing, moral or practical, has also been imputed as a motive for foreign aid by the critics of left and right: the assumption that aid is owed to poor developing nations because the rich became rich only at their expense. There was the looting of India and Latin America, the exploitation by way of slave-grown sugar and cotton; industrial investment created from slave-won profits.

This has merged into general theories of economic imperialism and the assumed inevitable deterioration in the terms of trade of primary producers against the industrial exporters in the international economy. In practical terms the circle of assumption is then completed by the argument that foreign aid is designed to rescue the country which received it from threat of revolution, or counter-revolution, to save foreign capital, protect foreign enterprise, profits and export markets and in general to stop the windows of the donor countries from being smashed by the irate mob of the poor nations in the international community. For some left-wing critics aid, like the supplementation of wages in early nineteenth-century England, induces the continuation of labour at even less reward, and succeeds in driving down the wage levels or, in the modern parlance of macro-economic relationships in the world economy, lowering the terms of trade of primary producers.

VII

Such theories of exploitation explaining poverty in the international economy, of course, mirror a long tradition of explanations of poverty within nations by the exploitation of class or ruling élites — not alone the Marxist thesis. In the eighteenth century Tom Paine offered a simple thesis that poverty was caused by the burden of taxation: it was a question of 'whether the fruits of his [man's] labours shall be enjoyed by himself or consumed by the profligacy of governments? Whether robbery shall be banished from courts and wretchedness from countries?'[18] Abolishing taxation, of course, meant collapsing the superstructure that it maintained — monarchy, peerage, government, even the landed interest, who had all climbed onto the back of the nation. Robert Owen, wilder radicals like Thomas Spence and J.F. Bray, Marxist and socialist thinkers widened and consolidated this tradition of explanation of poverty. The environment shaped cultural responses and determined consciousness. Drunkenness was a response to poverty, not its cause — the quickest road out of Manchester. Poverty derived from institutional patterns developing within society, demanding an institutional change for its cure, whether political, economic, and social change or the integrated dynamic of society that Marxist and other sophisticated socialist thinkers offered. And from this analysis, applied to the microcosm of a single national economy,

with Rosa Luxemburg, J.A. Hobson and the Austrian Marxist
•Hilferding, was deployed the macro-economic theory of economic
exploitation and imperialism in the world economy, giving greater
intellectual sophistication and integrated historicist theory to earlier simpler accusations of the wicked rich exploiting the poor in
far-flung lands.

Across this scenario falls the long shadow of Malthus, recognized as a primary intellectual enemy by Marx and Engels in their
generation, no less than Malthusianism remains a bogey for
left-wing interpretations of poverty in the Third World in our own
day. For, if the Parson was right that numbers press always upon
the level of resources, that elemental fact of the human condition
— the passion between the sexes — must undercut any institutional
explanations of mass wretchedness, leaving the poor poor under
any social or political system.

Malthus made a dynamic theory out of a widely acknowledged
law of large numbers. 'The labouring classes are only poor', wrote
Edmund Burke, 'because they are numerous. Numbers in their
nature imply poverty. In a fair distribution among a vast multitude
none can have much. That class of dependant pensioners called the
rich ... is so extremely small that if all their throats were cut and a
distribution made of all they consume in a year, it would not give a
bit of bread and cheese for one night's supper to those who labour,
and who, in reality, feed both the pensioners and themselves.'[19]
Certainly this is the grim truth of the logistics of any economic
system with low productivity, whether that of eighteenth-century
(or *a fortiori* medieval) Europe, or twentieth-century India. Redistribution of income cannot significantly change the level of well-
being of the masses of the nation, only a change in the economic
system which will bring higher productivity techniques. This vision
of a high-wage economy, a promised land where, for the first time
in the world's history, a cumulatively increasing standard of living
for all was possible, dawned only with the Industrial Revolution in
the eighteenth century. Regressive taxation, the burdens of standing armies, lavish courts, grasping landlords, or the capture by
social élites of the meagre surplus produced by land and trade,
brought greater pressure on the poor, to which cultural monu-
ments, extremes of luxury in the churches, courts and temples of all
great civilizations bear witness. But with low productivity, low
output per head in traditional agriculture, any economy dominated

by unmechanized agriculture, and the trade and handicraft production flowing from agriculture, does not produce a great surplus.
Even without the Malthusian assumption of increasing population
and diminishing returns from the land, an equilibrium between
numbers and resources will be balanced at a very low level; and to
laud an increase in real wages in the aftermath of famine, is to
count it a success in raising *per capita* national income by lessening
the numbers of people rather than by expanding the economy.
Malthus, by his two overriding assumptions about the rates of
growth of numbers and resources, projected present reality into an
eternal pessimism; offering a future without hope of a dawn.

In reality, both Malthus's assumptions were being negated within
his own society and others (although not in Ireland) at the
time —the green countryside surrounding Cambridge and Hailey-
bury, where he wrote, did not bear evidence of the factories and
industrial towns bringing in the new age. And so it has proved, even
within advanced agriculturally based economies, for the modernized societies ever since. But in the wider horizons of teeming Asia,
Malthus's theory was to win a currency in the twentieth century of
which he had no conception. Even here, however, Malthusianism
does not exhaust the diagnoses of underdevelopment; and the
inevitability of a Malthusian fate for many underdeveloped countries is, to my mind, very questionable. The assumption that world
poverty can be cured by an effective birth control campaign is as
naive an optimistic belief, though very widespread, in our own day,
as its mirror image, the absolute pessimism of a 'belief' in Malthus
as a single-course explanation for poverty, was in the early nineteenth century.

VIII

In conclusion. This chapter has not been primarily about facts but
theories; not so much an attempted analysis of the actual causes of
poverty, objectively determined, but a review of how the causes of
poverty have been conceptualized by different social cultural and
economic *milieux*. An historian is brought to realize — to his
disenchantment — more inescapably than other social scientists or
policy-makers the gap between fact and concept, objectivity and
assumption. Over time, doubtless, entrenched assumptions get
eroded by the glacial pressure of awkward facts, but those awkward

facts are not just thrown up autonomously, but often lie within the rationale of a new paradigm, a conflicting set of assumptions. Facts are sought in the light of beliefs and theories.

Over the centuries, the long debate about the causes of poverty in Western nations has experienced this continuing tension between a search for facts as they were and the prior assumptions of a value system which gave conceptual clarity to facts, an objective for policy and signals for action to policy-makers. With the hindsight of history, the only professional advantage which the historian enjoys, we can see how wide was the gap which often prevailed between social philosophies and the entrenched facts of poverty.

The wider ironies of this great sweep of social theory do not need stressing — of a widespread theory blaming poverty on personal character responses flourishing through centuries where the elemental logistics of the economy precluded anything except mass poverty; where pauperism required social action but poverty was endemic by definition. It might be added, more tendentiously, that this always challenged, but widely accepted, social dogma about the causes of poverty collapsed as a creditable thesis at the end of the nineteenth century and in our own century in generations when, with high productivity, and the assumption of efficiently managed demand and employment levels, mass poverty potentially can be eliminated in the advanced nations. In such a context, disprivileged minority groups apart, the diagnoses of personal motivation have become much more relevant as an explanation for the causes of poverty.

Responses to poverty also varied very greatly between different social groups, and different local contexts in Western society. They changed quite quickly over time when the local context changed. When Irish men or Italians, like Indians or Chinese, condemned to laziness and indolence in the eyes of contemporaries in other nations by the stultifying effects of their cultures and religions, emigrated what happened? They took their religion and their culture with them, as a cohesive force. But the Irish and Italians outworked the indigenous population consistently in just those regions and cultures from which the commentators had been condemning them; while the Indian minorities in East Africa and the Chinese throughout south-east Asia, dominate the enterprise sectors in their host countries as an entrepreneurial élite *par excellence*.

No absolute truth is offered to the present by the study of the past, but an appreciation of the complex relations between fact and assumption in one past debate may check the temptation to offer easy universal hypotheses as a nostrum for explanation in the contemporary dialogue. The study of the past in this indirect sense can widen the range of awareness with which we approach the present. The historian might thus say to the development economist, and to the administrator: beware the universal cause, the general residual hypothesis, which fits conveniently within the general scheme of a social philosophy and has acted as a substitute for analysis in real terms. Social theory is not autonomous, absolute, universal, but is given significance and relevance — even truth — in relation to a specific context of time and society. The blanket of a universal hypothesis, whether that of Calvin or Marx, has smothered reality and darkened counsel. The truth has proved much more diverse, much more complex. And if this is inconvenient to acknowledge in the short run, whether for historian or for policy-maker, it becomes dangerous to ignore in the long run.

Notes

1 A. Smith (1776) *Wealth of Nations*, Edinburgh, Book V, chapter 2, Part II.
2 R.H. Tawney (1948 edn) *Religion and the Rise of Capitalism*, Harmondsworth, p.265.
3 State Papers, Henry VIII, vol CXLI, ff. 134-5 (quoted Bland, Brown and Tawney, *Tudor Economic Documents* (1924), II, p.303).
4 Quoted Tawney, op. cit., p.254.
5 T.H. Green (1911) *Principles of Political Obligation*, London and New York, pp.225-6.
6 See the long list of examples quoted in E.S. Furniss (1957 edn) *The Position of the Laborer in a System of Nationalism*, New York, chapter VI.
7 J. Townsend (1786) *A Dissertation on the Poor Laws*, quoted by J.R. Poynter (1969) *Society and Pauperism: English Ideas on Poor Relief, 1795-1834 (Studies in Social History)* London, pp.xvi-xvii.
8 Bland, Brown and Tawney, op. cit., vol. II, pp.354-5, 418; J. Howes (1582) *A Familiar and Friendly Discourse* .... Compare an equivalent list of 1597 in H. Hart (1597) *Provision for the Poor.*
9 M.E. Rose (1972) *The Relief of Poverty, 1834-1914 (Studies in Economic History)* London.
10 Tawney, op. cit. pp.263-4.
11 Ibid., p.264.

12 B.H. Harrison (1971) *Drink and the Victorians*, London; P. Mathias (1958) 'The brewing industry, temperance and politics', *The Historical Journal*, I.
13 Chapter 8, pp.150-2.
14 P.T. Bauer (1971) *Dissent on Development*, London, pp.78, 519-20, 526-7. Given the prevalence of women's rôle in agriculture over much of the underdeveloped world the latter point seems groundless in fact, quite apart from the question of causation.
15 Op. cit., pp.96-113.
16 W.E. Moore (1951) *Industrialization and Labour*, Ithaca, NY, pp.302-6.
17 Chapter 8, p.163.
18 T. Paine, *Rights of Man* (edn H. Fast, *Selected Works of Tom Paine*, New York, 1945, p.246).
19 E. Burke (1795) *Thoughts and Details on Scarcity*.

LEISURE AND WAGES
IN THEORY
AND PRACTICE

I

There is a very large literature reporting on the existence of 'leisure-preference' in history, and a further extensive bibliography of strikingly similar comments made in our own day about the same phenomenon. The idea is simple, even where it has a theoretical formulation as a 'backward sloping supply curve for labour'. In brief, the concept implies that an increase in the demand for labour, expressed through an increase in its price with a rise in wages, will result in a lowering of supply. In one of the most famous expressions of this maxim Arthur Young, the eighteenth-century commentator on economic affairs, claimed that 'everyone but an idiot knows that the lower classes must be kept poor or they will never be industrious'. This is contrary to the normal expect-ations of the working of a free market; and is the antithesis of standard market theory. In competitive conditions, assuming no absolute limitations on supply — either of existing labour willing to increase their working hours or extra labour willing to come into the market — the assumption governing the 'rational' operation of a market is that extra demand, bidding up the price of a factor, will call forth extra supplies, and that a fall in demand leading to a decline in price will lead to a fall in supply. A large corpus of basic economic argument, and more operational assumptions about a free market system, lie behind this assumption of 'rational' responses to price movements, which provide the signals for action and the incentive system in a commercial context. Deviations from this norm thus, by implication, raise important questions in their turn about the motivations of individuals in a commercial context, their economic rationality or irrationality, and the nature of the competitive context within which such responses occur.

The issue, as so many issues in history, can be studied at two levels. In the first place, we can seek to assess the objective truth of the assertion, to see what significance it has as an accurate, 'value-neutral', factual record of labour reactions; to ask whether the actual functioning of the labour market followed this pattern, or to what degree, or when applied to what occupational groups; or to what extent these responses changed over time; or were relevant to short-term or long-term responses to change. The second approach is to seek to assess its significance as opinion; not so much to test the objective truth of the assertions but to see what they reveal of the value-systems of the time. What do they tell us about the attitudes of upper classes to the poor; of what general social philosophies are these opinions a logical part; are they characteristic of some social groups more than others; in what sorts of historical circumstance do they tend to be popular; are they, for example, more a characteristic of periods of rapid social change than of comparative stability?

The structural relationship between ideas and their historical context is always complex and subtle. The relationship between these ideas as the reporting of objective fact and 'normative' subjective opinion is also not straightforward: because they are part of a value-system held by actors in a historical situation they have an 'objective' importance in that historical context, influencing attitudes and policies, even though they may not be entirely true objectively, in the sense of reporting the prevailing facts about leisure-preference in an accurate, value-neutral way. This chapter will consider, first, contemporary ideas about leisure-preference as a theme of intellectual history, and then, second, offer certain observations about the incidence of leisure-preference as an objective characteristic of the labour force. Many historians have considered the question, but rather incidentally, in the course of other enquiries.[1] Over fifty years ago Edgar Furniss quoted more than twenty contemporary commentators holding this view in the late seventeenth and eighteenth centuries.[2] It has also been much studied in a different, non-commercial context of self-subsistence economies, dual economies and the domestic mode of production by anthropologists studying primitive peoples, Dutch economists in the interwar period considering the structure of colonial economies, and in relation to peasant studies; for example in A.C. Chayanov's, *The Theory of Peasant Economy* (tr. 1966).[3] Most modern development economists see the problem as only one of short time-lags before appetites for consumption catch up with the opportunities.

II

The tradition of comments about the labouring classes producing less work when offered more pay is remarkable. It acknowledges no frontiers and echoes down the centuries. More particularly, observers made such observations holding assumptions about particular social and occupation groups in their own countries and those in other countries in commercial connection with their own nationals. There is thus both an internal and an external, an indigenous and an alien, canon to the tradition. A few examples will show how widely the concept has ranged — both for commentators putting it forward as one point in a set of generalizations — virtually a cornerstone of a social philosophy — and others recording it as observed fact.

Arthur Young elevated his observations into a general law about the utility of hard times and low wages. 'Great earnings ... ', he commented, 'have a strong effect on all who remain the least inclined to idleness or other ill courses by causing them to work but four or five days to maintain themselves the seven; this is a fact so well-known in every manufacturing town that it would be idle to think of proving it by argument.'[4] 'Where the price of labour is highest and provisions are the cheapest,' wrote Joseph Townsend, 'there the poor rates have been the most exorbitant.'[5] These sentiments were echoed for the working masses in general and for the textile areas in particular, by a long canon. Among other commentators in this vein are Bernard Mandeville, John Weyland, Thomas Manly, John Houghton, William Petty, Josiah Child, John Law, David Hume, Jonas Hanway, John MacFarland, William Temple, Pollexfen, Joshua Gee, John Gary, Daniel Defoe (in some places, but not in others), William Allen, Josiah Tucker,

Francis Fauquier, Henry Fielding, Bishop Berkeley, Roger North.[6] Of Scottish labourers in Sutherland Thomas Pennant summed up the problem succinctly in 1772: 'Till the famine pinches they will not bestir themselves.'[7] This was part of a more general aversion — even horror — that 'civilized' eighteenth-century gentry and townsmen felt for rude peasants. *The Gentleman's Magazine* of 1766 spoke of the common people in Scotland as 'brutalised in appearance ... in their lives they differ little from the brutes except in their love of spirituous liquors.... They would rather suffer poverty than work....'[8]

The analogue is direct between attitudes to peasants on the geographical periphery of 'civilized society' within the island, and those groups beyond the frontiers of settlement of Western society. Mr White, Clerk of the Hudson's Bay Company depôt in Albany, upper New York State, reported to London in 1749 that 'he believes the Indians would kill no more beasts than what is sufficient to purchase commodities for the year ... and he does not know whether, if they could have an advanced price for their goods, they would not bring down fewer skins than they do at present'. He claimed that their 'necessities and desires' were fixed — all, that was, except for liquor. This assumption thereupon became enshrined in an official Company memorandum which ran: 'The giving Indians larger Price would occasion the Decrease of Trade'.[9]

Over a century later, in another continent, when William Lever was describing the difficulties of trading with Africans in Nigeria, he spoke in exactly equivalent terms: 'The fact is', he wrote, 'the native has few wants, a little salt and a little cloth are his indispensables. After this beads, brass rods and other luxuries. Twelve months ago he [Chief Womba at Leverville] and his people were poor and few in number and were keen to bring fruit. After twelve months of selling fruit he is rich and lazy, has ten wives ... but he gathers little or no fruit.... '.[10]

Indian coal owners and managers were expressing similar views about tribal labour in the 1920s and 1930s. In the present debate about increasing the wages of black workers in South Africa letters in the London *Times* echoed the traditional eighteenth-century view — and virtually in the same words — that higher wages would produce greater absenteeism rather than a higher standard of living.

In the British economy during the nineteenth century and after miners were said to have a particular propensity for working less when wages rose. Two assertions can illustrate the continuum of comments to this effect. A correspondent of Josiah John Guest, master of the famous South Wales Dowlais ironworks wrote to him in 1835: ' ... higher wages will of course be demanded, and as men grow scarce, will no doubt be obtained, so as to cause a reaction alike injurious to both Masters and Men in their employ. For I never yet knew high wages obtainable but Drunkenness, idleness, and loss of time were sure to be the consequences, as young men whose wages exceed their reasonable wants of food, lodging and clothing, generally spend the surplus in the Ale Houses ....'.[11]

'It is not that the men want to get very large wages', commented an Inspector of Mines about Monmouthshire colliers in 1873, 'I do not believe that they do; but they want short hours and more leisure, and a higher price for their piecework....'[12] Sir T.E. Watson, a coal exporter, told the Sankey Commission in 1919: 'Our constant experience has been that increases in wages have been accompanied by diminution in output per man.'[13]

Other occupational groups also frequently mentioned are casual workers, such as dockers, and always Irishmen. It is noticeable that these observations are not made about one style of occupation, nor about a uniform economic context. Miners were always a high-wage group amongst the working classes; dockers' earnings were high when work was abundant and overtime available, but much subject to seasonal and other forms of underemployment and much afflicted by cyclical variations. Many of the eighteenth-century complaints against textile-workers were also directed at higher-earning occupations compared with farm-labourers in regions without manufacturing work. At the same time another chorus concerned the very poor, with fears of increasing poor relief costs at the back of the complaints. Some high-wage groups were not so involved: skilled spinners in cotton mills were less subject to these accusations than hand-loom weavers; skilled 'puddlers' in iron works less than face workers in collieries.

The phenomenon is also not just that which is to be observed at the interface where representatives of a commercially responsive, market-orientated society, where 'rational' economic motivations rule, have business dealings with groups outside this value-system, and largely outside a market economy. This is, indeed, *one* main explanation for the phenomenon — whether the interface between commercial society and non-commercial motivations is an 'external' frontier (as with American Indians in the eighteenth century or Africans in the nineteenth) or an 'internal' frontier — for example, when a peasantry conditioned to a largely subsistence existence first find themselves placed within a market economy, which would be the position of some Irish immigrants to Great Britain who evoked these observations, or even more when the outriders of a market economy seek to have business dealings with them on their own ground. To this extent the observations represent the bewilderment and frustration of those accepting the logic of a commercial market economy, of production for sale rather than for use, coming up against a form of economy where these rules do not apply. By applying the logic of the market economy the explanation for such a negative response to incentives was laziness, and sloth — deviations in moral character from the correct norm.

But this is not the only sort of situation: rural outworkers and colliers were at the heart of the industrial economy when these comments were being made about them, and in no sense characterized 'first-generation' responses to market values. Coal mining was a rural-based industry in the main, with pit villages being largely self-contained communities, very traditional in social habits, with little alternative employment and very limited opportunities of competitive spending. The same was doubtless true of much rural-based industry in eighteenth-century England. There is also a structural difference in the incidence of leisure-preference. One manifestation of the phenomenon is that of the temporary, seasonal bonanza time in a traditional rural economy after the harvest, or in a year when prices were low and work plentiful. This response was possible in an economy innocent of rapid technical change, regional disparities or sectoral change. But a different manifestation of leisure-preference occurred exactly in response to the impact of economic development: with technical progress leading to the emergence of higher productivity in expanding sectors in the economy with offers of higher wages; and with regional differences in wages rates and earnings developing with such sectoral and structural change.

III

The implications of 'leisure-preference' as an historical phenomenon, assuming for the moment its existence, are profound, affecting interpretations of the sources of economic growth and the standard of living controversy and having important consequences for economic and social policy. Each deserves a comment.

One of the main sources of impetus for economic development in Great Britain during the process of industrialization is assumed to have been the extension of the internal market. This came partly from rising population after 1750 (there was little self-subsistence in the British economy to be squeezed out) and partly from rising real incomes. Of course, foreign markets were also important with exports expanding at 4 per cent per annum or more in some periods such as the 1740s, 1783-1803, 1840-70. But the expansion of foreign trade was intimately associated with the extension of effective internal demand, through the sterling credits pumped into the international economy in payment for imports to the United Kingdom (exports to the West Indies, for example, were largely a dependent variable to imports of sugar to the United Kingdom, and that fluctuated in response to effective demand within Britain). And in certain periods, including 1720-40, 1765-83; 1815-40, and 1870-95 exports of British products were not expanding in value at a high rate. For these periods in particular a great onus is placed on the extension of the internal market as the sustainer of growth on the demand side. Before the cumulative rise in population began in the 1740s one main mechanism for such expansion of demand is said to be the fall in agricultural prices, between 1720 and 1750, which released purchasing power for other products by increasing the real income of wage-earners. There is controversy about how such purchasing power was distributed (more particularly for the 'middling income groups' of society whose purchasing has been considered particularly strategic for the mass-produced goods of the Industrial Revolution) but, if 'leisure-preference' was operating to the extent that so many contemporary observers claimed, there would have been little extra purchasing power at all to distribute.[14] An equivalent point applies to the expansion of the internal market after 1750. Although numbers were rising, the increase in the level of effective demand was also enhanced by higher wage rates (particularly in industrial employment and the industrializing regions), higher earnings from the increasing volume of employment and changes in the structure of employment with a relative growth of higher wage sectors. Equivalent arguments apply to phases of growth in the nineteenth century, whether from increases in money wages in the period 1850-75, or gains in real wages from falling prices over the following twenty years. To the extent that it operated, 'leisure-preference' would have undercut the element the growth of effective demand which depended upon the *deepening* of demand by rising spending *per capita* (particularly on a widening range of articles) rather than the *widening* of demand by increasing numbers.

The 'standard of living' controversy is also at risk because the concept of a rising standard of living — in narrow economic terms of real wages and the extension of purchasing power — is largely meaningless under assumptions of 'leisure-preference'.[15] The 'leisure-preference' concept makes the basic assumption that the level of purchasing is largely fixed, according to a 'traditional' — and largely elemental — basket of goods. There is no potential desire to expand the range of consumption which extra purchasing power would allow to be realized. If real wages rose, enabling that traditional 'basket of goods' to be earned in fewer hours, the gain would be taken out in time rather than in the extra consumption of purchased commodities and services, or by extra leisure supplemented by forms of spending which do not traditionally feature as desirable constituents of a rising standard of living — particularly drink. In nineteenth-century Britain drinking was joined by another great industry of the poor, equally denounced by social reformers — betting on dogs and horses. When extra income was spent in ways deemed socially disadvantageous by critics from the upper classes (and also by reformist movements of the working classes themselves which adopted very 'bourgeois' virtues) the strict idea of 'leisure-preference' — that higher wages would result in no higher money income and no increase in spending but simply in extra time being taken from work — becomes transmuted. A very prominent moral overlay, in fact, covered the debate. Throughout it the condemnation of 'leisure-preference' associated these two characteristics: more idleness and the asumption that the extra leisure 'bought' with higher wages would be shared with socially (and morally) reprehensible extra expenditure — particularly on drink. There was an intimate connection between the two, of course: carousing implied absenteeism. But this also did not fall within conventional definitions of an 'improving standard of living'.

The implications for social policy of believing in a 'leisure-preference' response to higher wages are much bound up with these moral criteria. If the destination for extra income was to be less work or morally reprehensible extra consumption there was no economic, social or moral justification for the offer of extra money income. Indeed, at its most extreme, belief in 'leisure-preference' invited proposals that everyone would be better off if wages were lowered: the workers because morally dangerous leisure and socially disadvantageous consumptions of drink and other undesirable forms of spending would be reduced; employers because wage costs would go down and the supply and regularity of labour be increased. The dangerous habits induced by higher wages might even lead to an eventual increase in destitution — if the habits became ingrained while the higher money wages which originally induced them proved temporary — and this would produce a further evil of an increase in poor relief spending. Harriet Martineau reported this common belief in 1816, in the course of parliamentary debates on poverty and poor relief. Mr Curwen an 'intelligent agriculturalist' had a theory that the 'extension of manufactures, having raised the average rate of wages, had produced general improvidence; that improvidence was the main cause of distress and poor rates....'[16] It is apparent that belief in leisure-preference formed a central pillar of a widespread social philosophy. The ideological role which the assumption held within this social philosophy — and which the social philosophy required — largely accounts for its strength and the extent of its appeal. This is the power of myth — the role that an assumption plays within a value system — distinct from its objective truth, or at least buttressing the intellectual convictions it derives as a consequence of being believed as observed fact. To this role of 'leisure-preference' as part of a social philosophy we now turn.

IV

The general social philosophy, of which an assertion that 'leisure-preference' values characterized the responses of the poor formed a particular aspect, was widespread in the seventeenth and eighteenth centuries. It struck roots as a Puritan ethic in the sixteenth century but blossomed into the bourgeois virtues in the eighteenth and nineteenth centuries as a transcendently religious debate became secularized. The values which Tawney and Weber characterized in an older debate as Calvinist, in association with the emergence of capitalism, in Europe of the Reformation, now stayed in the wings of European history for a further two centuries, waiting to come on stage in England with Protestant Nonconformists and the bourgeois ethic of the Industrial Revolution.

The assumption of 'leisure-preference' was highly convenient for employers, more particularly those whose fortunes were committed to success in foreign markets. Their costs were principally made up of raw-material costs and wage payments: in circumstances of artisan production when technology advanced very slowly, rising productivity was not a means of equating low-cost production with high wages. Thus, in a context of great inflexibility over wage costs, low wages were felt to be a very necessary condition for success in export markets. Most textile areas in England were committed to export markets in some degree — some predominantly so — and this dominated the consciousness of employers in their attitudes to wages. A general thesis with the premiss that higher wages would lead to less work, which was economically disadvantageous to the employers, and at the same time would result in socially and morally adverse consequences for their workers was thus highly convenient. The further implication was equally welcome: that lower wages would lead to more work being sought by a more disciplined and more sober labour force, who would receive moral and social benefit from high wages foregone and would suffer no 'real' economic disadvantages themselves while employers would gain on all counts.[17] Characteristically the question of maintaining the level of effective demand at home did not receive such attention (which was a further logical consequence, of course, of believing in a 'leisure-preference' theory).

More generally this fitted into wider, more comprehensive attitudes to the poor and the labouring masses of the nation, forming part of what Furniss named the 'utility of poverty' doctrine — that low wages and high prices benefited the nation and that the national interest demanded that the bulk of the population be kept poor. It was equally important, of course, that they should not become destitute. In practice a narrow, and fluctuating margin separated the condition of destitution, where people became a charge upon the public purse, and poverty, where they remained poor but viable, making their own way in the world. Paradoxically (as we would now think) the schema equated the belief that low wages were advantageous with the assumption that poor relief costs would be lowered at the same time. One might believe that a social philosophy which succeeded in squaring this circle, in a context of a very low-income economy, could move mountains conceptually. The argument was that the salutary motivations to work and discipline occasioned by low wages and longer hours of work ensured less dependence on the public purse — taking for granted that sufficient work would be available and ignoring all the problems of the absence of savings and the causes of indigence occasioned by any interruption in the power to work. But the question of motivations lay at the root of this diagnosis of poverty, and the theory of 'leisure-preference' provided the psychological basis for a defence of this particular social order. The point was put succinctly by a rural incumbent, J. Townsend: 'The poor know little of the motives which stimulate the higher ranks to action — pride, honour, and ambition. In general it is only hunger which can spur and goad them on to labour. The wisest legislature will never be able to devise a more equitable, a more effectual, or in any respect a more suitable punishment, than hunger is for a disobedient servant.'[18]

Such a motivational structure established the psychological underpinning for a deferential, traditional, hierarchical society, where the position of the poor was to be explained by their own actions, where redistribution of public money, or fundamental institutional change, would not resolve the problems of destitution. 'Leisure-preference', as well as providing logical defence against claims for higher wages, also countered potential aspirations for social mobility, egalitarian trends in social habits and most other cultural, social and economic trends subversive of the deferential society. It is important to recognize that the value-system supported by these assumptions was a sedulous amalgam of the traditional and the bourgeois. A 'work ethic' lay at the back of it, with the bourgeois virtues of work and discipline. This was as hostile to current aristocratic cultural values as it was to these imputed attitudes which characterized the poor (or at least the undeserving poor). The poor with a high leisure-preference had some attitudes in common with the gentlemen of leisure, through this rejection of the virtues of work and redeeming the time, though from opposite ends of the social spectrum. The leisure of opulence, of attained material consumption from inherited wealth in unearned income, met the leisure of poverty, of the absence of material goods. An ethic of leisure faced an ethic of laziness; and bourgeois values were hostile to both.

Perhaps the clearest insight into these antagonistic social philosophies comes — as so often — from Alexis de Toqueville, exposed to these paradoxes and sharpened in his perceptions of European society by his visit to the United States, although prone, as always, to see contrasts in rather extreme terms. He compared the supposedly stable, aristocratic, hierarchical European society with the progressive, egalitarian, competitive, American social world, and specifically considered the 'Influence of Democracy on Wages'.[19] The passage deserves quotation:

Amongst a nation where aristocracy predominates in society, and keeps it stationary, the people in the end get as much accustomed to poverty as the rich to their opulence. The latter bestow no anxiety on their physical comforts because they enjoy them without an effort; the former do not think of things which they despair of obtaining, and which they hardly know enough of to desire.... When, on the contrary, the distinctions of ranks are confounded together and privileges are destroyed — when hereditary property is sub-divided and education and freedom widely diffused, the desire of acquiring the comforts of the world haunts the imagination of the poor and the dread of losing them that of the rich.

He spoke even more explicitly about the dissolution of the psychological basis of leisure-preference under the impact of egalitarian social habits:

... as the gradations of the social scale come to be less observed, whilst the great sink and the humble rise, and poverty as well as opulence ceases to be hereditary, the distance, both in reality and in opinion, which heretofore separated the workman from the master, is lessened every day. The workman conceives a more lofty opinion of his rights, of his future, of himself. He is harassed by new wants. Every instant he views with longing eyes the profits of his employer; and in order to share them, he strives to dispose of his labour at a higher rate ....[20]

We should doubtless give more weight to the labour market setting bargaining powers for labour, enabling successful bids for higher wages and the consequent enhancement of expectations, rather than the reverse sequence, which de Toqueville underlines, of enhanced expectations leading to demands for higher wages. But the clarity of insight about opposed social philosophies grounded in contrasting social structures is of direct relevance to the persistence and pervasiveness of the 'leisure-preference' doctrine in Europe. In the United States this analysis was projected upon the black labourers, who were commonly identified with a motivational structure (as slaves or ex-slaves) similar to that of the unregenerate poor in Europe.

The strength of the doctrine was, in part, independent of its truth exactly because it was consonant with a social philosophy of wide appeal, which signalled a set of social attitudes important in these social groups irrespective of their truth, although a superficial credibility was doubtless a necessary gloss for more deeprooted and instinctive satisfactions. It could be argued that, over the centuries, attitudes to the poor and diagnoses of poverty have been more directly consequential upon the implications of general value systems held by the non-poor, who shape policies, than upon empirical enquiries, where enquiry was ostensibly value-free, with controls built in against bias. In turn such 'subjectively' held opinions have 'objective' influence. Prescription rests upon diagnosis. Legislation depends upon the assumptions of causation which shape the objectives of policy; and those assumptions become integral with prevailing social philosophies.

V

Up to this point the discussion has avoided the question of whether the assumptions of 'leisure-preference' were an accurate representation of the functioning of the labour market in the eighteenth century as well as being a widely held and influential belief. In short, was it true?

No simple, or brief, answer is possible and space does not permit a lengthy discussion. In any case the data on earnings, consumption patterns and hours and intensity of work are not systematic enough for the British economy as a whole to allow the question to be resolved in a satisfactory quantitative way. The absence of homogeneity in the labour market would preclude absolute national generalizations. The economy was experiencing so much structural and inter-sectoral change, with marked sectoral, regional and occupational differences, with such contrasting experience in the short run, in different phases of cyclical fluctuations, that evidence has to be strictly related to particular circumstances in time and place and not selected as piecemeal facts to fit into a spurious homogeneous national framework. In many ways national generalizations are less possible during this first century of industrialization than either before or since: there was neither the greater uniformity provided by a more completely agricultural, rural-based, very slowly changing economy pre-1700; nor the greater institutional uniformities brought by centralizing forces in the century after 1850. The same problems bedevil the 'standard of living' controversy.

Some things, however, can be said. 'Leisure-preference' was certainly not the representative, long-term response of the labour force to a rise in real wages. Employers did not, in fact, reduce wages when they wanted to increase the supply of labour. They acted, despite complaints about the ill-effects of higher wages, 'rationally' in the market, offering increased wages when labour was scarce and lowering wages when the state of the market, and their bargaining power, allowed them to do so. This reaction was representative of all parts of the labour market, as comments and complaints (particularly complaints) make abundantly clear. It is not conclusive proof: employers could have found themselves caught in a vicious circle and could only have escaped from it by effective collective action, which proved impracticable. But the evidence does not suggest that wage increases were progressively cumulative in the short run, as they would have needed to be in the face of a truly backward-sloping supply curve for labour.

Second, two strongly held views often maintained in association by proponents of the leisure-preference thesis are mutually contradictory, and are to be reconciled only by a joint moral condemnation rather than by any economic logic. This is the double complaint that higher wages invoked greater absenteeism but also were associated with the poor indulging in extravagances, forgetting their due station in life and aping their betters in diet, clothing and pleasures. The process by which fashions introduced at the summit of the social and income pyramid eventually reach the poor was much in evidence amongst the same social groups in the same centuries, noticed and bewailed by the same critics who lamented (and believed in) leisure-preference. This did not stop at the increased consumption of liquor (itself, as a bought commodity, the refutation that *all* increments in earning were taken out in extra leisure), but embraced tobacco, snuff, tea, sugar, silks, linen, muslins (particularly cottons imported from the East Indies), fashionable hats, ribbons, trimming, and the like. Continental visitors complained that they could not tell maids from their mistresses on the streets of London; that servants in England were intolerably overpaid and insufferably arrogant. Tea, in particular, was singled out by such as Jonas Hanway as the apotheosis of luxury spending on needless extravagances by the poor. He was shocked to find that even labourers mending the roads demanded their daily tea. In economic terms such commentators cannot have it both ways — having one's leisure and consuming it, so to speak.

The figures for consumption of commodities such as tea and sugar tell their own tale.[21] In the first decade of peace, 1715-24, retained imports of tea were less than 0.10 lbs per capita per annum and retained imports of sugar about 0.1 cwts per capita per annum, for England and Wales. Between 1785-1800 the corresponding figures for Great Britain were over 1.5 lbs for tea and about 0.2 cwts for sugar.[22] Wage rates moved up strongly (particularly in industrializing regions) between 1760 and 1780.[23]

During the last fifteen years of the century the rate of consumption of excised commodities, in mass demand, such as tobacco, soap, candles, printed fabrics, spirits and beer was increasing more than twice as fast as population.[24] Although it is impossible to judge movements in total effective demand from changes in the consumption of individual commodities, or groups of commodities, these trends, after a period of rising money wage rates, surely tell their own story. Regional growth was strongest, in numbers and demand, where the processes of industrialization gave most impetus, and it was in these regions that wage rates moved ahead most strongly. Future research will doubtless document such trends in local expansion more systematically. A widening range of commodities was coming onto the market; a widening range of shops and development in the distributive system provide direct evidence of the institutionalizing of this growing internal market. It may well have been that the demand of the 'middling orders' of society — from skilled artisans upwards — proved more critical in the patterns of market growth and differentiation than the elemental demands of the labouring masses, as Dr Eversley and others have argued, but trends in food and drink markets and basic textiles indicate that, on trend, higher real wage-rates were not all being taken out in increased leisure.[25]

This, however, does not end the matter. There is the mass of comments on the other side from observers reporting experiences without moralistic overtones. Indeed, a counterpoint of commentary in terms of humane scepticism survived alongside the moralizing. Adam Smith remarked, in characteristic vein, 'our ancestors were idle for want of a sufficient encouragement to industry. It is better, says the proverb, to play for nothing than to work for nothing.'[26] His general conclusion was as follows. 'That a little more plenty than ordinary may render some workmen idle, cannot well be doubted; but that it should have this effect upon the greater part, or that men in general should work better when they are ill fed than when they are well fed, ... seems not very probable.'[27] Almost a century before this, in 1691, Sir William Petty commented of the Irish, the targets for so many accusations of 'leisure-preference'; 'Their lazing seems to me to proceed rather from want of Imployment and Encouragement to work than from the natural abundance of Flegm in their Bowels and Blood'.[28] In the 'moral economy' of the working classes, which Edward Thompson has analysed in relation to expectations about prices, wages and relations with employers, undoubtedly expectations about levels of consumptions and hours of work had an important place in the short run. Time-lags relating wages to the expectation of *wider* purchasing patterns were very important.

The essence of the matter, which enables these observations to be equated with the longer-term trends of consumptions, seems to be that 'leisure-preference' was a relatively short-run phenomenon. Observations which were factual for the short run were then taken up and incorporated into a theory of the universals of human behaviour by those seeking documentary evidence to give credence to a social philosophy and a theory of motivations. Data from the world of history, legitimate within their own terms of reference, were illegitimately transposed into a normative world of social theorizing — in ways which historians will find depressingly familiar in our own days. Increased real earnings were doubtless shared between extra leisure and extra consumption; and that extra consumption shared between traditional products and commitments to new ranges of purchasing. Time-lags occurred in both these movements. In nineteenth-century Britain I suspect that such time-lags in actual leisure-preference, following increases in money wage-rates, were matters of weeks or months, rather than years; and that a 'rachet' effect occurred successively; initial gains being taken out more in leisure and drink but then being absorbed back into wider purchasing and employment patterns. There is certainly a correlation between short-term wage movements and beer consumption, for example. The productivity of miners in South Wales did, it appears, dip in response to wage increases.[29]

There is a further aspect to the reconciliation of factual observations about preferences for leisure, the seemingly 'rational' responses of employers in the labour market of successfully offering higher wages, when they need to attract more labour, and the extension of demand in the internal market. This is so obvious as to have been often overlooked. It is that there are two separate demand and supply curves for the labour in question: that of individual workers and of the potential labour force as a whole responding to the offer of wages by employers. Undoubtedly individual workers placed leisure amongst their priorities with higher income and responded accordingly. But other workers were attracted into the market at the level of wages which tempted others to increase their leisure. The fluidity of the labour market in eighteenth-century England accommodated such a variety of responses — which provide piecemeal evidence enough to offer superficial support for any general proposition. One man's leisure preference proved to be another man's employment opportunity.

With first-generation migrants into a market-oriented commercially motivated society, doubtless, time-lags were longer and traditional motivations much more strongly entrenched. Intergenerational change might well prove a precondition of changing motivational structures in such a context; although the transformation of 'laziness' in the Irish — or any other country's supposedly racially, nationally or religiously determined behavioural characteristics — judged by the experience of emigrants from that country to Great Britain or the United States during the nineteenth century, underlines the speed at which such changes can occur. Apart from consistently outworking the indigenous inhabitants (exactly in the countries from which moralistic protestant condemnations had been loudest) a steady flow of remittances went back to their native lands.

The expectation of continuation of reward at the higher level was also necessary to invoke the response of widening and extending one's spending patterns. If higher wages came unexpectedly, spasmodically, and might disappear as quickly or as unexpectedly as they came, increased permanent commitments in spending, or more expensive social habits, could prove disastrous. In such a context preserving a basic, minimal level of commitment to the market at a 'traditional' standard and pattern of consumption was an important psychological safeguard — and ironically in terms of moralistic denunciations, pouring away a surplus in drink or leisure, could be thus defended as a rational response to context. Of course, savings would be a more constructive response to the occasional surplus; but the availability of local institutions for encouraging savings were slow in coming, and did not exist in village society. Indeed, the site for such spontaneous self-help — the friendly societies — being traditionally the public house, did not encourage socially useful savings; while the apparatus of the consumer-orientated society did not extend far into rural society in eighteenth-century England. Conditions of high risk, high uncertainty for the future and high mortality, paradoxically, did not encourage a 'savings' mentality. But this is yet another aspect of the way in which the exploration of 'leisure-preference' both as a real phenomenon in history, and as a conceptual presupposition in social theory, leads towards very wide historical horizons.

Notes

1 A.W. Coats (1958) 'Changing attitudes to labour in the mid-eighteenth century', *Economic History Review*, XI; (1967) 'The classical economists and the labourer' in E.L. Jones and G.E. Mingay (eds) *Land, Labour and Population in the Industrial Revolution*, London; A.H. John (1965) 'Agricultural productivity and economic growth in England, 1700-1760, *The Journal of Economic History*, XXV;

D.C. Coleman 'Labour in the English economy of the seventeenth century, *Economic History Review*, 2nd Series, VIII, April; E.J. Hobsbawm (1968) 'Custom, wages and work-load in nineteenth-century industry', in *Labouring Men*, London; K. Thomas (1964) 'Work and leisure in pre-industrial society', *Past and Present* XXIX; E.P. Thompson (1967) 'Time, work discipline and industrial capitalism', *Past and Present*, XXXVIII; I. Blanchard (1978) 'Labour, productivity and work psychology in the English mining industry, 1400-1600', *Econ. Hist. Rev.*, XXXI.

2 E.A. Furniss (1919) *The Position of the Laborer in a System of Nationalism*, New York, chapter 6.

3 M. Sahlins (1974) *Stone Age Economics*, London; (1961) *Indonesian Economics*, The Hague; A.C. Chayanov (1966) *Theory of Peasant Economy*, New York; W.E. Moore (1952) *Industrialisation and Labour*, Ithaca, pp.302-6.

4 A. Young (1770) *Northern Tour*, I, London, p.197.

5 J. Townsend (1787) *Dissertations*, p.84.

6 All these are quoted by Furniss, op. cit., Contemporaries who declined to accept these assumptions formed a much shorter list, but the names included: Sir W. Harris, M. Postlethewaite, N. Forster, J. Vanderlint, Sir John Nickolls, R. Gould Smith, and J. Howlett.

7 T. Pennant (1790) *Tour ...*, II, London, p.315.

8 *The Gentleman's Magazine*, London 1766, p.211.

9 E.E. Rich (1960) 'Trade habits and economic motivation among the Indians of North America', *Canadian Journal of Economic and Political Science*, XXVI.

10 Ch. Wilson (1974) *The History of Unilever*, I, London, p.176.

11 E. Pickering to J.J. Guest, 6 March 1855, quoted in M. Elsas (ed.) (1960) *Iron in the Marking*, Glamorgan, p.68.

12 *Parl. Papers*, 1873, X. Select Committee on Coal Industry, p.52. I owe this, and the following reference to Dr R.H. Walters of Jesus College, Oxford.

13 *Parl. Papers*, 1919, XI, Sankey Commission on Coal Industry, p.541. See also equivalent assertions in *Parl. Papers*, 1847, XV, p.401; 1873, X, p.53; 1907, XV. p.367; 1919, XI, p.681; *Colliery Guardian*, 3 June 1909, pp.1064-5.

14 A.H. John (1961) 'Aspects of Economic growth in the first half of the eighteenth century', *Economica*; D.E.C. Eversley (1967) 'The home market and economic growth, in England, 1750-1780', in Jones and Mingay, op. cit.

15 Gains in total satisfaction, of course, are not to be questioned. If leisure is given a transcendent priority and rising real wages enable more time to be devoted to leisure then the net total of satisfaction will have increased, assuming that the level of consumption of other commodities consumed is maintained. But that is true by definition.

16 H. Martineau (1872) *A History of the Thirty Years' Peace, 1816-1846,* I, London, pp.110-11.

17 Coleman, op. cit., explains the objective characteristics of the labour market in the seventeenth century in which these attitudes were prevalent. An alternative way of reducing the real wages of the labourers was by increasing the costs of necessities by excise taxation, although this would not have such directly favourable consequences for employers as lowering money wages.

18 J. Townsend (1786) *A Dissertation on the Poor Laws,* London, quoted in J.R. Poynter (1969) *Society and Pauperism,* London, p.42.

19 A. de Toqueville, *Democracy in America,* Part II, Book II, Section 37.

20 Ibid., Sections 32 and 37.

21 There are complications. The servants were probably wearing some of the cast-off clothing of their employers; while selling used tea leaves was a traditional perquisite for cooks and housekeepers.

22 E.B. Schumpeter (1960) *English Overseas Trade Statistics, 1697-1808,* Oxford, Table XVIII.

23 The wage rate figures per day for unskilled labourers are: Oxfordshire 1700-1770 14*d.*, 1770-1800 16*d*; Lancashire 1700-1760 8-12*d.*, 1760-1780 18*d.*, 1780-1800 22-24*d.*; London 1700-1800 22-24*d.* E.W. Gilboy (1934) *Wages in Eighteenth Century England,* Cambridge, Mass. This trend is more likely to have been reinforced than diminished by movements in the volume of employment.

24 The figures, from fairly reliable import and excise statistics, are as follows. Population in England and Wales rose by 14 per cent between 1785 and 1800. Percentage increases for this group of commodities were: candles 33.8, soap 41.7, tobacco 58.9, strong beer 33.4, small beer 30.6, spirits 73.9, tea 97.7, printed fabrics 141.9.

25 Eversley, op. cit; N. McKendrick (1974) 'Home demand and economic growth', *Historical Perspectives* ed. N. McKendrick, London.

26 A. Smith (1796) *Wealth of Nations,* 8th edn, London, Book I, chapter 8.

27 Ibid., p.226.

28 Sir W. Petty (1691) *The Political Economy of Ireland,* quoted B.E. Supple (1961) 'Economic history and economic development', *Canadian Journal of Economic and Political Science,* XXVII.

29 A.E. Dingle (1972) 'Drink and working-class living standards in Britain, 1870-1914', *Economic History Review,* XXV; Dr R.H. Walters, of Jesus College, Oxford has constructed an index of labour productivity for the S. Wales coalmining industry and considered the various correlations.

PART II

TOPICS

9

THE SOCIAL STRUCTURE
IN THE
EIGHTEENTH CENTURY:
A CALCULATION BY
JOSEPH MASSIE

I

It is by now a commonplace that Gregory King, despite the many textual variations which mar his calculations, has weathered criticism more successfully than many later social and economic arithmeticians, whose great progenitor he was. His cross-section of the social structure of England and Wales, derived from the hearth tax returns, illuminates the state of the nation on the eve of the eighteenth century, as Patrick Colquhoun's complex calculations from the income tax, census and poor-relief records delineate it more precisely in the first decade of the nineteenth century.[1] From such men as these even guesses and interpolations, based on a wealth of demographic knowledge interpreted with perception born of experience and trained intelligence, are valuable as a record of probable fact, or at least of informed contemporary opinion which in its turn might well influence action. In short, they can give historical enlightenment without quantitative accuracy. For these reasons — the belief that King, Colquhoun, Beeke, Eden, Young, Chalmers and their fellows have added much to historical enquiry — a further calculation for the mid-eighteenth century drawn up specifically in the terms of Gregory King's main table, as was one similar enquiry of Colquhoun, deserves an audience. Dependent upon the perception and sense of responsibility of its author, the potential value of such a calculation (which is more directly comparable with both those mentioned than any other) made at the onset of developments which so radically changed the structure of British society is obviously very high, even though it has been ignored as much as the man, Joseph Massie. And if it does not prove to merit such responsibility as a guide to actuality there remains its value for the history of opinion — in showing assumptions current in the mid-eighteenth century about the structure of society.

Joseph Massie's incursions into political arithmetic stemmed always from robust polemical intentions. From what printed work remains he shows up as a disappointed government publicist writing in support of Pitt's policy during the Seven Years' War (during which time 22 out of 25 tracts — excluding the wartime broadsheets — were dated) and inveighing against the sugar planters, the cider tax, and against any increase in the malt and beer excises — the last plea reconcilable only with difficulty to his first loyalty. Yet, despite such overt intentions, one thing is certain: Massie stands out from the general press of pamphleteers both in ability and assiduity.[2] In content his work was much more responsible than the titles he chose suggested. Had Massie never written his score of pamphlets, few of which reach fifty pages, the important library of commercial and economic literature which he assembled (of which only the catalogue now survives in the British Museum) would have made him a man whose views merited consideration.[3] Had he published the elaborate history of commerce on which he had been working for more than twelve years his name might have overshadowed many more eminent contemporaries. Even more, had he in fact been appointed as official economic historian to the government (for such was his aim) neither man nor precedent could have been ignored.[4] As things stand, however, we must enquire briefly but critically into what writings do remain in order to judge the better that calculation from which the tables on pp.186-9 have been compiled. The important thing, quite apart from the objective validity of the estimate, is that here is an intelligent, well-informed observer, intimate with economic literature and commercial experience, who set himself to think out what changes he considered had come to English society and wealth in the seventy years since a similar complete survey had been attempted, and who evidently realized that a completely new estimate was needed, such being the scale of change which had occurred in the meanwhile.

Although very little is known about Massie's life in London, it is possible, as W.A. Shaw remarks, that he was personally interested in the sugar trade as a merchant or factor, since his main pamphlets bitterly oppose the endeavour of the West Indian planters to set up their own marketing organization.[5] An extensive knowledge of the trade and the conditions of sugar estates is set forth in a remarkable series of computations on the running costs per acre of a plantation, with profit and loss tables for the sugar islands as a whole.[6] Intrinsically reasonable, such calculations are important in giving evidence of his ability to marshall a large volume of facts in conformance with a preconceived pattern. The same bent is shown in tracts upon the reorganization of naval and marine detachments which display in tabular form the cost of all articles of equipment for men 'of each Class, Rank and Degree'.[7] Here is, in little, the cross-section of a deliberately articulated society, with its appurtenances, laid out in a methodical plan such as he delighted to devise, whether it be for the nation as a whole, or for such smaller and more formal hierarchies as a regiment or a charity institution. Similarly, he investigated in great detail the incidence of taxation on a family of each degree and income group (using most of Gregory King's social categories but not many of his income estimates) and that of excise taxation upon maltsters and brewers at every scale of production.[8] These essays in method show Massie's bent as a political arithmetician — he is as indefatigable a calculator and table-maker as Gregory King himself — and establish his claim to be considered as a competent, reasonable, even an ingenious reckoner. They are important for a further reason: unmistakable evidence is given of his acquaintance with unpublished information which, like King before him, he could only have obtained from access to the papers of the Treasury Board, the Navy Office, the Excise Commissioners and the unprinted session papers of the House of Commons.[9] Being at this time almost certainly in the pay of the ministry (although he published all his work through T. Payne of Castle Street, Charing Cross, independently and, he claimed, at his expense) this would not be surprising, while for such calculations as those of the broadsheet which forms the basis for the tables printed here, it would have been invaluable. As Massie himself observed, with King's work in mind: 'The tax upon Houses and Windows seems to have been originally considered rather as an *Index* whereby to form a Judgment of the *number of People* in this Kingdom and of their various *Circumstances* than as a *Fund of Supply* ...'.[10]

To such diligence in collecting and deploying statistical data shown in his later wartime tracts, Massie brought a strong interest in theory, which is most effectively revealed in the 1750 tract on the natural rate of interest. In purpose this is undoubtedly his least polemical publication, being dated well before the controversies to which he sold his pen, and it has rightly been given greater publicity by students of the history of economic thought than have his other works by economic historians.[11] Two years before Hume, this delivered a head-on challenge to Petty and Locke, the last an opponent of formidable stature, by maintaining that the evidence showed that the rate of interest did not vary according to the quantity of money, but rather depended upon the rate of profit in trade which in turn was a variable of the number of traders in relation to the state of trade.[12] Unlike Hume's *a priori* attack on Locke, this was an attempt to prove him wrong from empirical observation of corn prices and interest rates. The objective and the mode of attack, as the principle for discovering the true answer (or at least disproving a false one) were secure, even if his precise technique was naive.

A grasp of theoretical patterns in the light of which data might be assembled for testing, with an ability to display evidence on an imposing scale, distinguishes the serious student of economic and commercial phenomena from the *ad hoc* deliberations of ephemeral pamphleteers. The comments of Massie himself upon this double interest in pattern and facts accompany his discreet plea to be appointed official historian of the rise of British commerce, where he confesses an ambition to write:[13]

> ... an Historical Account of the Several Branches of Manufacturing and Trade belonging to this Kingdom and also ... another Treatise wherein I shall endeavour to establish upon fixed Principles that Branch of commercial Knowledge which may properly be called elementary, because it is deducible from self-evident Truths, and not at all connected with either the historical or the practical Branches.[14]

That Massie should have been so precise in formulating such an aim — common in other fields of scholarship in his time but precocious in the study of commerce and economics — that he should have set out self-consciously to become the Newton or the Locke of economic history is indeed remarkable. The result was to belie expectations. His draft of an open letter to the principal landholders of England in 1768 shows an embittered and disappointed man, whose high potential was never fulfilled and whose labour of 'above Twelve Years' collecting materials remained incomplete.[15] Only the tracts which do survive as polemical works reveal glimpses of such a stature, and thus help to give responsibility to those of his statistical investigations which are to be considered here.

II

The broadsheet in question is summarized in Table 9.1 after transposition out of Massie's original terms of reference where it was entitled *A Computation of the Money that hath been exorbitantly Raised upon the People of Great Britain by the Sugar Planters, in One Year from January 1759 to January 1790; shewing how much Money a Family of each Rank, Degree or Class hath lost by that rapacious monopoly, after I laid it open* ... [16] As with some of his other calculations elaborated for political debates, the figures remain more sober than his language. Its original form consists of a table showing all the social and economic ranks in society, similar to, although a little more elaborate than, Gregory King's, divided up in terms of whether their occupiers drank tea, coffee or chocolate — and so consumed sugar — once or twice daily, occasionally, or rarely, with the information for each group in society given as follows:

 (i) their annual 'Incomes or Expences'[17]
 (ii) the annual average consumption of sugar for one family in each group;
 (iii) 'money exorbitantly raised' by such consumption on each family;
 (iv) money exorbitantly raised on all the families in the group.

These calculations in sugar and money, with the arbitrary estimate of sugar consumed and, more particularly, the assumptions of the 'monopoly' proportion of the retail price, form the polemical part of the story — although even here his total conversion rates seem reasonable, the estimated consumption for England and Wales being 56,282 hogsheads, that of Scotland another 3,717 hogsheads, to make the round total 60,000 hogsheads 'the usual quantity consumed yearly'. He prices this at 23s.4d. per 112 lbs of muscado, both figures being reasonable averages consonant with customs entries and wholesale prices. From the information supplied here for each category it is a simple matter to convert the totals given in sugar and money back to the income and demographic patterns from which they were composed. The result of dividing (iv) by (iii) gives the number of families in each category. That multiplied by (i) gives the 'annual Incomes or Expences' for the whole group. When these groups are variously rearranged into occupational categories they form just such a table as King's and Colquhoun's, to the first of which in form they are quite clearly indebted.

The estimates of numbers in the groups stand open to judgement by all circumstantial evidence available, whether from potentially definitive categories such as naval and military officers, registered inn-keepers and ale-sellers, or by known information about wage-rates in London and the country. On the whole — although opinions may conflict on all groups — they seem likely enough to bear printing. The weekly rates, for example, follow Mrs Gilboy's estimates fairly closely, although I have posited for convenience a working year of 50 weeks' paid work which probably exaggerates the annual earnings of this group.[18] If Massie's single category 'Ale-sellers, cottagers' is placed with his other group 'Inn-keepers and Ale-sellers' their total numbers, 42,000, approximate to the registered total.[19] One may think that his figures for Common Soldiers (18,000), Military Officers (2,000) and Naval Officers (6,000) are low for a year of mobilization, but it may well be that only those actually in England at the time are considered, the object being to establish the pattern of sugar consumption at home. At the top of his scale the definable groups of peers are not listed separately, Spiritual Lords, Temporal Lords, Baronets, Knights, Esquires and Gentlemen together being given twelve income categories ranging from £20,000 to £1,200 which prevents an individual check. However, the upper bracket of £120,000 seems more apposite than King's average of £2,800 for temporal lords. On the other hand a clear anomaly seems to lie in his very large estimate for the lowest category of tradesmen — 125,000 with a total income of £5m. — far larger than any other single group. Colquhoun estimates a total of only 74,500 shop-keepers and tradesmen in

1812. By contrast Massie's estimates for group B in Table 9.3 (Professions) may appear wrongly depressed in comparison with that group in 1688. The income of Massie's 12,000 lawyers is £1.2m. as against King's £1.4m. for 10,000; and Massie's 16,000 Civil officers receive £0.96m. against King's 10,000 receiving £1.8m., which two categories more than account for the differences in the group as a whole. It is difficult to assess the merits of either judgement in absolute terms, but the contraction indicated by their comparison seems unlikely.

There are two parts of Table 9.1 which, when split up into the commonly accepted groupings according to function, as in Tables 9.2 and 9.3, need more comment. Within the agricultural group Massie assumes that freeholders have enlarged their numbers since 1688, which would certainly not conform to accepted conclusions. He gives 210,000 as their total (in three income groups) as against 155,000 farmers, 200,000 husbandmen and 200,000 labourers in the country (as opposed to London), this last group perhaps not being considered to have been employed on the land. Gregory King assumed there were 180,000 freeholders, 150,000 farmers, while in addition he has an undefined labour grouping of 364,000 'Labouring people and outservants' with 400,000 'Cottagers and Paupers'. Apart from the dangers which would be involved in accepting Massie's opinion about the numbers of freeholders, the doubtful comparability of King's categories of labour with those of Massie and Colquhoun (who both indicate in which sectors of the economy their labouring groups are working) leads to confusion. The whole concept of 'freeholder' in this context is uncertain. The scale of this is large enough to rob the neighbouring groups C and E — agriculture and industry — of meaning when developments between 1688, 1760 and 1804 are investigated, so that the alternative alignments must be considered. These are given in different allocations of Massie's figures in Tables 9.2 and 9.3, the first in accordance with King, the second with Colquhoun.[20]

Such a necessary procedure raises the issue of the comparability of results which is further discussed below. The significance of Gregory King's two general categories for labour should be a warning in itself: that in his day there was no clear-cut distinction between the agricultural and industrial 'sectors' of the economy, in this respect the nature of the putting-out system being precisely to distribute 'manufacturing' work to the less intensively employed families working on the land. The common complaints from employers in industry right through to the nineteenth century that their hands commonly deserted their workshops for the fields during the harvest season illustrates the same point. Similarly, King and Massie do not distinguish between merchant seamen and naval seamen, so that an arbitrary decision was necessary to place this category within group F (Trade and Distribution) rather than B (Forces).

The broad movements shown in Table 9.3 do not need stressing in a written commentary. Perhaps most important is the general fact that, in 1760, Joseph Massie thought that Gregory King's assumptions of numbers and wealth needed to be generally revised and increased, and that the new categories and wages for labourers might be separately considered. The decline in the total proportion of families earning their living in agriculture, and the even greater decline in the proportion of total income accruing to all families going to those in agriculture is clear. The upper social and income groups in group A and within groups B, E and F seem to have increased their wealth more rapidly than those in other sectors. From other evidence one would certainly posit a steepening pyramid of wealth, although lack of data on the numbers in each household do not allow *per capita* calculations to be made for direct comparison between King and Colquhoun.[21] The numbers in groups B and E increased the most rapidly after 1760. In group F (Trade and Distribution) Massie's reckoning on a much larger number of tradesmen (162,500) than Colquhoun (74,500), which was noted as an anomaly, raises the 1760 estimate above that for 1812, with the share of total income allotted to it. Such a gloss as this, with the high number of Massie's freeholders, raises an issue relevant for judging the objective veracity of all such calculations in ages or conditions where the reliability of the original figures may be questioned. From other non-quantitative evidence, the broad movements occurring within the economic and social structure of the country coming with the onset of the Industrial Revolution and concomitant commercial developments are testified historically. To give what precise figures contemporaries may have conceived for the cross-section of society in their own times, may not, as we have stressed, be superfluous historiographically. But, on the other hand, the *potential* weakness of their estimates is so great that, if the conclusions drawn from them are not those which have been already drawn from other kinds of evidence, the possibility — or even the probability — is that it is the figures which are wrong. They may be mistaken in conception or through miscalculation and misprinting; they may be selective, or fragmentary, or wrongly interpreted; while, if the new conclusions merely reinforce normally accepted ones, the exercise is historically, after all, only a demonstration of the obvious — a journey to an already known John O'Groats by way of a tediously distant Lands End. The hope that demonstrations of method have validity apart from their practical conclusions may be an equally forlorn compensation for historians.

III

In conclusion, some of the differences between these calculations of the incomes and expenses of all families in England and Wales, and modern concepts of national income accounting, with some of the dangers lurking in the no-man's land of exact comparisons between years so far apart as 1688, 1760 and 1803 need to be stressed: the figures cannot be squeezed very vigorously to extract twentieth-century conclusions. They show only the social distribution of wealth created by families, not national net 'added value' for the year. Colquhoun's other tables where, following Arthur Young, he tries to establish the net value accruing to all the various sectors of the economy are very different.[22] In turn, such a division of wealth as this, seen according to the social stratification, masks much of the more sophisticated economic significance which national income estimates provide. No clues are given here about annual increments not distributed to families, or not withdrawn for consumption: the increase in fixed capital or stocks, undistributed corporate wealth produced during the year whether by foreign-trading companies or domestic joint-stock companies, added values remaining abroad on private account, revenues of colleges, trusts, crown lands and the rest. Silence on saving and investment (which Massie avoids discussing by the simple device of making his totals 'annual Incomes *or* Expences' whereas King gave separate estimates for income and spending in each case), the absence of any mention of 'transfers' by taxation, poor relief or interest from government debt, make the 1760 figures less useful than either King's — with his astonishing conclusion that more than half the families in the land decreased the net wealth of the country — or Colquhoun's with more accurate calculations for rentier categories. The latter addition of £5 m. (or 2.25 per cent of total revenue recorded) for 50,000 persons living on such incomes and 'transfers', with certain other persons not found specifically listed in either Gregory King's or Joseph Massie's social structure — the sovereign and his household, pensioners of Chelsea Hospital and Greenwich Hospital, lunatics and the rest — may distort their comparability to some extent, but they fit in with the general groupings more reasonably than the larger outstanding category of labour. To conform with Gregory King's estimate of income, the £4.26 m. received by paupers from parochial rates in 1803 has been deducted from Colquhoun's totals.

Other combined functions which will be obvious to the most casual observer of eighteenth-century England affect group A, in which will be found prospering many persons taking a most successful part in the activities accorded to groups B-G: the merchant-, banker- and brewer-knights, the unpaid noble and gentle administrators and legislators, the magistrates, statesmen and multitudinous 'office-holders' of trusts and charities who escape record as such and get caught, at leisure, upon their estates. Were this not the case, bishops should be in the same group as their priests and deacons. This is true of all those who become 'landed' through the traditional metamorphosis of wealth derived from trade, industry and office (for whom group A is rather the club open to membership of those graduating most successfully from groups B-F); of those who were active in exploiting the mineral wealth beneath or who directly supervised the home farms upon their freehold land. Conversely, many of the freeholders who are classed in group C with others employed in agriculture may rather have been 'gentlemen and esquires' in their economic function — Adam Smith's 'mere' landed gentry, or those gentlemen farmers raising little except their hats.

One further major qualification must be made between the groups purporting to represent the contributions of agriculture and industry respectively to the total employment and total remuneration of families in England and Wales. Apart from the merging and coalescing of some agricultural and 'industrial' labour (mentioned above), certain important categories of artisans and skilled metal workers — although in their individual functions clearly not employed upon the land or with the harvest — as directly serve the agricultural sector and should therefore be properly caught in the agriculture group (C) rather than the industry group (E). They are, of course, the blacksmiths, wheel-wrights, certain mill-wrights, thatchers and their fellow-workers in villages and small market towns throughout the length and breadth of rural England. It would be impossible to determine accurately the dividing line between agriculture and industry which runs through these categories of employment, and certainly to make the attempt would mean violating the categories of the three estimates being considered here. Moreover, having once taken the first steps along this road it is difficult to know the most judicious stopping point, for the attorneys, bankers and land agents of those same market towns as clearly serve and profit from the agriculture which sustains them as blacksmith and farmers. One might then consider the maltster and brewer — as did all contemporaries — in the same light, and, at only single stages further on, the baker, the butcher, the soap-boiler and the tallow maker, the wool-merchant, even the wool- and worsted-manufactures themselves, at the heart of industrial England. To consider such a progression, with that side of the metal industries whose final products also went to serve domestic agriculture, is to emphasize that, before the nineteenth century, agriculture was the great prime mover of the economy and that most of the nation's industry was processing materials drawn from the harvest of crop, beast, or timber or in some way directly serving these harvests.

To force these issues to extremes would be as foolish as to ignore them altogether: in the end, members of society are as interdependent in their economic life as in their political union. They deserve stress here partly because it is so easy to transfer contemporary assumptions, instinctively held in the case of twentieth-century Britain, about the dichotomy of industry as against agriculture back into centuries where a fundamentally different economic structure makes them largely meaningless. The tables have been given in current prices, to which the application of a price index would have serious effects upon comparing the totals of *income* over time, as opposed to the *proportions* going to the various groups in society. This applies more particularly to Colquhoun's, which is that of an inflated year without convertibility, where a simple calculation might reduce the figure of £217.74m. to a level of about £132m. in 1760 prices.[23] Even this could not indicate any alteration in the structure of prices between the various sectors of the economy which had taken place in generations since 1688 or 1760. Such a consideration leads into the more recondite doubts about those increases in, and the appearance of, the income groups supplying goods and services which can be identified in money terms, and so added to the total of annual value accruing to society, which previously were included within a household economy, escaping both the market and the count: the home-brewing, home-baking, soap-making, butter-making, cheese-making and so forth with the changing proportion of clothes made up at home. The average consumption of beer per head, for example, does not seem to have increased greatly while an 'industry' developed which augmented the national income by no insignificant amount. Similar implications apply to the appearance of 'added value' in domestic service which these figures for households and families avoid as neatly as they do that of the unpaid contributions of housewife and farmer's wife which have harassed later economists. To this should be added the larger question of perquisites supporting money wages which has for long bedevilled attempts to evaluate economically meaningful wage-rates. All these things, with the consideration, too, that many services which appear and grow more important throughout the process of a society adapting itself to more vigorous industrial, commercial and, above all, urban life are not responsible in any real sense, for 'adding' to the wealth of that society, while some merely lessen the inconveniences which such a process entails, rob the comparisons between years far apart of some reality. Economic categories do not bear a fixed and frozen structural relationship to one another for very long, in which time changing quantities in any one category may be presumed to operate within the same frame of reference. Qualitative change is always affecting the assessments of quantitative measurement.

Notes

1 Gregory King, *Two Tracts*... ed. J.H. Hollander (1936) Baltimore; P. Colquhoun (1806) *Treatise on Indigence*. More detailed computations for the national income of Great Britain and Ireland were made (for 1812) by Colquhoun (1815) *Treatise on the Population and Resources ... of the British Empire*. There is a critical discussion of

King's work by P.E. Jones and A.V. Judges (1935-6) 'London population in the late seventeenth century', *Econ. Hist. Rev.*, VI; D. Glass (1946) 'Gregory King and the population of England and Wales ...', *Eugenics Review*, 37; (1950) *Population Studies*, II; J.P. Cooper (1967) 'The social distribution of land and men in England, 1436-1700, *Econ. Hist. Rev.*, 2nd Ser., XX; G.S. Holmes (1977) 'Gregory King and the social structure of pre-industrial England', *Trans. Roy. Hist. Soc.*, 5th Ser., XXVII.

I have used the versions reprinted in M.D. George (1953) *England in Transition*, Harmondsworth, correcting the slips in transcription: King assumes 5,000 Naval Officers (not 4,000) and 30,000 people in the families of Esquires (not 3,000); Colquhoun 5,000 shipowners letting ships (not 50,000). Although for the purpose of their general implications a comparative study of the various printed versions of King's table would be unnecessary, some discrepancies should be noted. The versions printed by Chalmers (1802) *Estimate of the Comparative Strength of G.B.*, Colquhoun, *Treatise on Indigence*, and Hollander are very different in detail.

Hollander's is the most accurate in relation to the B.M. Harl. MS. which appears to be the immediate basis for all of them. Colquhoun's, nevertheless, appears to be from a separate, although broadly similar, calculation, distinct in several cases for both numbers and incomes. There are several arithmetical inconsistencies in the version Hollander prints. To make the totals correct the income for each family of Esquires should be £400 (not £450), that of Gentlemen £240 (not £280). There in a slip in transcription for Cottagers' income which should total £2.6m. (not £2m.) — the higher figure being used by King when making the additions for his totals. In the other discrepancies noted, the income assigned to the individual family rather than the total income for all families in the social category or the total number of families, is mistaken. King, of course, never checked his manuscripts for publication. Any person who has seen his work (P.R.O. T.64/302) will endorse Chalmer's remark (op. cit., pp.112): 'He who was consulted on difficult occasions by a Board of Trade where Mr Locke sat could have been no mean man'.

2 Cunningham, who possessed many of Massie's tracts, said of the mid-eighteenth-century generation: 'The one man who united a profound knowledge of economic literature ... with a keen interest in the practical economic difficulties of his time, was Joseph Massie'. *Economic Journal*, I, 1891, p.81.

3 A list of Massie's writings, with an appreciation of him as a writer and calculator, appears in the introduction to the *Catalogue of the Massie Books and Tracts*, ed. W.A. Shaw, 1937. This is the main printed source for the meagre facts known about his life. Another appreciation and bibliography of Massie is given in Palgrave, *Dictionary of Political*

Economy. His library of fifteen hundred tracts and over five hundred other works was dispersed in 1760, but he continued to extend and revise the catalogue (B.M. Lansd. MS. 1849).

4 Massie remarked in one pamphlet (*A Representation Concerning Commercial Knowledge*, p.6): 'I am persuaded that no judicious Man will make any Difficulty of admitting that the Knowledge of Trade as a National Concern is *perfectly liberal.*'

5 Shaw, op. cit. pp.3-5.

6 J. Massie (1759) *A State of the British Sugar Colony Trade*; (1759) *Calculations ... relating to an additional Duty on Sugar ...*; *2 Broadsides* (on sugar and the trade of the sugar colonies).

7 J. Massie (1758) *A Proposal for Making a Saving to the Public ... in the Charge of Maintaining H.M. Marine Corps ...*

8 J. Massie (1755) *Plan for the Establishment of Charity Houses*; (1759) *Further Observations ... on the Foundling Hospital*; *Broadsides ...*; (1756, 2nd edn 1761) *Calculations of Taxes for a Family of each Rank, Degree or Class in 1 year.* In contrast to other writers Massie here is quite clear that, even if some of the figures have to be estimates, to discuss the percentage of income taken by taxation one needs to know (i) number of people, (ii) pecuniary amount of their income and expenses, (iii) the rise in prices caused by taxation, (iv) the total sum paid in taxes.

9 This is also apparent in his *Ways and Means for Raising the Extraordinary Supplies ...* (1757) which he dedicated to Pitt and Henry Bilson-Legge 'with great Deference and Humility'. He displays here intimate knowledge of published economic literature: the tract is really another set of annals of trade and industry *post* 1688.

10 J. Massie (1758) *Observations concerning the Tax upon Houses and Windows ....*

11 J. Massie (1750) *Essay on ... natural rate of interest* (reprinted and ed. J.H. Hollander, Baltimore, 1912); (1750) *Observations relating to the Coin of Great Britain.*

12 For Shaw (op. cit., pp.i-ii) this showed Massie at the height of his powers, 'a profound and acute thinker on abstract economics'. This is overstated, but Massie merits a place in any pre-Adam Smith survey of the field and has recently been accorded it by J.M. Low (1954) in *Manchester School of Economic and Social Studies*, XXII. From Massie's assumption of increasing numbers of traders he suggests that in the long run the rate of interest will tend to fall, being one of the first writers to have any conception of a long-term trend in interest rates.

13 J. Massie (1760) *A Representation Concerning Commercial Knowledge*, pp.17-8.

14 Ibid., p.1.

15 B.M. Add MS. 33,065, fol. 285, dated 9 January 1768. The letter complains of the failure of Pitt to pay the £1568 owing to him, doubtless for

pamphleteering. This letter gives one of the few references to where Massie lived in London — New Street, Covent Garden. Shaw mentions another address from Holborn; *Brief Observations* ... (1765) is written from Westminster, and the obituary notice in the *Gentleman's Magazine* of November 1784 gives Holborn as the place where he died.

16 Dated 10 January 1760. The broadside is bound up in an almost complete collection of Massie's tracts presented to the University Library, Cambridge by Dr Cunningham. Almost certainly this is the actual volume which the *D.N.B.* mentions as being sold in the Breadalbane Sale at Edinburgh in 1866.

17 A very similar scheme is also laid out in Massie (1756) *Calculations of Taxes for a Family of each Rank, Degree or Class* ... and (1765) *Brief Observations and Calculations on the present high Prices* .... In no case, to my knowledge, did Massie divide up any such table according to occupational categories, or categories of economic function.

18 E.W. Gilboy (1934) *Wages in Eighteenth-Century England*, Cambridge, Mass. p.220.

19 This was 40,166 for 1760: it had been above 45,000 before 1756. *Excise Statistics, 1162-1806*, (MS. Kings Beam House).

20 Colquhoun includes the estimate of labourers in manufacturing only with that of artisans. This prevents a direct isolation of the labouring force in industry which might be transferred to a 'general labour' group for direct comparisons with King.

21 Trying to calculate national income per head *within* the categories, even where numbers in each household are posited, raises nice problems about the payments to the hierarchy of servants. Where income was so unevenly distributed as in eighteenth-century England, and where data is so imprecise, 'welfare' calculations about national income per head seem pointless.

22 Colquhoun (1815) *Treatise on the Wealth, Power and Resources of the British Empire* ... Miss P. Deane has compiled a composite N.I. estimate from the various tables of Colquhoun to give a total of £404.95 m. for Great Britain and Ireland in 1812, at current prices (*Economic Development and Cultural Change*, IV, 1955). See also her 'Contemporary estimates of national income in the first half of the nineteenth century', *Econ. Hist. Rev.*, 2nd ser., VIII, 1956.

23 With E.B. Schumpeter's price index, *Rev. of Econ. Statistics*, XX, 1938, p.35.

Table 9.1 Joseph Massie's Estimate of the Social Structure and Income, 1759-1760, with that of Gregory King, 1688

Joseph Massie, 1760

Rank	Annual income or expenses per family £	Number of families	Total income £m
Temporal Lords	20,000	10	.2
Spiritual Lords	10,000	20	.2
Baronets	8,000	40	.32
Knights	6,000	80	.48
Esquires	4,000	160	.64
Gentlemen	2,000	320	.64
(n.b. These categories not distinguished individually in relation to their numbers or wealth)	1,000	640	.64
	800	800	.64
	600	1,600	.96
	400	3,200	1.28
	300	4,800	1.44
	200	6,400	1.28
Clergy, superior	100	2,000	.2
Clergy, inferior	50	9,000	.45
Persons professing the Law	100	12,000	1.2
Persons professing liberal Arts	60	18,000	1.08
Civil Officers	60	16,000	.96
Naval Officers	80	6,000	.48
Military Officers	100	2,000	.2
Common Soldiers	14	18,000	.252

Gregory King, 1688

Rank	Annual income per family £	Number of families	Total income £m
Temporal Lords	2,800	160	.448
Spiritual Lords	1,300	26	.338
Baronets	880	800	.704
Knights	650	600	.39
Esquires	450	3,000	1.35
Gentlemen	280	12,000	3.36
Clergymen	60	2,000	.12
,,	45	8,000	.30
Persons in the Law	140	10,000	1.4
Sciences and Liberal Arts	60	16,000	.96
Persons in offices	240	5,000	1.2
,,	120	5,000	.6
Naval Officers	80	5,000	.4
Military Officers	60	4,000	.24
Common Soldiers	14	35,000	.49

Category			
Freeholders	100	30,000	3.
,,	50	60,000	3.
,,	25	120,000	3.
Farmers	150	5,000	.75
,,	100	10,000	1.
,,	70	20,000	1.4
,,	40	120,000	4.8
Husbandmen (6s. per week)	15	200,000	3.
Labourers, country 5s.	12.5	200,000	2.5
,, London 9s.	22.5	20,000	.45
Manufacturers of Wool Silk etc., country 7s. 6d. per week	18.75	100,000	1.875
do. in London, 10s. 6d.	26.25	14,000	.375
Manufacturers of Wood, Iron, etc., country 9s.	22.5	100,000	2.25
Do. in London, 12s.	30	14,000	.42
Master Manufacturers	200	2,500	.5
,,	100	5,000	.5
,,	70	10,000	.7
,,	40	62,500	2.5
Merchants	600	1,000	.6
,,	400	2,000	.8
,,	200	10,000	2.
Tradesmen	400	2,500	.5
,,	200	5,000	1.
,,	100	10,000	1.
,,	70	20,000	1.4
,,	40	125,000	5.
Seamen, Fishermen	20	60,000	1.2
Inn-keepers, Ale-sellers	100	2,000	.2
Ale-sellers, cottagers	40	20,000	.8
	20	20,000	.4

Category			
Freeholder (better sort)	84	40,000	3.36
Freeholders (lesser)	50	140,000	7.0
Farmers	44	150,000	6.6
Labouring people and outservants	15	364,000	5.46
Cottagers and Paupers	6.5	400,000	2.6
Artisans and Handicrafts	40	60,000	2.4
Merchants and Traders by sea	400	2,000	.8
Merchants and Traders			
Shopkeepers and Tradesmen	200	8,000	1.6
Common Seamen	45	40,000	1.8
	20	50,000	1.0
Vagrants	2	30,000 (persons)	0.6

Table 9.2.   Groups and Categories

Gregory King	Joseph Massie		Patrick Colquhoun
Group A 1 Temporal Lords 2 Spiritual Lords 3 Baronets 4 Knights 5 Esquires 6 Gentlemen	As Gregory King, but the 6 categories divided up only by differences in income: i.e. the number of families in *each* category is not distinguished		As Gregory King, *plus* Sovereign's household and the incomes of those living with other families who receive interest from Funds
Group B 1 Clergy (all categories) 2 Persons in the law 3 Liberal arts and sciences 4 Office holders (civil and military) 5 Common soldiers	As Gregory King		As Gregory King, *plus* teachers, entertainers, keepers of institutions, naval seamen, revenue men
Group C 1 Freeholders 2 Farmers	(i)* Freeholders Farmers	(ii)* Freeholders Farmers Husbandmen	Freeholders Farmers Labourers in husbandry
Group D 1 Labouring people and outservants 2 Cottagers and paupers	Husbandmen, labourers in London and the country, manufacturers of wool, silk etc. wood, iron etc. in London and the country.	Labourers in London and the country	Pauper labourers Pensioners who work
Group E 1 Artisans and handicrafts	Master manufacturers	Master manufacturers, manufacturers in wool, silk etc., wood, iron etc., in London and the country	Manufacturers employing capital in various trades, artisans, labourers in manufactures, building mines, canals
Group F 1 Merchants and traders 2 Shopkeepers and tradesmen 3 Common seamen	Merchants, tradesmen, innkeepers and ale-sellers, cottagers and ale-sellers, seamen and fishermen		Merchants, bankers, tradesmen shopkeepers, shipowners letting ships for freights, warehousemen, clerks, hawkers and pedlars, innkeepers and publicans, merchant seamen
Group G 1 Vagrants			Vagrants, etc., lunatics, debtors in prison

*See p. 177 for the explanation of these alternative groupings in groups C, D, E.

Table 9.3 Comparison: Gregory King, Joseph Massie, Patrick Colquhoun

Group	King 1688 Families '000	Income £'000	Families %	% Total Income %	Massie 1760 (i) Families '000	Income £'000	Families %	% Total Income %	Massie 1760 (ii) Families '000	Income £'000	Families %	% Total Income %	Colquhoun 1803 Families '000	Income £'000	Families %	% Total Income %
A Nobility Gentry, Rentiers	16.6	6,286	1.2	14.1	18.	8,720	1.2	14.3	18.	8,720	1.2	14.3	27.2	32,800	1.4	15.1
B Professions, govt. service, forces, service pensioners	90.	5,770	7.6	12.9	83.	4,822	5.6	7.9	83.	4,822	5.6	7.9	172.5	31,300	8.9	14.4
C *Agriculture	330.	16,936	24.3	37.9	365.	16,950	24.8	27.7	565.	19,950	38.4	32.7	660.	48,540	34.2	22.3
D *General Labour	764.	8,060	56.2	18.	648.	10,870	44.1	17.8	220.	2,950	15.0	4.8	290.7	2,910	15.0	1.3
E *Manufactures	60.	2,400	4.4	5.4	80.	4,200	5.4	6.9	308.	9,120	20.9	15.	541.	51,080	28.0	23.5
F Trade, Distribution	100.	5,200	7.3	11.6	277.5	15,400	18.9	25.3	277.5	15,400	18.9	25.3	242.9	48,725	12.5	22.4
G Vagrants etc.	30. (persons)	60		.1					(persons)				234.5	2,385		1.1
Totals	1,360.6	44,712	100	100	1,471.6	60,962	100	100	1,471.6	60,962	100	100	1,934.3	217,740	100	100

England and Wales only.
Current prices.
Incomes received into families only.
Public receipts by poor excluded in King and Colquhoun, unmentioned by Massie.
*See Table 9.2 and p. 177 for the explanation of the two assessments of these groups in Joseph Massie's calculation for 1760.

10

THE PEOPLE'S MONEY
IN THE
EIGHTEENTH CENTURY:
THE ROYAL MINT,
TRADE TOKENS
AND THE ECONOMY

I

In Restoration England John Evelyn, the diariest, considered that his country had seen the last of tradesmen's tokens. Just then issues of copper halfpennies and farthings from the Royal Mint were driving them out of circulation. 'The tokens', he wrote,

> which every tavern and tippling house (in the days of late anarchy and confusion among us) presumed to stamp and utter for immediate exchange, as they were passable through the neighbourhood, which, though seldom reaching further than the next street or two, may happily in after times come to exercise and busy the learned critic what they should signify and fill whole volumes with their conjectures.[1]

One part of Evelyn's prophecy has certainly been true for a long time: literature about tokens began long ago. But in another sense he was mistaken. One of the most important and historically interesting outbreaks of token issuing came long after his death, in the late eighteenth and early nineteenth centuries. Only the latter series is described here. In fact, the appearance of every wave of tokens implied that the Royal Mints were failing to issue enough regal coins of small denomination to provide adequately for the nation's small change. There is an early example in the reign of Edward I, when token money was used for paying wages to labourers building castles in North Wales.

Trade tokens are well known to numismatists, and excellently documented by them. But they are not as familiar outside specialist circles as they might be.[2] The aim of the present chapter is to explain why informal currency — coins not of the realm but of the locality or the region — deserves wider recognition historically. They sometimes provide more direct evidence, and usually more vivid evidence, of historical events than regal coins. Unlike the coins of Greece and Rome in classical times, which recorded many historical events, those of Great Britain show nothing of the kind. Not one national event does an English coin after the Norman Conquest portray. It is otherwise with tokens. 'Issued by the people', wrote a Victorian antiquary, 'they tell of the people, and become imperishable records of that most important estate of the realm.... They indicate to us their occupations and their skill, their customs and modes of life ...'.[3]

The demands which occasioned the issues of tradesmen's tokens in the eighteenth century meant that the coins provide an unusually clear picture of the industrial and commercial activities they helped to promote. They become intriguing evidence for the history of Britain during this period, while for economic history, at a time when the foundations of a new industrial society were being laid they are of peculiar significance: they virtually provide an illustrated history of the Industrial Revolution.[4] This essay, however, is concerned to explain the needs which produced the tokens and the role they played in the economy.

II

By the end of the eighteenth century copper had been the Cinderella of the regal coinage for a long time, uncherished by the Mint and unprotected by the law. Queen Elizabeth had declined to authorize any issues of regal coins in base metal, as this was below the dignity of a monarch. With the great price inflation of the sixteenth century, fractions of a penny became inconveniently small when issued in the traditional silver coins. Hence the appearance of a wave of tradesmen's tokens in the early seventeenth century — mainly farthings, mainly issued by retailers in the larger towns in a strange assortment of metals. They received a reluctant blessing from the Crown in a proclamation of 1613. This underlined the function that tokens had in retail trade. 'Whereby such small portions and quantities of things vendible as the necessity and use specially of the poorer sort of People doth often times require', ran the announcement, '...the use of Farthing Tokens hath in itself a good end, tending to parsimony, and to the avoiding of waste in petty contracts and pennyworths; in which respect it cannot be but a great comfort to the poorer sort of the People.'[5] Here was the continuing justification for tokens: a recurrent failure by the Mint to provide enough coins for small change.

Striking copper farthings became a lucrative monopoly for favoured individuals able to obtain a royal licence in early Stuart times (falling under the general condemnation of such monopolies by Parliament). Their issue was still quite separated from the activities of the Mint. Only a decision by the Privy Council in 1672 for a large regal coinage of farthings and halfpence to drive the tokens out of circulation brought copper presses into the Mint at the Tower of London.[6] From then on regal base-metal coins — sometimes in an odd mixture of metals — kept down issues of private tokens, save in the more remote districts of the country. But the Mint usually stamped 'blanks' which had been prepared by some commercial firm, and sometimes even in making the dies they acted just as agents to contractors.

All this did not change the logic of the situation. Lack of initiative on the part of the Treasury (who gave orders to the Mint about how much copper had to be struck and when), therefore, produced all the old incentives for private issues of unofficial coins. Public policy after 1672 insisted that regal copper should be of full weight. This meant that its current value was broadly equal to the intrinsic value of the metal plus the cost of fabrication, rather than being of 'nominal value' (the exchange value being considerably higher than the intrinsic value). Such a policy gave a standing incentive for clipping, melting Mint issues, and forging lighter counterfeits, although the profits from so doing were lower than they were with gold and silver coins. Moreover, with every rise in the price of copper, which took the value of the metal in the coins above their exchange value, there was profit to be made in melting or exporting them. Re-coinages thus had to be frequent if regal copper coins were to be kept in circulation, and successive issues had to be of varying weights and sizes. The problems did not stop here. Copper was bulky in relation to its value (very much more bulky than gold and silver) so that there was a considerable burden of transport and distribution costs if regal copper was to be efficiently spread over the country. But the Mint possessed no distribution system of its own. There was no provision made in its coinage budgets for distribution costs.[7] A country banking system grew up only in the second half of the eighteenth century and even then did not usually handle copper for distant transfers. If a local business man wanted his banker to provide him with copper, he might have to pay heavily for the service.

A Committee of the Privy Council concerned with the coinage commented in August 1799 that 'an insuperable Difficulty has always occurred in getting them [*regal copper coins*] into Circulation in all parts of the Kingdom. Those who live at a Distance will not send for them and it is owing probably to this circumstance that the Counterfeits have been made use of in preference to those hitherto coined at the Tower.'[8]

This fact was important when different regions of the country were developing economically at very different rates, and hence were generating very different demands for coin, particularly for wages. When retailers in a large town might be burdened with an excess of copper, industrialists in fairly isolated mining or manufacturing communities could be desperate for small change.

In 1782 the state of the Mint was investigated by two Birmingham experts, Samuel and Francis Garbett (Samuel Garbett was a partner in the great Carron Iron Works of the Clyde, established in 1760, and knew very well the problem that industrialists faced in getting cash for wage payments).[9] Their report pinpointed the weaknesses of the whole system of issuing the copper coinage, and recommended that there be a strict enforcement of laws against counterfeiting copper coins. Magistrates were to be given the power to deface counterfeits. It was proposed that a new Mint issue of higher quality copper coin should be made, and an allowance granted to customers of the Mint for carriage, for interest on their capital, and for their pains in distributing copper. This allowance was an essential complement to the other measures, for without it there was very little demand on the Mint for copper coinage. Had the advice of the Garbett brothers been taken there might have been no tokens to form the subject of this enquiry.

Many public authorities in eighteenth-century England were inefficient and corrupt. This was one of the prices the nation paid for the patronage system in politics. But there was a special reason why the Mint did not take its responsibilities for providing the country with copper coins very seriously. The fact was that, throughout the eighteenth century, coins in the base metal were not thought of as proper currency at all, even though the Mint had long overcome the Tudor reluctance to coin any copper. In 1757, Joseph Harris, an Assay Master, could remark: 'Copper coins with us are properly not money, but a kind of *token* passing by way of exchange instead of parts of the smallest pieces of silver coin; and useful in small home traffic.'[10]

The magical qualities of the two precious metals were in no sense shared by copper, which was rather condemned as the favourite agent of their debasement. It was a common metal, without easily agreed standards of purity, yet with many utilitarian uses. There was a fluctuating supply, which led to disturbing price changes. In a sense, therefore, all copper coins were 'token' money, and substitutes for gold and silver coins. Much of the regal copper coinage had little to do with the Mint. Indeed, the greatest recoinage of regal copper in the eighteenth century (that of 1797-9) was completely contracted to Matthew Boulton, the famous Birmingham manufacturer. Two reasons for this failure to fulfil the normal responsibilities of a Royal Mint were offered by investigators into its faults: firstly, 'the Mint not being sufficiently efficient', and secondly, 'the copper coinage not being considered as properly belonging to the Mint'.[11]

Potential token issuers in the eighteenth century had the way cleared for them by official practice and opinion. Moreover, they had the good seventeenth-century precedent to go on, whereby their activity although a 'notorious abuse of the royal prerogative', was 'winked at'.[12] Even towns began to issue them under acts of Common Council with the authority of the Mayor. In any case, legal penalties for forging copper were slight compared with the fate of forgers of gold and silver money, who could face death at Newgate gaol.[13] Up to 1744 the offence was merely a misdemeanour. Following a new statute of that year, it became punishable with only two years' imprisonment. Even though penalties were increased in later years, the authorities never possessed adequate power to search premises for the illegal moulds and dies, nor did the possession of counterfeit copper become an offence. In all, few prosecutions were initiated by the public authorities (despite the Mint's demand in 1742 that forging copper be made a felony).

Striking coins which did not *exactly* resemble the regal issues remained unpunishable. Thereby the way was still open for coining 'evasive' halfpence, as they were called, which were not exact copies of the Mint coins, and thus not legally forgeries.

All things considered, it was as though the upper classes — those ranks of society mainly represented in Parliament and sitting as Justices of the Peace — not being much involved with copper currency in their own dealings were not concerned about the state of the regal copper coins, their forgery or the issue of private substitute coins. The sanctity of the guinea was to be preserved at all costs. Silver also needed protection (and when a rush of silver tokens appeared in 1811-12 the government took quick action against them) — but copper went largely by default. It was against this background that the token-makers operated.

A large coinage of copper farthings and halfpence (coins struck both by the Mint and private contractors) in the last decade of the seventeenth century satisfied public needs for some years.[14] No new copper coins were issued from the Mint between 1702 and 1717, but almost every year from 1718 until 1754 (apart from 1825-8) saw between £1,000 and £10,000 issued in copper. These issues of regal coins did not prevent the appearance of light-weight forgeries or, after 1742, of the new 'evasive' halfpence. Contemporaries said that the forgers merely 'published their works in a new edition'. Occasional outbreaks of official hostility to them were supported by brief flurries of Mint issues, in 1762-3 and 1771-5 (when 200 tons of halfpence and farthings worth £46,000 were issued). Apart from these years, no regal copper coins appeared between 1755 and 1779. The Mint, in fact, complied with a request from the butchers, bakers and grocers of London who were swamped with copper coins. They were not legal tender above 6*d*, hence impossible for settling debts or taxes. Nothing was worse than too much copper, for such tradesmen, except it be too little. This strongly suggests that the main difficulty was the maldistribution of copper in the face of an increasing demand for it from growing provincial centres — for the main issuers of tokens in the seventeenth century had been in fact the London 'Vintners, Tapsters, Chandlers, Bakers and other like Tradesmen and their customers'.

This excess and the leniency of the law meant that the lightweight forgeries drove many Mint coppers into the melting pot. There were estimates that about half the copper coins in circulation around 1780 were 'Brummagens' (as the 'Birmingham halfpennies' were called).[15] The Mint thought that the numbers of this fraudu- lent coin had exceeded their own copper by 1787 and Matthew Boulton reckoned to receive two-thirds counterfeit halfpence in change at toll gates on the turnpike roads between Birmingham and London. Other estimates were even higher — and everyone agreed that fraudulent issues were 'beyond calculation'.[16] Most blanks for the forgeries were struck in Birmingham, but London was the main centre for imposing the final image on them. 'Scarce a waggon or coach departs from the Metropolis,' remarked a magis- trate, 'which does not carry boxes and parcels of base coin to the camps, seaports and manufacturing towns' (the places where demand for coin was highest).[17]

Such a large-scale trade became highly organized and much subdivided, in common with other offshoots of the parent Bir- mingham industry of button-making. It was also very profitable. Patrick Colquhoun, the famous London J.P., spoke of one successful forger who retired from business after seven years, during which time he had produced £200,000 in counterfeit silver. But the trade brought riches only to those few who were lucky, highly skilled and self-disciplined. 'Prudence', said a commentator, 'rarely falls to the lot of men who live by acts of criminality.' Dealers in a large way of trade employed artisans to do the actual coining of counterfeits at a commission of 8 per cent. As in legal minting the blanks were first turned on a lathe. They were then stamped, often with slightly worn dies. After that came processes unique for the forging trade. The coins were 'rubbed with sand- paper and cork; put into *aquaforte* to attract the silver to the surface; rubbed with common salt and next with cream of tartar, warmed in a shovel ... before the fire, and, last of all, rubbed with blacking to give the money the appearance of having been in circulation.' Two persons could produce £25 a day in forged silver. Various other forms of forging used casting processes rather than striking and minting. Most of these sophisticated devices would be lavished on imitations of silver coins (produced in a mixture of silver and copper or in copper coated with silver). It was less economic to lend such an air of age and probity to the spurious copper money, which was usually imitated in the same metal. Its general character was clear: ill-conceived, shoddily produced and deficient in weight. Imitation copper coins of 36*s* face value could be bought new from a forger for 20*s*. Not only was this a 'token' coinage in the way that even regal copper was not (being lighter than its real worth), but it was a bad token coinage at that.

III

Such a complete failure to provide adequate small change in reputable coins lay behind the re-emergence of tradesmen's tokens in the 1780s — and justified it. A proposed Mint re-coinage of 1787 was thwarted by a sharp rise in the price of copper (which would also have increased the incentives to melt existing regal copper) and this seems to have been the deciding factor for Thomas Williams of the Anglesey Copper Mines Company.[18] Its first penny token, with the Druid's head on the obverse and the cypher 'P.M.Co.' (for Parys Mines Company) on the reverse appeared in that year. It was not quite the first of the new tokens, although it was the first to be struck in large quantities. In common with some other concerns, the Adelphi Cotton Company had been counter-marking ordinary halfpennies from the Mint, undertaking to redeem them at 4*s* 6*d* each. The Anglesey coin was a rather different sort of 'token', however, for all Thomas Williams' coins, in common with those of the other reputable issuers, were of full weight, finely struck, and well designed. One or two very isolated mining communities had a longer tradition of private currency than this — there are halfpenny tokens of the Lowther Colliery, Whitehaven, struck before 1784, and a similar one for the Curwen Mine, Workington, actually struck at the Mint when Isaac Newton was Master in 1725. There is a Suffolk halfpenny token of 1750. All these were spasmodic, widely scattered, small-scale issues. Thomas Williams' 1787 token was the immediate forerunner of a vast series.

It was no accident that this first major issuer of tokens (and the largest of them all) was an industrial magnate operating mines in Anglesey, smelting works in several widely scattered places and even his own coining presses in Birmingham.[19] The second was John Wilkinson, one of the greatest iron masters of the eighteenth century, operating blast furnaces and foundries in four different sites. He also began a long series of tokens in 1787, some of the later ones being struck by Matthew Boulton at Birmingham (himself with large-scale interests in copper mining and smelting).[20] In contrast to the seventeenth-century issues, the main impetus behind this new beginning came from industrialists. As Lord Liverpool wrote in 1805 in a famous treatise on coins: 'Many principal manufacturers are obliged to make coins or Tokens to enable them to pay their workmen and for the convenience of the poor employed by them; so great is the demand for good Copper Coins in almost every part of the Kingdom.'[21]

The central feature of the industrial changes which were gathering strength in the second half of the eighteenth century was the application of bigger fixed capitals to production, as water-power and then steam-power became the prime motive forces for mines and mills. Technology was becoming massive in scale in certain key industries. These changes involved the bringing together of large numbers of workers in the single industrial plant. With much of this industry sited by the availability of coal, ores, or water-power, industrial communities often grew up in isolated districts. By their growth they dramatically altered the economic and social patterns of localities. At the centre of the bond between worker and master was a money wage — and money wages in the rising industrial districts were higher than in agricultural areas. For obvious reasons payments in kind usually formed a lower proportion of a worker's income. The shortage of cash, and the absence of shopping facilities in isolated sites, increased the incentives for industrialists to provide 'truck' payments at the shop — and to provide the shop. They might also be led to pay wages at intervals longer than a week — and to provide their own cash to do it. For doing any of these things industrialists incurred great blame. Yet they were not necessarily suffering from a double dose of original sin. In the hands of unscrupulous employers, indeed, all these devices (equally with company housing and other sponsored facilities) increased the opportunities for exploitation. For honourable men they mitigated the disadvantages of living in such newly grown communities.

Less directly, the new industrial communities provided the basis for the unprecedented growth of towns and the urban way of life (particularly in mill towns where many women and girls had factory employment) itself increased the need for money. In village England many commodities were not usually purchased in shops or markets, for jam, butter, bread, beer, cheese, clothing, vegetables and other things were often made at home. In town the list of things bought steadily increased, and with it the need for ready money for these retail transactions. The Industrial Revolution and its consequences bred the need for small change to satisfy wages and retail purchasing on a scale quite unknown in Britain up to that time. The regal coinage, as we have described, was bad enough to make the need for private coinage felt very widely. But industrialists, such as Thomas Williams and John Wilkinson, experienced more immediate and stronger pressures for cash than other sorts of people, being responsible for vast weekly wage bills in rapidly growing enterprises.

The changing economic and social circumstances which industrialization brought with it demanded equivalent change in traditional institutions. The response of the public authorities in providing small change — as in so many other aspects of public responsibility at this period — was quite inadequate to cope with the problem. There was no plan or institution with responsibility for distributing copper rationally according to need. In the absence of public provision, industrialists and others were forced to create for themselves private institutions and devices which enabled the momentum of industrial change to be maintained. The social and economic needs of the community were strong enough to invoke a response by determined men. Their issue of private tokens was a minor instance of this general truth. Many tokens actually recorded the need which called them into existence (even where their light weight suggests that coiners and issuers made handsome profit from the issue) — 'For Change not Fraud', 'To Facilitate Trade', 'For General Convenience', 'For the Accommodation of the County', 'A Remedy for the Shortage of Change' and many other variants.

The copper companies had, of course, a more particular inducement to issue tokens than other industrialists, deriving profit from enlarging the market for copper and stimulating demand. The extent to which this motive dominated their activities is not clear, but it undoubtedly influenced Boulton as a man connected with copper mines and smelting.[22] Copper companies, as iron works, were usually operating on a large scale with mines and smelting operations in different places. Their demands for wage payments were therefore large, and they were producing raw materials for tokens. It was, therefore, fairly simple for the copper magnates to supply their own cash as tokens. The actual weight of metal in the token issues of the Anglesey Copper Company must have been only a small fraction of their total production of copper, and hence the manufacture of tokens was not particularly important to them as a market for copper. Moreover, because Williams kept scrupulously to 'full weight' policy he rejected the opportunities for making unscrupulous profits from light-weight coin. Apart from the advantages to the firm in supplying cash for wages, the other gains from tokens, when they escaped from the industrial communities into general circulation, were the more subtle ones of prestige and advertisement, for the coins were well made and popular. In 1789, for example, the magistrates and traders of Stockport asserted at a public meeting that they would 'take no other halfpence in future than those of the Anglesea Company'. All these reasons combined to make the copper companies one of the most important group of token-issuers. For Boulton, and the copper companies from which he bought, the main prize to be sought was always the exclusive contract for a re-coinage of regal copper. This would put the large number of token-strikers out of business and bring all the profits of issuing copper coin, and all the demand for copper that entailed, into the hands of one firm.

The disadvantages of using local tokens as a form of national currency were still manifold. Some were an inevitable consequence of any local currency. Travellers beyond the natural circulating area of particular tokens would have the inconvenience of exchanging them for coin of the realm, or the risk that they might only be accepted at a discount, or for their intrinsic value as metal rather than their face value as coins. Shopkeepers had to keep complicated sorting boxes in which tokens could be classified according to their issuers in neighbouring towns and they could be a nuisance for bankers transferring them back to their places of origin for redemption. The workman paid in such tokens might find himself at a disadvantage if they were of light weight and redeemable (or acceptable by shopkeepers) only at something less than their face value. His security, and that of all who accepted them, might lie in the intrinsic weight and fineness of the coin, or might rest in the promise of convertibility made by the issuer (and usually announced, with his name, on the coin). If this was upheld, then the probity of the issue could survive a weight lighter than its intrinsic value. But it needed a bold workman to present tokens to his master and demand their face value in coin of the realm.

In general, the personal issues of known individuals lived up to this responsibility and were far better money than the fraudulent copies of regal coins. Indeed, largely because of the flood of private tokens the Government was enabled to prevaricate for another decade before finally taking the plunge and ordering a copper re-coinage. But the tokens suffered the traditional fate of success by attracting imitations and counterfeits. All the inducements for coining false regal copper applied to the counterfeits of trade tokens. The fraudulent tokens were lighter and cruder than the originals. They might not be redeemed at their par value. Less responsible manufacturers issued their own tokens without the standards upheld by the originators of the movement, seeking to make a direct cash profit out of the issue. Then the fashion spread for quite other reasons. The lesser advantage of self-advertisement became the main object of the game for many retailers, their tokens being little more in function than hand bills, but often circulating as coin despite this. With such issues there was seldom any promise of convertibility and seldom full weight. A wave of other tokens, which had no precise source, appeared when the acute shortage of small change from the Mint had produced a burst of public enthusiasm for the substitutes. These had no known issuer and no known person to whom they might be presented for their face value in cash. If they were much lighter than their intrinsic value, or if the price of copper subsequently dropped, such tokens would be a liability to their possessors, should a day of retribution come when they were prohibited by law or lost their currency.

Yet other issues owed their existence to the craze for collecting tokens which rapidly followed the original appearance of 'genuine trade tokens'. Here tokens merged in function with medals struck to commemorate special events, a very much older tradition. Particular coin dealers, like Thomas Skidmore of Holborn or Peter Kempson of Birmingham, put out whole series of architectural studies, of churches, public buildings, Oxford and Cambridge colleges and the like. Thomas Spence, a wild radical, conducted his own political propaganda in this medium in great style. Patriotism took a hand during the French wars and several military and naval heroes found themselves, and the names of their victories, enshrined on halfpenny tokens passing current 'for the convenience of trade'.

Finally, token-striking for collectors became a justification (and

a trade) in its own right. Dealers and collectors persuaded medal-
lists to match up dies with different obverses and reverses into what
were called 'mules' to increase the permutations possible from
existing sets of tokens, thus creating artificial 'rarities' for their
cabinets. Descriptive literature for collectors first appeared in 1795
in the *Virtuoso's Companion*. Charles Pye of Birmingham published a collectors' guide in 1796 engraving 180 different examples
'from the originals in his own possession'.[23] He thought the last
two years had seen the appearance of 'prodigious quantities' of
tokens, many executed 'for the sole purpose of furnishing the
collectors'. All these extensions from original trade tokens —
counterfeits, mules and collectors' pieces of different sorts — mean
that the present-day collector has to check any token carefully in
the catalogues. At the time they increased the difficulties of using
tokens as money by encouraging a deterioration in standards as
widespread in its own way as the original failings of the regal
copper coinage.

Token-mania coincided with a sharp rise in the price of copper
following the threats of war in 1792. British 'cake' copper rose
from under 90s to over 100s per cwt. Such a price rise enlarged the
profits to be made from melting full-weight coins and tokens, and
increased the slide towards re-mintings of ever lighter, more
irresponsible money. By 1797, things had become so bad that only
a large official re-coinage could put them right. This came in July
1797 with Boulton's massive contracts from the Treasury, buttres-
sed with more terrible legal threats against counterfeiting. Over
1,000 tons of twopenny pieces (veritable 'cartwheels' weighing two
ounces apiece), pence, halfpence and farthings poured out of the
Soho Mint in the next two years, effectively driving most tokens
out of circulation, and preventing new issues. Boulton had seen to
it that an allowance had been made for distribution costs in his
contract.[24] But copper continued to rise in price during the war,
reaching 200s per cwt. in 1805-6. Because the new coins were still
issued at 'full weight' on Treasury orders, they went rapidly from
mint to melting pot once more. Boulton's contract of 1799 for
halfpennies and farthings had enabled him to coin them slightly
lighter to take account of this; but the new weights did not
anticipate a continuing rise in copper prices. Already, by 1802,
petitions had been addressed to the Committee of the Privy Council
on Coin from traders in Edinburgh, Glasgow and Aberdeen. In

April 1804 they had evidence of a great shortage of copper 'particularly from the Northern parts of the Island'. By 1805 Boulton's work needed to be done again, and he was commissioned to coin a further 1,000 tons of coppers in 1805-7, as well as 600 tons for Ireland.

This issue seems to have done its work too well. Reports to the Committee claimed that 'no other Copper Coin has been seen in circulation in the Country to the North of Stamford'. By May 1808 petitions had started coming in from London tradesmen (particularly the brewers) that stocks of Boulton's coins, unwanted and unusable, were piling up in their vaults. Boulton was told not to send any more into the capital until the brewers had 'disburthened themselves' and his agent John Woodward had taken nearly £10,000 in copper from four leading brewers by February 1809, which he distributed to persons who had been ordering from Boulton at the Soho Mint. The brewers were particularly liable to receive large quantities of coppers because they were London's largest scale cash-traders at this time, selling a cheap product in mass demand. They brewed about one-and-a-half million barrels annually, which represented a consumption of over fifty gallons per head in London, sold at 5*d* per quart (but not all of this was drunk in London).

Other complaints of a surfeit of copper — all Boulton's — came in from Canterbury and Liverpool, so completely had the tables been turned. Not only had most tokens been driven out, and new issues prevented, but even the Mint became embarrassed. Under sharp advice from Sir Joseph Banks arrangements were made, but not in fact put into force until 1814, to have the badly worn 'Tower halfpence' (issued between 1719 and 1775) called in.

In time the wheel turned again, and gluts in some places could still coincide with shortages in others, despite Boulton's more efficient methods of distributing his issues over the country. More copper tokens appeared, mainly in 1810-12 as evidence of the recurrent shortages, even though surpluses of regal coin with the London brewers were again transferred to the provinces. Many more penny tokens appeared in the 1810-12 issues — possibly because of the example given by the regal coinages of 1797, when copper pennies were struck for the first time. Issues of pennies were perhaps encouraged by the continuing rise in prices under wartime inflation, which made relatively more retail purchases demand the bigger coins. Fewer retailers' copper tokens seem to have appeared in this new wave of issues, which was much smaller than that of 1787-97. Some civic bodies, such as Workhouse Boards of Guardians and Overseers of the Poor, took part in the movement.

IV

By far the most interesting theme of the 1811-12 tokens, however, was that considerable numbers of silver coins, particularly shillings, appeared, whereas previous issues had been virtually confined to the baser metal. One of the only private silver coins of the previous decades had been a version of John Wilkinson's famous token, with his bust on the obverse and a ship on the reverse. It was issued for 3s 6d, but a hundred only were struck, so it remains doubtful if they were meant for currency. Striking private currency in a precious metal was a far bolder breach of the royal prerogative, of course, than issuing copper. Only a desperately poor regal silver issue and a recent precedent of Bank of England tokens struck in silver provided sufficient inducements. Silver tokens, like their copper counterparts, can only be understood in relation to this context. Since 1758 there had been virtually no Mint issues of silver, save for an isolated £55,000 coined in 1787. The same hazards applied to these regal silver coins as to regal copper — with meltings, clippings and counterfeiting. The price of silver often stood above its price when in currency (at the weights the Mint were issuing silver coins), giving a standing incentive for melting and exporting it. By the 1790s the silver coin was 'notoriously defective', according to the Committee on Coin, with an average deficiency in weight of 45 per cent in the smaller denominations. It was a moot point whether the silver or the copper coins of the realm were in the worse mess.

Silver was probably more important than copper in wage payments, although not as important in retail transactions. Unskilled labourers received between 10s to 15s per week, at this time, and skilled from perhaps 20s to 30s depending on their trades. 'Silver Coin', remarked the Committee, 'is the Coin which the Poor principally use....'[25] The interesting question, therefore, is why there was no flood of silver tokens to complement the copper issues after 1787, particularly as industrialists, with the problem of getting cash to pay wages, were behind so many of the token issues.

There is no certain answer to this, but a variety of restraints probably operated. The legal position was not as clear-cut, and the penal deterrent was higher if the authorities decided to take action against the infringement of the royal prerogative. Further, the burden of distributing silver (transport costs as a proportion of its value) was much less. It flowed very much more freely through the banking system in response to local needs and therefore the great problems of distribution which so affected copper were largely avoided. Further, manufacturing 'interests' in silver were not as powerful as the copper companies, always on the watch to boost sales.

Proposals to mint new silver in 1797 came to nothing. The crisis was scotched, but not finally resolved, by the extraordinary expedient of letting the Bank of England issue captured Spanish dollars (for 4s 9d) counter-marked with a small impression of George III's head.[26] A city wit immediately coined the couplet:

The Bank to make their Spanish Dollar pass
Stamped the head of a fool on the head of an Ass.

These were quickly recalled (only a fraction of the 2.3 million stamped were ever issued) as well as a few privately commissioned shillings, but further large issues of 5s pieces were made in 1804. Counterfeiting the small inset stamp of the king's head proved too simple, so Boulton was called in again to completely overstamp the Spanish dollars as 'Bank of England dollars' in their own right.

Several other large issues were made until 1815 (some of them still with the 1804 dies) and they were supplemented in 1811 with Bank of England silver tokens of 3s and 1s 6d, the nominal value of the larger coin being 5s. Undoubtedly these Bank of England tokens did a great deal to resolve the problem of shortage of silver currency, but the emphasis had been deliberately on the larger coins. The authorities were persuaded that a direct challenge to the bulk of defective coin in circulation, which was both silver and copper in the smaller denominations, would bring hardship upon its holders — the poor — if it suddenly ceased to be current. This explains the decision in 1797 to coin only pennies in copper, and not halfpennies. Originally, the hope was that the larger coins would gradually influence the circulation of the defective issues of lower denominations, but, in both cases, this had to be abandoned for a more directly competitive issue of smaller coins. In the event, the Bank tokens of 3s and 1s 6d whetted the public appetite for such unofficial silver coin. They did not satisfy all the demands for it. Thus these smaller Bank tokens directly prepared the way for the private issues. As was said at the time: 'Since Ministers have transferred to the Bank of England one of the prerogatives of the Crown ... every other Bank, Banker, Agent, Merchant and Shopkeeper has taken it for granted that an equal right ... is the privilege of all.'

V

These issues of silver tokens began the attack on the whole idea of the state (and the Mint) contracting out of its responsibilities for providing the nation with its small change, leaving such provision mainly to spontaneous local market forces and private initiative. Although some Bank of England issues went on, general — if tacit — permission for issuing private silver tokens was withdrawn by an Act of Parliament in July 1812. Petitions from Newcastle and elsewhere pleaded for a re-coinage of both silver and copper because the light-weight local tokens were becoming more depreciated as time went by. Action soon followed. Huskisson, with the weight of responsible business opinion behind him, put pressure on the Chancellor of the Exchequer in the House of Commons in April 1812. The Mint, meanwhile, had been completely re-equipped and modernized under Matthew Boulton's direction. He supplied the steam engine, the bulk of the new machinery, and even the skilled fitters to supervise it.[27] At last it was prepared to undertake its old duties again. The final date of outlawing private silver tokens had to be postponed. Then at long last in February 1817, twenty-three artillery train waggons, drawn by six horses apiece and accompanied by a military escort, rumbled north from London to distribute the new Mint coins. One chapter in the token coinage had virtually closed.

The move to close in on the copper tokens began in Parliament at almost the same time, where they were accused of intensifying the banking crisis of the year before. A bill was passed in July 1817 forbidding further manufacture of copper tokens and ordering that all in circulation be presented to their issuers for redemption by January 1818 — with a few exceptions granted to 'poor-relief' tokens which were extended into the 1820s. As with the silver tokens, however, legal prohibitions were not very effective until massive issues of regal coinage took place, and these did not begin until 1821.[28] They were the first from the Mint since 1775. Then the end came quickly, and with it social hardship for those caught with their savings in the form of anonymous, and therefore unredeemable, copper tokens. In practice it could prove equally impossible to redeem tokens which had strayed far away from their place of origin or whose issuers had moved out of the district or had died. Coiners, out for what profit they could get, had once more brought all tokens into discredit. A movement which had begun by being a genuine private response to a failure in public responsibility ended in a sordid liquidation. Moreover, the holders of copper coin were usually humble people who could ill afford such depreciation of their savings, where they had any. The message inscribed on such a number of tokens, 'For change not fraud', was now belied in the eyes of many. Only collectors and historians were left to profit — as they so often do — from the makeshift arrangements forced upon a harassed generation.

Notes

1 J. Evelyn (1697) *Numismata.*
2 For catalogues see R. Dalton and S.H. Hamer (1910-17) *Provincial Token Coinage of the Eighteenth Century*; J. Atkins (1892) *Tradesmen's Tokens of the 18th Century*; W.J. Davis (1906) *Nineteenth-Century Token Coinage*; and specialist numismatic journals.
3 L. Jewitt in *J. of Brit. Arch. Assn.*, XXX, 25.
4 For an illustrated survey of the coins, and the evidence they provide of economic activities, see P. Mathias (1962) *English Trade Tokens: The Industrial Revolution Illustrated* London, pp.31-62; F.D. Klingender (1943) 'Eighteenth-century pence and ha'pence', *Architectural Review*, XCIII.
5 Quoted J. Craig (1953) *The Mint*, Cambridge.
6 C. Oman (1931) *The Coinage of England*, Oxford, pp.334-5.
7 Craig, op. cit., p.142.
8 P.R.O. BT.6/126, 1 August 1799.
9 *Parl. Papers*, 1837, XVI, Select Committee on Royal Mint, App.34.
10 J. Harris (1757) *Money and Coins*.
11 *Parl. Papers*, 1837, XVI, Select Committee on Royal Mint, App.34 and Q. 1868.
12 T. Snelling (1766) *A View of the Copper Coin and Coinage of England*, preface.
13 F.P. Barnard (1926) 'The forging of English copper money in the eighteenth century', *Numismatic Chronicle*, pp.341-60.

208   *The Transformation of England*

14 For sequence of regal issues see Craig, op. cit.; R. Ruding (1840) *Annals of the Coinage*; W.A. Shaw (1896) *History of Currency*.
15 F.P. Barnard, op. cit.
16 Lord Liverpool (1805) *Treatise on the Coins of the Realm*.
17 P. Colquhoun (1797)...*Police of the Metropolis*.
18 For copper prices see T. Tooke (1838) *History of Prices*, vol. I, p.400.
19 J.R. Harris (1964) *The Copper King*, Liverpool.
20 T.S. Ashton (1924) *Iron and Steel in the Industrial Revolution*, Manchester.
21 Lord Liverpool, op. cit., pp.198-9.
22 See *Parl. Papers*, 1799, 1st Ser. X, Committee on Copper Mines.
23 C. Pye (1796) *Provincial Copper Coins or Tokens issued by the Years 1787 and 1796*.
24 Much of the following text for 1798-1809 is based on MSS. in P.R.O. BT.6/117-127, Committee of Privy Council on Coin.
25 BT.6/127 10 Feb. 1798.
26 See M. Phillips (1900) *The Token Money of the Bank of England, 1797-1816*; and E.M. Kelly (1976) *Spanish Dollars and Silver Tokens*, London.
27 *Parl. Papers*, 1816, VI, p.403, Report from Committee on New Silver Coinage.
28 *Parl. Papers*, 1837, XVI, Select Committee on the Royal Mint. App.35, p.228.

11

AN INDUSTRIAL REVOLUTION IN BREWING,
1700-1830[1]

That the brewing industry is of the utmost importance
to Great Britain is sufficiently evidenced by the very
considerable portion of the public revenue thence
arising, by its commercial advantages, as an article of
trade, and by its essential utility to individuals....

J. Richardson, *Philosophical Principles of
the Science of Brewing*, 1805, p. iii

An early eighteenth-century ballad boasts the verse:

There's many a clinching verse is made
In honour of the blacksmith's trade,
But more of the Brewer may be said
Which no-body can deny....[2]

which at least has the merit of redressing the balance of the old
world of the Industrial Revolution's historiography, concentrating
on iron and textiles, to the exclusion of other industries passing
through their own form of industrial development. In no industry
is this form of change more pronounced than in brewing, where, in
idealized terms, the structure of the industry in London moved from
a situation in 1700 where innumerable small producers mostly sold
beer which they themselves had made, to one of oligopoly by 1830,
when a few large concerns, consciously leading prices, dominated

the market. At the latter date Charles Barclay (one of the partners of Barclay Perkins Brewery, then the greatest in the country) could tell a parliamentary committee that the first twelve 'capital brew-houses' of the metropolis produced 1,200,000 out of the 1,400,000 barrels of beer from tax-paying brewhouses within the London area, and remark, 'We are the power-loom brewers, if I may so speak.'[3]

I

This essay will not analyse in detail the structure of ownership of the London breweries during this period, nor will it concentrate on the sources of capital which made expansion possible. But in discussing the industrial and commercial changes which occurred in the brewing industry — mainly in London and in similar urban centres — it is impossible to take these aspects of the rise of the great breweries for granted. The familial structure of ownership in almost every case gave the cobweb of personal relationships from which capital was drawn into the firms; and in no industry is this familial structure more marked or more tenacious than in brewing. This has been true both of Europe and America, and remained a dominant feature of the control of the brewers into the 1960s even when it lay concealed behind the mask of incorporation: nearly every name in London was that of a family who founded a brewery before 1800, and one before 1700.

These familial groups — interpreted in the widest sense, and including the close friends of the family 'clan' — provided most of the financial strength of the breweries in the eighteenth century. Above all, the need was for short-term capital once the crucial years of the growth of the firm to a reasonable size had passed. Then the business itself was lucrative and extensions of plant could come out of accumulated profits. At the end of the century more long-term capital was needed for investment in real estate when the race for 'tying' the trade, and securing outlets for retail sale, had begun in earnest, but until that period the real problem was the need for cash in occasional years of bad harvests. When such years of dearth came, the brewers were competing for malt at an inflated price without being able to raise their prices to the publican, the traditional arrangement being that they stood the loss in a scarce year, and took the gain in a season of glut and low prices. For one of the 'capital houses' in London by 1790 this bad year might entail an extra outlay of £75,000 on malt alone, on the reasonable assumptions of an output of 150,000 barrels and an intake of 75,000 quarters of malt with a price increased from 40*s* to 60*s* per quarter. When this coincided with the blight striking the hop-gardens in a season when the house had anticipated making heavy purchases, the total extra outlay for the primary raw materials of trade alone might be £100,000. Moreover the need tended to arise suddenly and in its very nature had to be satisfied quickly.

The larger breweries opened their coffers for deposits from a wide variety of humble investors and trade connections — employees, personal servants, publicans, merchants in trade with the house, sickness, burial and 'Christmas' clubs attached to public houses in trade and so forth. The investments sought were those which would be an adjunct to commercial cohesion (as with the clubs at the public houses which would promote a regular clientele), steady deposits earning a regular 5 per cent, or perhaps with the clubs a 4 per cent interest, mutually beneficial to both parties. Deposits of this kind rose to about £20,000 in some years at Barclay Perkins, and to £47,000 in 1796 at Whitbreads.[4] Despite these funds which could be put to work in the firms, extra commitments on the scale indicated meant that the owners of these breweries would have to turn to their relatives and friends for help. Nor was it simply a matter of high malt prices, for the bad harvest had a complex influence upon the whole economy. Very often it coincided with financial stringency in the City, which might mean a run on the banks in general, and consequently upon the brewers as bankers in particular. Further, it was often associated with a drop in demand, as declining employment hit purchasing power and high food prices curbed outlays on drink. This is typified in the case of Henry Thrale who had a large personal expenditure — living a social life in London, Brighton and Bath, travelling in Europe, and with all the expenses associated with being a Member of Parliament in the eighteenth century — and ploughed all the rest of the year's gains from trade back into buying raw materials and expanding plant, without keeping reserves of cash or securities which could easily be liquidated. The firm therefore tended to suffer a liquidity crisis at every commercial disturbance. In 1772 Mrs Thrale set about collecting enough cash to save the business. As she confided to her diary:

... first we made free with out mother's money, her little savings
— about 3,000£ 'twas all she had; and big as I was with child, I
drove down to Brighthelmsone to beg of Mr. Scrase 6,000£ more
... Dear Mr. Scrase was an old gouty solicitor, retired from
business, friend and contemporary of my husband's father. Mr.
Rush lent us 6,000£, Lady Lade [i.e. Thrale's sister] 5,000£....[5]

Six years later, when most of these debts had been repaid and
most arrears of payment to malt factors and hope merchants made
up, Thrale was again in difficulties through 'speculation', which
Mrs Thrale described as 'brewing more beer than is necessary
merely because malt is cheap, or buying up loads of Hops in full
years, thereby expending one's ready money in hopes of wonderful
Returns the ensuing season....' Her comment on this over-commit-
ment is significant in the same sense as her previous description of
the people to whom she turned in the emergency of 1772: over-
production, she realized, had caused an 'artificial scarcity' of
money in the family's budget because of higher raw material
costs.[6]

These financial strictures gave way to resilience once the Barclay
and Perkins families had taken over the business in 1781. John
Perkins had married Amelia Bevan, the heiress of one of the
Quaker banking families on Lombard Street, so that on both sides
the brewery was able to draw on the capital of one of the most
important Quaker kinship groups in England — those of East
Anglia and London. Many of the cousins who invested money in
the brewery (£143,000 out of £167,000 deposited in 1790 came from
within this family circle) happened to be bankers — the Gurneys,
Lloyds, Barclays and Bevans — but to call this a case of 'institutional financing' as such is more misleading than to see it still as
capital from within the family circle, where the members of that
circle happened to be bankers. It is the kinship tie which explains its
presence in the counting house of the firm. This wide net of
financial strength — some of its origins being outside London and
unaffected by a local rush for liquidity there — proved the greatest
asset when long-term capital was needed at the end of the century,
and during the years of unprecedentedly high prices during the
French wars.

Whitbread the younger, meanwhile, was being forced to take the
most extreme measures to save the trade. In any case he lost the

lead in production, being forced to curb buying through lack of capital. Extensive partnerships begin to provide the resources which were unavailable within his personal circle, and in the worst years of 1797 and 1801 he was forced to borrow in the most expensive way from his Whig friends and relatives, whose social group he entered after his marriage to the sister of Charles Grey. In any case his new social and political life was drawing him away from active management of the business, but here, ironically, his seducers saved the brewery. They lent him money by selling out their holdings in government Funds, on condition that he gave them the same yield as their holdings in the Funds afforded them, and promised to replace the same amount of nominal capital in the Funds when the emergency was over. In every case security on the loan was taken in freehold land, itself a capital stock accumulated from the profits of trade since 1761. Altogether £97,000 worth of stock was lent to the firm, on all of which interest was high, because the prices were low at the sale; and for the same reason the brewery stood to make a capital loss when replacing the nominal capital back in the Funds. But the times were desperate for the firm, and this expensive remedy at least ensured survival.

The different reactions of these two breweries in changing economic circumstances, emphasize the importance of the social 'milieu' in which eighteenth century firms grew up. Economic pressures worked through this social structure, and while all responded to the purely economic pressures the reactions were tempered in different ways by the various family groupings of the entrepreneur-capitalists. To ignore this social situation — to see the businessman only in his role as entrepreneur or capitalist, and to divorce business history from the genealogical tables of the business men — is to deny an important reality.

II

Throughout rural England, and in the market towns which were a part of that same local economy, the 'brewing victualler' made almost all of the beer which was publicly sold. He was a legally distinct animal from the 'Common Brewer'. The latter could brew only for sale to publicans and customers away from the brewery, apart from the one permissible retail outlet of the 'tap house' at the brewery. Although this dichotomy remained within the industry until the twentieth century, it is in the eighteenth century that the brewing victuallers in London, and a few of the larger cities such as Bristol and Sheffield, became depressed into the function of publicans only, as the large breweries emerged; and in the next century and a half that the railroad and motor transport carried this same development over the rural districts of the country. In 1700 the brewing victualler served the same sort of market as the local baker, although he exercised the duties of maltster and brewer, manufacturer and retail seller. The typical figure in this undifferentiated pattern of organization was Peter Stubs of Warrington, who was a brewing victualler as well as owning his file manufactory.[7] He would buy barley from the local corn markets, or farther afield if there was a local scarcity; hops from a travelling hop-merchant up from the Shropshire gardens or the Stourbridge and Weyhill fairs. As maltster he would make for the customers in the country houses and farms who brewed their own beer (or had it brewed for them by peripatetic brewers) and for his own requirements as brewer. In the latter capacity he brewed for customers who came to take away, occasionally for sending out to clients in cask, and above all, for his own inn, which was probably the heart of his trade. Serving these many functions, the thousands of brewing victuallers prospered within their local markets and their narrow radius of sales.

The crucial circumstances which allowed differentiation to come to the brewing industry was the growing urban market. It was in these 'intensive' more than geographically extensive markets — above all that of London — that production split off from selling, and the manufacture of beer became industrialized. Similarly specialization between malting and brewing had developed for the London market. Beer was a relatively cheap and bulky commodity, deteriorating rapidly under certain conditions such as a rough sea voyage or a hot climate (unless specially brewed for these conditions), consequently limited both in a sea-transport market and in an inland marketing area through high transport costs. Under these conditions the ideal market was that within the three to five mile radius which could be exploited by dray (the brewer's two wheeled cart carrying three 108-gallon butts and usually drawn by a pair of horses in tandem). There was a bulk export market in Ireland until the end of the eighteenth century, shared by the London, Bristol and Liverpool brewers, and a small trade to other provincial centres in England accessible by water. Most of the beer sent abroad, following the English settlements, was not the mild beer or porter of the London market but a stronger and more expensive stout. This deteriorated less in transit and was technically more suitable for these markets, as well as having a wider economic marketing area through the transport costs being less in proportion to its value. Outside London, the Burton brewers were developing a considerable export market to the Baltic. [8] For the London brewers, however, the country and export trade was insignificant when compared with their London sales — on which their fate depended. And this market grew always during the century, both intensively and extensively, as population density increased and the built-up area expanded. Sometimes this growth was slow, when expensive credit curbed building during a war; sometimes more rapid, as the houses marched out into the fields beyond Limehouse and West-minster, forming into the Bloomsbury squares and terraces like an army, while the poorer multitudes pressed into once fashionable suburbs. The boroughs outside London, even before they became joined to the main body of the city, like Hampstead, Highgate, Finsbury, were still within the metropolitan marketing area of the porter brewers.

These marketing opportunities, which improved as the eight-eenth century advanced, could be seized by the brewers more completely than by most potential industrialists, for the industry was technologically very suited for large-scale production within the single plant; and above all, the techniques of large-scale manufacture did not have to wait for steam power or the railroad before this market could be exploited. Steam power consequently did not work the revolution in brewing that it did in cotton, although it was adopted at once, when in an efficient form, by the great brewery to aid a process which had been actively at work for over a generation. While technological invention is not exogenous to economic circumstances, the absence of the necessity for any invention or process before which brewing could not be industriali-zed, meant that there was no technological time-lag in its industrial or commercial development. In this purely technological aspect, baking could not go the way of brewing until the invention of the gas-fired and steam oven in the later nineteenth century, remaining very much in the 'brewing victualler' stage of development of serving a very narrow market.

For the brewers, in essence, the problem was simple. To take advantage of the larger market, the scale of manufacture had to be increased. This was most economically done by increasing the size of the utensils, which itself gave economies of scale in costs of construction and materials, and the number of workers did not increase proportionately with the size and capacity of vat, copper or 'back'. Moreover, because the handling of a liquid in manufacture was simpler than processing a solid such as cloth or iron, planning the brewery led directly to major economies. When malt and water were at the top of an efficiently laid-out brewery, gravitation could carry the liquid down from one utensil to another through the various processes of mashing and boiling, fermentation and cooling. Only one man was needed at the valve-cock to transfer the contents of the largest vat to the utensil below, and one pump could get water to the top of the building or the 'wort' from one side of the brewery to the other. By 1800 an Archimedean Screw was raising the malt mechanically to the top of the brewery. Not until the beer came to be racked into barrels, stored and distributed, was there need for many labourers and — as in an equivalent modern industry handling liquid, the petroleum industry — labour costs were, and still are, less in relation to capital employed than in most other industries; and in the eighteenth century less probably than in all other industries operating on a large scale.

III

Although the Common Brewers did not dominate the trade in London until the end of the eighteenth century, the capital city did not offer this intensive market in that century alone, and there had been Common Brewers at least since Tudor times. Stow remarked on what he considered quite large breweries situated at St Katherine's Hospital on the Thames near the Tower; which had mainly grown up on the export trade and the market for victualling ships.[9] From 1672 there was a positive fiscal incentive given to the Common Brewers against the brewing victuallers, which remained present throughout later years and must have given a steady advantage to them above and beyond the economic advantages of large-scale production. They received an allowance of three barrels in thirty-six free of duty for 'wastage' from the Excise

Commissioners, in whose interests it was that the industry should be concentrated in a few large concerns. Where the scale of production warranted it, an excise officer could be attached to the brewery permanently to guard against fraud, whereas the same official could visit the countless brewing victuallers only occasionally. Excise officers were evidently supervising the bigger breweries continually on a six-hour shift as early as 1724.[10] In retrospect the point is made quite clear when the Excise Commissioners applied in the courts to withdraw the allowance from the Golden Lane Brewery in 1808:

> The Legislature thought it was better for the Crown to have these breweries conducted on a more extensive scale, and that it was considered a great object to prevent as much as possible brewing privately and in small quantities — The Legislature felt perhaps that from the magnitude of the concern in the one case it would be easy to collect the duty and difficult to evade the payment of it; whereas in the other the collection of the duty would be troublesome and expensive and the revenue daily liable to be defrauded.... It is important that the breweries should be confined as to their numbers but extensive with regard to their concern....[11]

With this encouragement, and the general fact that payment of duty implied advantages for the person who had capital, the Common Brewers became more important. Obliquely, their wealth and social position from this time onwards suggest the ownership of businesses producing greater and greater wealth, and more particularly, representation in Parliament is a good indication both of the general economic importance of the industry and the eminence to which it could carry its greatest entrepreneurs. From the election of Sir Charles Cox in 1695, the Borough of Southwark became traditionally represented by its brewers — John Lade, Meggott, Edmund Halsey, Ralph and Henry Thrale. More specific evidence from within the records of the firms themselves is scanty at this time, but some details showing the growth of one of them may be apposite.

The Anchor Brewery (at Dead Man's Place, Park Street, Southwark) stood on a site paying £21.10s per annum ground rent in 1633, and its buildings were apparently sold for £400. The first surviving record of the firm is a 1692 cash book (in that year the owner, James Child, became Master of the Brewers' Company and his daughter had married Lord Cobham — both events being economically significant). It is at this point that the brewery becomes large enough to support in his station an eighteenth-century gentleman living — in Horace Walpole's phrase — 'handsomely but without ostentation'. Edmund Halsey was the poor apprentice who found a father-in-law in his master and inherited the business — the first of three times before 1781 when the success story of the apprentice who lived to own the firm was repeated. It was more, in fact, the tragedy of successive masters who had no sons who could carry on their trade — as Johnson remarked on the third occasion, when Henry Thrale owned the brewery: 'A son is almost necessary to the continuance of Thrale's fortune; for what can misses do with a brewhouse? Lands are fitter for daughters than trade.'[12]

Edmund Halsey's cash book lists certain payment for 'Rideing horses at the Liveries Stable, Man's Livery, wine for hunt, wigs' which indicate the social position he must have held, moving in the small political and social group of the City — as a Member of Parliament related to the Cobhams, Lord of the Manor of Stoke Poges, Master of the Brewers' Company (1715), and Governor of St Thomas's Hospital (1719). He died a rich man. Selling the brewery for £30,000 to a poor nephew, Ralph Thrale (who was a clerk in the firm and bought it over eleven years out of the profits of trade), Halsey left, apart from the regular provisions of his will, £500 to his daughter, £300 to one clerk, £100 to another, and £10 each to every other clerk, workman and servant in brewery and household so that they might show their grief at his death in suitable mourning. The 1692 cash book gives only scanty information about the actual trade. The brewery bought and controlled at least one dependent inn for the sale of its beer; £1,700 was invested in the business by friends and relatives; and £1,000 was held in the government funds by the firm. In 1700 there were payments for what appears to be the erection of a new building with brewing utensils, £3,546 being paid for construction, £254 for carpentry and £408 to the coppersmith, which suggests a fairly large establishment in all. Blind horses were being bought, which implies that the pumps and mills were being driven by horse-power, and there is one entry showing that a consignment of a strong export beer had been sent to the Barbadoes.

All this is fragmentary and limited to the particular but, as the first detailed commercial record available for the London brewing industry at the moment, it deserves attention, as showing some details about the commercial life of one of the few larger breweries in London at the beginning of the great expansion period, and in relation to the more prevalent evidence about the owners of the trade at this time.

IV

The Anchor Brewery — with a few other firms such as Calvert and Truman — were exceptional in the pattern of the London trade of 1700. Functioning on a very small scale when compared with what they later became, they nevertheless seem to have already the characteristics which were developed. Altogether, registered Common Brewers in London numbered 199 in 1684, compared with 625 in the remainder of England and Wales and over 20,000 brewing victuallers, while the rest of the country still had 20,575 brewing victuallers and only 1,488 Common Brewers.[13] This shows very much the pattern to be expected, confirmed by the district reports which began in 1831, that the Common Brewers were prospering in the areas where population had clotted and the brewing victuallers were still dominant in the rural areas. More important than the numbers of Common Brewers, or their individual outputs, was the changing pattern of trade which resulted when a rising proportion of total output became controlled by the few great brewers knowing that they can influence prices. This movement, which the following section will describe, is illustrated in Table 11.1, but unfortunately before 1776 individual outputs are known only for the years 1748-50, 1758 and for 1760.[14] From the table it will be seen that the decades from 1750 to 1790 show the change-over: in 1750 less than half the beer sold was being made by the first twelve porter breweries, after 1780 above 75 per cent and by 1830 85 per cent.

The great names of the London trade arose on the production of porter, a heavy beer, dark in colour and slightly bitter to the tongue. Its invention and development were technological innovations of the first importance which cannot be ignored. From the first, when supposedly introduced by Ralph Harwood, who never became one of the great brewers, it undercut the brown and pale

Table 11.1. Production of Strong Beer in London.[1] (figures all in thousand barrels)

Year	Total brewed	First 12 houses	% of total	Whit-bread	Barclay (Thrale)	Truman
1748	915.5	383.0	41.9	?	35.5	39.5
1750	979.5	437.0	43.6	?	46.0	46.0
1760	1,114.5	525.5	47.1	64.6	32.6	55.5
1776	1,289.0	707.0	54.8	102.5	75.4	83.0
1780	1,319.5	680.0	52.8	97.4	65.6	80.1
1787	1,251.0	965.0	77.1	150.2	105.5	95.3
1795	1,326.5	978.2	73.7	159.0	122.3	99.1
1800	1,359.9	994.5	73.2	137.0	136.3	109.7
1810	?[2]	1,320.5	?	110.9	235.1	145.0
1815	1,768.5	1,401.5	77.7	161.7	337.6	172.2
1817	1,532.5	1,226.5	80.0	151.9	281.5	168.8
1830	1,441.5	1,200.0[3]	85.0	131.3	231.3	150.3

Source: Total, from excise returns, where available.

First 12 houses, MSS and printed lists at the Breweries.

[1]The total is composed of all strong beer on which duty was paid, and therefore includes ale brewed. The first twelve Houses brewed porter and stout alone, so that the final percentage is including, in the total figure, a section of the market for which they were not competing. By 1820 the amount of porter brewed by the others was admitted to be 'very trifling'.

[2]Returns for 1810 are unknown to me at present.

[3]Figure based on the evidence of C. Barclay to Committee on Retail Sale of Beer, (*Parl. Papers*, 1830, X, p. 21).

ale brewers in price (selling for 23*s* a barrel and 3*d* per quart) and allegedly combined the virtues of the mixtures of beer being sold as 'three threads'.[15] In fact the method of brewing must have differentiated the product very strongly. The malt was roasted from the drying kiln to a dark brown, which gave the colour and flavour to the beer, and the bitterness remarked on by everybody must have come from the fact that all the saccharine matter contained in the malt and extracted during the process of brewing had been converted into alcohol. This left none of the sweetness as in the old ale which had not been fermented to the same degree. Part of this taste may have come from heavy hopping, but it seems probable the porter was technically an efficient product in this way — that the raw material had been fully exploited to utilize all its strength possible.[16]

The introduction and eventual success of porter was part of the general commercial revolution in the industry. As a contemporary wrote, the general pattern of trade at the end of the seventeenth century was that beer was

> ... mostly fetched from the Brewhouse by the customers themselves and paid for in ready money so that the brewer entertained but few servants, fewer horses, and had no stock of beer or ale by him, but a trifling quantity of casks and his money returned before he paid either his duty or his malt.[17]

No valuations exist for any of the larger breweries at this time so it is impossible to judge the accuracy of this description of the distribution of beer in the case of a business as Halsey's in Southwark. Middlemen were developing the practice of buying beer from the brewers, maturing it themselves, and then selling at a profit, because they had the capital to be able to do it. But from the beginning, porter was completely in the hands of the brewers — made by them, matured in vat and cask and distributed by them. By the mid-century the publicans being served were on a regular basis of monthly credit, paying the collecting clerks of the brewery each month when the new stock was delivered, while this new stock was itself supervised for fining and 'staling' by the abroad coopers from the brewery.

Fiscal advantages for the Common Brewer combined with technical and market opportunities to encourage the growth in scale of production — as described previously. It is with the self-conscious and deliberate search for economy, improvement and expansion that the few greater porter breweries could become industrial enterprises of almost unparalleled size and capitalization in the economy of eighteenth-century England. Contemporary publications stress the size of the concerns and the professional attitudes already developing. Apprenticeship fees were usually above 100 guineas and sometimes as high as 300 guineas for learning the business from one of the great,[18] and already there was difficulty for a newcomer setting up from the beginning in the porter brewery. Most new blood entered existing concerns as partners: 'in Proportion what cash they can advance, which is the most common way of their coming first into trade, for to erect a common Brewhouse and lay in Stock answerable, will sink many Thousands before they see any Returns.'[19]

Progress in the actual construction of a brewhouse — a search for efficiency in design — is also made clear at this time. The brewery was to be erected with the fermenting chamber open to the air, yet slatted to keep out direct sunlight. One solid wall on the south-west warded off both the sun and the prevailing wind. Writing in 1742-3 the author of *London and Country Brewer*,[20] himself evidently in the trade, described these improvements as of 'recent years'. Malt was ground on the floor above the mash-tubs and slid down a shoot into the water; underback and cooler were similarly arranged so that the wort could be run off by gravitation into wide and shallow cooling chambers which would speed the process as much as possible. And in the same pursuit of speed and economy horses were to work the pumps and the mills. With these methods two men did the work where four had been previously employed: 'This better Management saves the loss of a great deal of Time, Waste and Men's Labour.' The whole book has the air of advising the London brewer and instructing the country brewer in the realities of the profession. Already the 'capital brewhouse' was as different from the village ale-wife as the cotton factory from the spinning wheel.

There was another interaction between fiscal regulation and the techniques of production which threw emphasis upon the regularity, quality and strength of porter. Beer, as of old, came under the Assize of Ale, which meant still that its price was fixed and that a rise in price had to be negotiated with the government. From the introduction of porter until the increase in duties for the Seven Years War in 1761 the retail price had been 3*d* (1.25p) a pot (of one quart capacity). From 1762 until the fluctuations in duty during the French Wars at the turn of the eighteenth century it remained at 3½*d* (1.46p) a pot (sold to the publicans at 1.5*d* a barrel). At a fixed price, therefore, the advantages of the Common Brewer over the brewing victualler, and the large-scale brewer over the smaller, were reflected in the difference in quality and strength, which their lower costs enabled them to exploit — besides providing a handsome rate of profit. The product could be 'differentiated' merely by the addition of water, so that the maintenance of the superior product at a fixed price became the secret of the success of the great brewers. This explains the quest for the best materials, which were also the most economical for them to use, the price range not reflecting fully the range in quality, an insistence upon quality

malts, and the attempt to find these in the malting areas of Hertfordshire and Norfolk rather than relying on the grain which was
brought to the public markets at Bear Quay and Mark Lane. In
itself, brewing on a large scale improved quality and allowed
greater regularity of product:

> The Great Brewer has some advantages in Brewing more than the
> small one ... [he] can make more Drink and draw a Greater
> Length in Proportion to his malt, than a person can from a lesser
> quantity, because the greater the quantity the more is its untied
> Power in Receiving and Discharging, and he can brew with less
> charge and trouble by means of his more convenient Uten-
> sils....[21]

The point is also illustrated well by an entry in the Property Book
of Samuel Whitbread.[22] Whitbread typifies the first generation
of entrepreneurs in whose lifetime the industry changed its face. He
was apprenticed in 1736, took a sleeping partner to buy a small
brewery in Old Street in 1742, and had saved up enough money by
1750 to set up — with the help of a few of his Bedfordshire
friends — a larger brewery in Chiswell Street. This had become the
largest in London by the 1780s, and received the accolade of its
degree of eminence, a visit from the king and queen. Whitbread's
conscious search for economy and 'good management', an independent application of reasoning to a problem without the curb of a
traditional method,[23] made him take full advantage of his
opportunities.

> 1775. Having built two very large Vaults under the Great Store-
> house in 1774 my next consideration was how to occupy them to
> the best advantage by making them contain the greatest quantity
> of beer. My first thoughts were upon Vats to be made of differ-
> ent Dimensions but at length a very singular idea occurred to my
> mind, and that was to fill a part of the Vaults themselves with
> Beer, putting up such partitions as should be thought necessary
> to divide any part of them into different cisterns by walls; which
> I apprehended would certainly be making the most of the room,
> and from their situation in the earth be beneficial beyond any
> Cask whatever to the quality of the Beer, and attended with less
> Fermentation than Casks which are more exposed to the Air and
> on the whole admit of a longer length in the Beer brewed from an

equal quantity of Malt and Hops when kept in Casks; which have all turned out as at first conjectured....

By 1787 the capacity of the cisterns installed was over 500,000 gallons, and Whitbread ended his description with a minute calculation of the direct financial gain — apart from the advantages of the improvement in quality:

> Suppose they [i.e., the cisterns] lasted 7 years, the use of them would have profited about £4,200 and the 4,000 Butts would probably sell for about £4,200. So that in seven years the Amount of the Capital advanced in building the Cisterns is secured and all further use very profitable indeed....

The logical conclusion of this search for regularity, and the calculation of 'strength' was reached, it not utilized, in 1784. In that year John Richardson published a tract describing his saccharometer, an instrument giving exact knowledge of the specific gravity of the 'wort' — the extract from the malt — and, through that, the amount of fermentable matter contained in a unit weight of malt or barley.[24] Although Baverstock claimed to have applied the hydrometer to brewing in 1768, certainly it was Richardson's saccharometer which was ultimately used by the great brewers, after some resistance.[25] Unfortunately, I know of no evidence which describes the gestation of this invention or the particular incentives which existed for Richardson, apart from those general for one who was in the trade himself. Its advantages were apparent. Once the amount of fermentable matter could be discovered in any particular parcel of malt, the amount used could be adjusted to maintain the same strength in the beer. When financial economies were needed in an expensive year the savings in the outlay on malt could be translated in advance to find out what decline in strength it would entail in the beer. And if it was thought that the market would stand a weakening of a certain degree, this could now be made out in money terms prior to the operation. It opened a new world for the exact manipulation of the rate of duty according to strength, and an exact method of pricing products. With the thermometer, which Michael Combrune introduced into his own brewery by 1762, and which had been generally accepted for normal use by 1780, the saccharometer brought the possibility of exact calculation to an industry in which the scale of production was demanding more and more accuracy of measurement.[26]

V

When such a ferment for expansion and improvement existed amongst the London brewers it is little wonder that they took the advantages of steam power as soon as it was offered them in an efficient form. Nine engines were installed in breweries in the London area before 1796, and another five before 1801, so that all the 'capital houses', except for Truman Hanbury, who did not begin to install their engine until 1805, seem to have power-driven machinery.[27] The great advantage given by steam power was that it enabled the mill horses to be put aside, and further speeded up the processing. The Rest Books of Charrington show the numbers of horses dropping from 51 at Midsummer 1784 to 35 by 1788, at Truman Hanbury 14 mill horses became redundant between 1805 and 1809. The same economy is described by Joseph Delafield, the brewer at Whitbread; writing to his brother in March, 1786:

Last summer we set up a Steam Engine for the purposes of grinding our Malt and we also raise our Liquor [i.e., water for brewing] with it.... The improvements that have at various times been made on the Steam Engine, but particularly the last by a Mr. Watt ... are very great indeed and will bring the machine into general use where the strength and labour of Horses is largely and particularly wanted — you may remember our Wheel required 6 Horses but we ordered our engine the power of 10 — and the work it does we think is equal to 14 horses — for we grind with all our 4 Mills about 40 qrs an Hour beside raising the Liquor. We began this season's work with it and have now ground about 28,000 qrs with it without accident or interruption. Its great uses and advantages give us all great satisfaction and are daily pointing out afresh to us — We put aside now full 24 horses by it which to keep up and feed did not cost less pr Anm. than £40 a Head — the expences of Erection was about £1,000. It consumes only a Bushel of Coals an hour and we pay an annual Gratuity to Bolton and Watt during their Patent of 60 guineas.

This next summer we have it in contemplation to put all our Cleansing Works and other works upon it.... The brewhouse, as the possession of an individual, is and will be when finished still more so, the wonder of everybody by which means our pride is become very troublesome being almost daily resorted to by Visitors, either Strangers or Friends to see the plan....[28]

By 1805 the 'other works', besides grinding and pumping, included the 'mashing' of the ground malt in the vats, which had previously been done by men with oars, the 'rousing' of the worts in fermentation, and the raising of the malt by Archimedean Screw to the top of the brewery. So that virtually all the operations of brewing where labour was involved, before the stage of racking into barrels and delivery, had been mechanized.

VI

It follows from the previous sections that the London brewery had become organized on a scale which required, and produced, much wealth. From the books of three of the largest establishments some estimate of the amount of capital behind production can be found.[29] It rose from an average of about £1.7 per barrel in 1750 to £2.35 per barrel by 1800 and £5 per barrel in 1830 (when much capital had been put in real estate and loans to 'tie' the trade). This means, by calculation from known outputs, a rough increase in financial resources employed in the first twelve 'capital houses', who were operating on the same kind of plan with about the same scale of overheads, from £0.75m. in 1750 to £6m. in 1830. Profits were high, as diminishing costs of production from industrialization (outweighed only partially by gradually rising malt prices after 1770) were not reflected in falling beer prices. Great wealth accumulated in the hands of the owners of a large brewery — after 1790 above £20,000 clear profit in a good year — accruing from the exploiting of a mass market with a single product manufactured in bulk. It was one of the first markets to be monopolized by an industry organized along 'modern' mass-production, mass-marketing principles. As Sir Benjamin Truman wrote in the Rest Book of his brewery in 1775:

My Reasons for committing this to writing in this book [are] that it will be frequently under your Inspection, Grandson. It may be a matter of wonder to you as being a young Brewer, in Comparing this Rest with former times how so much money could be got in one year, consider the price of malt and hops. My committing this to writing is solely to inform your Judgement, to account for this large profitt and give you my reasons which I hope will never be forgot by you.... There can be no other way of raising a great Fortune but by carrying on an Extensive Trade. I must tell you young Man, this is not to be obtained without Spirrit and great application....

VII

Such an industrial development had wide implications. In the span of relationship between barley farmer and the publican, the centre of gravity moved towards the brewer as manufacturer (in the twentieth-century rather than the eighteenth-century sense) and away from the independent merchant in the corn markets. This emergence of the manufacturer, marking the change from a previous pattern of economic relationships, brought with it integration backwards to raw material sources after 1780, when the porter brewers began to deal directly with farmers, malt-makers and factors in Norfolk and Hertfordshire, and to malt for themselves. With the drop in demand after 1796, this movement was supplemented by a stronger race to integrate forwards to control retail outlets of trade. With rising wealth Common Brewers in the provinces often turned their profits to use in banking, while in London there was an association of banking capital with brewing, the connection personified in the Barclay, Bevan, Hoare and Hanbury families. The great porter brewers became natural associates of banking circles in London, and were represented, or were married to relatives of representatives, in the House of Commons, so that a Parliamentary 'interest' developed as trading interests consolidated. With control of manufacture and marketing by the few, and, until the abolition of the restrictive licensing system for the sale of beer in 1830, with the opportunity of monopolizing the retail outlets of trade,[30] the London brewing industry resembled precociously the business situation of later times, with integration, imperfect competition and pricing agreements.

These developments are, however, broader aspects, if not alone consequences, of the more narrowly industrial revolution in brewing which it has been the purpose of this chapter to analyse.

Notes

1 See P. Mathias (1959) *The Brewing Industry in England*, Cambridge.

2 D'Urfey (1709, 3rd edn) *Pills to Purge Melancholy*, London.

3 *Parl. Papers*, 1830, X, Evidence to the Report on the Retail Sale of Beer, p.16. The actual marketing position shows an even greater control than this 85 per cent of total production indicates. The great brewers made only porter — the bulk and standard product — and had wiped out all competition. The other 200,000 barrels were composed mainly of ale, in which section of the market the porter brewers were not competing.

4 Documentary evidence, unless from printed sources which are individually noted, comes from records held at the breweries. I was able to study this material through the courtesy of the managing directors of the companies concerned. In recent years much has been placed on deposit in the Guildhall Library and at County Hall; while the records of many provincial breweries have come into County Record Offices.

5 Hayward (1861) *Autobiography of Mrs. Piozzi*, Vol. II, p.25. Also C.K. Balderson (ed.) (1942) *Thraliana*, Vol. I, Oxford, entry for April-May 1778. See chapter 16, pp.311-16.

6 *Thraliana*, Vol. I, p.333. See chapter 16, p.312.

7 T.S. Ashton (1939) *An Eighteenth-Century Industrialist*, Manchester, pp.71-86.

8 *Irish Market: Bristol Port Books*, Bristol Reference Library; *Diary of R. Hadley*, sent by the Bristol Porter Brewery to develop the market in 1784 (all records of the brewery destroyed in 1940); Morewood (1836) *History of Inebriating Liquors*. Appendix gives statistics of Irish production, imports and exports. *Parl. Papers*, 1835, XXXI, Excise Reports, pp.157, 166. *Baltic Market*; Whitworth (1776) *State of the Trade of G.B. in its Imports and Exports*, pp.xx, xxiv. *Parl. Papers*, 1806, II, Evidence to Malt Report. ... p.335. A. Barnard (1889) *Noted Breweries of Great Britain*. ... p.117. The Country Trade ledgers of Whitbreads, Barclay Perkins, and Truman Hanburys also show regular shipments to Cork and Dublin merchants. Distribution appears to be by these merchants rather than by the exporting breweries.

9 A. Stow (1908) *Survey of London*, Oxford, pp.237, 242, 281 (Strype edn, Vol. II, p.204).

10 *Instructions for Officers in the London Brewery* 1724, p.4.

11 Allowance Acts run from 12 Ch. II, ch. 23, s. 22 to 6 Geo. IV, ch. 58, with varying amounts. The issue is discussed in *Parl. Papers*, 1819, V, Evidence to Report on the Public Breweries, pp.32, 99. Rex v. Brown & Parry (Golden Lane Brewery Co.) in Court of Exchequer, 1808: Evidence of Sgts, Vaughan, Nolan, Marryat (proceedings published verbatim, London, 1808. Guildhall Pam. 3802).

12 J. Boswell (1946) *Life of Johnson*, Oxford, Vol. II, p.69.

13 1684 figures from excise returns in MSS. at Barclay Perkins brewery.

Later returns quoted by S. Morewood (1836) *History of Inebriating Liquors*, and in *Parl. Papers*, 1831-2, Accts. VII, no. 223.

14 Production figures for 1748-50 are in MSS. in Barclay Perkins brewery, for 1758 in Truman, Hanburys, 1760 figures are printed in London Chronicle, Vol. VIII, No. 568, and in Barnard, op. cit. p.xiii. Figures for first twelve houses after 1776 were in MSS. at Barclay Perkins, until printed press returns begin.

15 Accounts of the origin of porter are numerous and appear to be derived from the same source. *Picture of London*, 1805, note to p.26; F.A. Accum (1821) *Art of Brewing*, p.6; H. Thomas (1803) *Antiquities of London*, p.154.

16 There is little contemporary evidence for this interpretation which is, however, supported by inference from literary sources describing the taste of porter, and by technical considerations. There is recognition of it in 1819 in evidence before Committee on Public Breweries. Aitkin, a chemist, says: ' ... the object of the porter brewers is to produce the most highly fermented liquor that is possible ... ale still having certain clamminess or sweetness showing that fermentation has been stopped before reaching its natural height.'

17 Broadley and Bullock, *Collection on History of Brewing*, held at Whitbreads Brewery. Entry from 1771.

18 Brewers' Company Records. Apprentice Books (Guildhall MSS., London). Fees to unimportant brewers were very small, reflecting the difference existing in the industry. Whitbread's apprenticeship to Wightman, Master of the Brewers' Co., in 1736 cost £300 (Guildhall MSS. 5450).

19 *General Description of All Trades*, London 1747, p.34.

20 *London and Country Brewer*, 1742-3, *passim*; especially pp.179-182 on the 'Great Common Brewhouse'.

21 *London and Country Brewer*, 1742-3, p.25.

22 Southill Park MSS., Property Book (i), 1750-95. I was enabled to see these records through the kindness of Major Simon Whitbread, of Southill Park, Beds.

23 This did not apply to some of the actual processes of brewing and fermentation. There the chemical and organic analysis of yeasts was unknown before the researches of Pasteur and procedure was formed from traditional experience.

24 J. Richardson (1784) *Statistical Estimates of the Materials of Brewing, showing the use of the Saccharometer*. The section is elaborated in his *Philosophical Principles of the Science of Brewing*, 3rd edn, 1805.

25 J. Baverstock (1824) *Treatises on Brewing by the late James Baverstock* The introduction of the thermometer and saccharometer is discussed in Clow (1952) *Chemical Revolution*, London, pp.544-5.

26 M. Combrune (1762) *Theory and Practice of Brewing*, p.30.

27 E. Roll (1930) *An Early Experiment in Industrial Organisation*, London,

pp.111-16; J. Lord (1923) *Capital and Steam Power*, London, Tables pp.167-75. Before 1795 only two other industries (cotton and coal) had a greater number of engines than the breweries (twelve, totalling 95 horsepower); in terms of horsepower, canals also were ahead of brewing. This was out of a total of 144 engines (2,009 horsepower).

28 A copy of this letter was in the possession of Mr J.E. Martineau, of Whitbread and Company, through whose kindness I was able to see and quote it.

29 I have included in this estimate all valuations of assets listed and debts owed to the firm in trade, less debts owed in trade by the firm.

30 Licenses for the sale of beer and spirits were issued by local authorities. After 1800 it was their policy, for the protection of public morality, not to allow an increase in the number of public houses, except in the newly built up areas. This meant that if the brewer could get control of the trade of a public house serving a locality a rival could not set up another house to bid for the same custom. Where the brewers had influence with the Justices this quest for control of retail trade was facilitated. Monopoly was also encouraged by the curtailment of building in London during the long wars between 1793 and 1815.

12

THE ENTREPRENEUR
IN BREWING,
1700-1830[1]

I

Recent study in economic history has, in several ways, sought to explore the diversities existing within national aggregates and generalizations. Research makes plainer every year that the eighteenth-century industrial entrepreneurs were far from belonging to a single ideal type in class, creed or attitudes.[2] When the industrial structure itself was so differentiated — as to such matters as the size of plant, the level of technique, or the relationship of enterprise to the ownership of landed estates or to foreign trade — it is no wonder that noble coal-owners, landed canal and railway projectors, wealthy merchants like the Finlays of Glasgow or the Reynolds of Bristol should qualify for the compliment of this title equally with traditional *elite* of the type — Quaker ironmasters, Unitarian cotton spinners, or even the dissenting yeoman turned industrialist. In turn, single industries which were virtually nationwide, like textiles or brewing (or even, in a different way, farming), possessed within themselves, at the same point in time, a complete spectrum of industrial organization from household production through cottage workshop to powered factory. Such industries show, in consequence, as diverse a collection of business leaders, of entrepreneurs and non-entrepreneurs.

In 1750 there were 996 Common Brewers in England and Wales, and 48,421 Brewing Victuallers — that is, almost 1,000 people who brewed only for sale to publicans and private customers away from their breweries, and over 48,000, who, like Peter Stubs of Warrington, brewed mainly for their own inn, but also for sending out to customers.[3] In London alone, where production had been dominated since the seventeenth century by Common Brewers, there were 165 of them, who together produced about one-quarter of the entire national output for sale. The differing roles of the entrepreneur in such an industry have, therefore, to be related to the several diversities contained within this national aggregate of firms. Only then will the common features, as well as the differences, become historically significant. Most entrepreneurs in the eighteenth century were opportunists — even if opportunists with vision to see opportunities not apparent to others equally anxious to get ahead, and with determination to organize things in such a way that potential opportunities became actual ones. Effectively controlling the relevant factors of production, for example, could enable them for the first time to gain effective control over the product and so design it for a particular market. A similar flair in trading might discover, develop or create a new market — success usually involving elements of all these three activities. As individuals they made a positive step by seeing opportunities for profiting in enterprise in a new way. But the more one emphaisizes the degree of opportunism involved, then the more importance one must attach, by implication, to the circumstances which conditioned their response, and offered them the possibility of success. These 'circumstances', of course, make up collectively the emptiest box one could wish to fill — the assorted factors within it ranging from technological invention to new transport, a changed law or a change in fashion — but such an approach has the merit of relating 'entrepreneurship' to its objective context, to the

Table 12.1.   Number of Brewers, 1700-99 [4]

Year	Brewing Victuallers		Common Brewers	
	England & Wales	London	England & Wales	London
1700	39,469	—	746	174
1750	48,421	—	996	165
1799	23,690	—	1,328	127

actual problems and opportunities facing the businessman. To develop hypotheses and concepts of entrepreneurship in the abstract, uncontrolled by concern with the limitations put upon the actors by real factors is a temptation to arbitrary theorising unsupported by historical experience.

Here there is space to look at only a few of the contrasts and common features in the brewing industry. Four have been selected: as contrasts, the nature of the enterprise over the country, and the kind of person entering the London porter market at different times; as common features, trading skills and social positions.

II

There is, firstly, of course, the vast gap in size between the few giants in London, where perhaps half a dozen were brewing over 100,000 barrels (all of porter) by 1800 (the greatest of these double that amount) and the anonymous multitudes of humbler producers in smaller towns and villages.[5] The story of most of these as brewers, if not as entrepreneurs, may be summed up by saying that they prospered upon and were limited by their local markets. Clearly, for a commodity of such low 'value density' as beer, high transport costs set strict boundaries to the possibilities of expansion as a brewer, save in special circumstances. John Smith of Oundle, for example, first seized his chance to develop from a brewing victualler when the prisoner-of-war camp was set up at Norman Cross; while John Gardner of Cheltenham and John Palmer of Bath enjoyed the patronage of the visiting *elite* who took ale as well as the waters.[6] For them, a metropolitan market, so to speak, brought itself to their localities each season. In other small towns another special factor channelled the response of persons eager to take what business opportunities were available to them as brewers. Francis Cobb, for instance, who established a brewery at Margate in 1760, became so dependent upon naval demand that he bought a second one at Deal to be closer to his market.[7] Heavy dependence upon public contracts survived the establishment of naval breweries at all the admiralty dockyards for many brewers in the south coast ports.[8]

The limitations of the local market gave the entrepreneur an incentive to employ his capital and his energies in other directions, ambition for enterprise necessarily overflowing from its source, unlike the situation in London where the market for the brewer was large enough to satisfy the ambition and absorb the capital of those most aggressive in expansion. Although this characteristic was by no means universal in London by the end of the century, [9] the decades of most rapid expansion after 1740 certainly saw it, and as will be apparent below, non-brewing wealth and enterprise became associated with the industry precisely because the need for capital in brewing became so urgent, and on such a large scale, that it could not be produced fast enough from the profits of the firms.

The Burton brewers had no demand on such a scale at their doorstep. They were mainly dependent upon selling to the Baltic until Napoleon, by closing the parts in 1807, forced a rapid deployment in the English market on them. [10] Their traditional market demanded a very strong and expensive ale to survive both the journey and the transport costs, its profitability being always dependent upon the fact that most vessels cleared to the Baltic from Hull in ballast. Owners and skippers were looking for any cargoes outward to replace the bulky inward freights for which the voyage had primarily been made. A very short brewing season, therefore, had to be sandwiched between January and May: that is, starting in preparation for the year's Baltic sailings but ending before the weather became too hot to brew with safety. The greatest Burton brewers, Benjamin Wilson, Thomas Salt, Worthington and Bass, brewed not more than 5,000 barrels annually at this time — even though their product was widely known for its quality — but their initial sales of beer formed the basis for a pyramid of transactions, with trading margins being taken at every stage to supplement already comfortable manufacturing profits. The shortness of their brewing season was useful, too, in giving them the time to profit by other enterprise.

Through the lack of a mass market in England, and through the need to accommodate the Baltic merchants to whom they sold ale, they were drawn into dealing in Baltic produce by ledger-barter and complementary purchasing of timber, staves, iron, flax and hemp. [11] They dealt in London as well as through Hull and the Vale of Trent. One group, at least — Benjamin Wilson and his sons — concentrated mainly on timber and staves at Burton, which was a distributing centre for their region of the Midlands. In addition, they owned parts of ships and were willing to take a profit by speculation and trading when buying any of their raw materials for brewing ale and in all the goods gained with the credits they piled up from selling it. Until the expansion of brewing in Burton in the next century, when the railways opened up London and the national market to them, little of their accumulating surpluses went into fixed capital for brewing, but was put out in these ways to other enterprises. The majority of them were amplifications and extensions by trade of the central business. Less linked to brewing was one further venture. Benjamin Wilson became a partner in a cotton mill near Lichfield in 1784. All this activity lay apart from his investments in those fields where 'enterprise investment' merged into 'status investment' and his motives included a desire for rentier profits — real estate, canal shares, government stock.

Parallels to this situation may be seen in Samuel Palmer of Bath developing two theatres, a tallow chandler's business and a spermacetti factory; Sir Edmund Lacon in Yarmouth investing heavily in malting for sale and in ships; the Cobbold family in Ipswich, and brewers on the north-east coast becoming prominent on the east coast as corn merchants, merchants in foreign trade and as shipowners.[12] These last two, amongst numerous other instances of the same link, also illustrate the widespread connection between banking and brewing.

The move by country brewers into banking in small towns may well have been an entrepreneurial response to profit from the status wealth brought and from funds it was less profitable (or less possible) to reinvest in brewing, as well as being a useful adjunct, seasonally to their breweries. All things considered, for such businessmen as these, limited by the narrowness of their local markets for brewing, the distinguishing mark of the entrepreneur was non-brewing activity, the unenterprising being content to slumber peacefully as brewers or rentiers in a traditional market in a traditional way.

III

The leaders of the industry were, generally speaking, not the first technical innovators. Here the pattern is that of Arkwright and Crompton, rather than such as Abraham Darby (or Bessemer), who made their fortunes on their inventions. The great quickly adopted innovations perfected by brewers, it is true, but brewers who were and remained in a small way of business. An obscure London brewer, Ralph Harwood, is said to have first brewed porter in 1722, the stability and efficiency of which made the mass-production plant

Table 12.2. Brewers and Bankers[1]

London

Family or person	Brewery	Family or person	Brewery
Bevan	(Barclays)	Shaw-Lefevre	(Whitbreads)
Barclay	(Barclays)	Clutterbuck	(Whitbreads)
Hanbury	(Trumans)	Wilshere	(Whitbreads)
Gurney	(Barclays)	Hoare	(Hoare)
T. Brown	(Whitbreads)	J. Cripps	
Hobhouse	(Whitbreads)	J. Curtis	

Provinces

Family	Place	Family	Place
Simonds	(Reading)	Weston	(Norwich)
Oakley	(Deal)	Dowden and	
Cobb	(Margate)	Lee	(Alton)
Smith	(Oundle)	Mildred and	(Diss,
Gardner	(Cheltenham)	Sampson	Norfolk)
Ramsbottom	(Windsor and London)	Crabb	(Hitchin)
		Lucas	(Hitchin)
Hector	(Petersfield)	Ashby	(Staines)
Greenall	(St. Helens, Warrington)	Searle	(Saffron Walden)
Christie	(Hertford)	Gibson	(Saffron Walden)
Lacon	(Yarmouth)		
Weston	(Norwich)	Hollick	(Cambridge)
Wells	(Biggleswade)	Angove	(Falmouth)
Cobbold	(Ipswich)	Threlfall	(Liverpool)
Worthington	(Burton)	Billingsly and	(Oakhill,
Tollemache	(Ipswich)	Jillard	Somerset)
Tawney	(Oxford)	Baldock and	
Clinch	(Witney)	Rigden	(Canterbury)
Bireham and Fox	(Reepham, Norfolk)	Farr	(Beccles)

[1]This list is by no means complete, but it is sufficient to show the intimacy of the connection between brewing and banking. Each case listed is of a person being brewer and banker, or partner in a brewery and a bank. In addition there is a possible, but as yet undocumented, connection between brewing and banking in the case of the following, whose names appear separately in directories as brewers and as bankers: Drew (Chichester), Tylee and Gent (Devizes), Wakefield (Kendall), Woodcock (Halesworth), Burdon (Newcastle on Tyne), Slocock (Newbury), Deane (Reading), Embury (Tewkesbury), Wells (Wallingford), Sanders (Witney), Dawes (Warwick).

a possibility in the industry: but he did not rise to industrial eminence himself.[13] It was almost the same with Michael Combrune and the application of the thermometer, James Baverstock and John Richardson with the hydrometer, similarly with the attempts to introduce an attemperator for controlling the speed of fermentation.[14] All these innovations are scarcely technical inventions in the sense of Wyatt's roller spinning, Watt's separate condenser or Hackforth's steam blast. They are more the quickwitted adaptation to industrial use of instruments already known in scientific circles, to achieve exact 'measurement control' of processes which were traditional (and of which the chemistry remained undiscovered).

Other important changes involved merely a simple alteration in a process of manufacture without any new device: such as making black porter malt by 'high drying' on the malt kiln, varying the hoprate with the season to improve stability, or employing the more rigorous extraction methods in 'mashing' which porter malt made possible to give more efficient use of raw materials. Only in certain aspects of innovation did the sheer problems of size force the opportunity of increasing productivity to the attention of the greatest, and improvement arrive from the top.

Important efficiencies resulted from planning the brewery rationally, which was being noted as a feature of the 'Great Common Brewhouse' in London by the 1730s, and from storage in bulk by vatting.[15] Mechanical innovation is the other field where technical change penetrated through the industry from above but only after the great expansion in fixed capitals was well under way, and as a consequence of steam power. In the 1780s steam-engines came to most of the 'capital houses' in the metropolis as a more efficient substitute for horse-milling and horse pumps. Once installed the gains from applying the engine to new jobs previously done by men — cleansing casks by steam, hoisting, mashing, rousing — which it had *not* been installed to replace, became as important as its superiority over horses in the functions it *was* designed to perform.[16] Its creative effects, so to speak, proved as valuable as its substitution effects.

Source: Much of this table has been composed from banking rather than brewing evidence, and for this I was indebted to Prof. L. S. Pressnell of the University of Kent and Mr C. N. Ward-Perkins of Pembroke College, Oxford.

IV

With such diversity in the scale of operations and the nature of the market, the capital requisite for entering the industry varied correspondingly, and with this the social origins and attributes of the entrepreneurs. At one end of the scale is Isherwood, a Windsor brewer, who, from being a servant in the Christopher Inn at Eton, married into some money, established a brewery and left his son between £8,000 and £9,000 a year from the business.[17] In London already the barrier to entry could be high. Ralph Thrale was the son of a farm labourer, it is true, but he had a successful uncle without a son and was enabled to buy his brewery from him for £30,000 out of the profits (over 11 years).[18] By 1736, Samuel Whitbread's apprenticeship cost him £300 and he needed all of his £2,000 patrimony as younger son of a prosperous — and dissenting — Bedfordshire yeoman, plus loans from friends at home, plus a sleeping partner, to set up porter-brewing on the competitive scale current in the 1740s.[19] By the next generation in the same market, it needed the resources of the Barclay-Bevan-Gurney Quaker banking clan to put up the £135,000 for Thrale's old business.

With them was the old manager who had saved his way up the salaried ladder of a lifetime to climb into the partnership on his master's death, and he still had to borrow from his master's widow in 1781 to make his stake a respectable one.[20] This man, John Perkins, had been one of the architects of success for thirty years, personifying a new race of men, the salaried entrepreneurs, little known in the brewing industry outside the capital in the eighteenth century. In London, however, they became more important as the unit of production became larger, so demanding greater capital and more partners, some of whom were less intimately associated with day-to-day control of production. In consequence of the increase in size more articulate management developed with a division of function between buying, brewing and accounting. This path of entrepreneurs from salary to partnership-profits was trodden increasingly. It was one way of overcoming from the inside the increasing barrier of capital required for ownership, feasible by middle age where a senior clerk's salary rose to £1,000 p.a. as it could do in a London 'capital house' by 1800. And usually these 'department managers' invested considerable savings (at 5 per cent) in the firms.[21]

Gyfford's brewery in Long Acre was bought in 1787 by a typical combination of talent, capital and kinship. Joseph Delafield moved from being an employee with twenty-three years of technical training and considerable savings behind him as a chief salaried brewer of Samuel Whitbread. Harvey Christian Combe, the second partner, was his brother-in-law. He was the son of an eminent attorney and

Table 12.3. Partners and Capital

Year	Barrels brewed	Loans to retailers and value of leases	Number of partners	Surplus capital invested in firm[1]
(i)	*Whitbreads*			
1790	175,000	£ 11,860	1	£ ?
1799	203,000	45,060	4	75,450
1810	110,939	114,500	7	66,000
1830	131,300	355,600	9	297,200
(ii)	*Thrale - Barclay Perkins*			
1780	65,460	7,800	1	1,206
1790	126,725	26,570	4	167,740
1800	105,905	39,180	4	139,150
1811	264,165	114,280	8	417,300
1830	231,340	356,050	8	702,864
(iii)	*Trumans*			
1780	80,730	18,810	2	2,135
1790	93,715	19,570	2	5,850
1800	101,560	37,970	3	51,050
1810	144,990	121,670	4	90,720
1830	203,530	345,590	6	288,925
(iv)	*Meux - Reid*			
1797	95,375	?	5	?
1810	211,010	266,440	20	166,340
1820	159,385	294,370	16	177,190

[1]Much of the surplus capital (that is, capital surplus to the joint partnership capital) was invested by the partners themselves, as reference to Table 12.4 will make plain. There is not enough space here to give a complete analysis of the capital, nominal and actual, of these concerns in a single table, nor is it possible in all cases. These figures have been extracted to illustrate the points made on pp. 238-41.

Source: Rest Books and other records at the breweries.

landed proprietor in Hampshire, having a rich uncle (who became also his father-in-law) who launched him in London grain markets as a factor. George Shum, the third, was just rich.[22] Rather different pressures were supplementing this growing barrier on entry by 1800. Brewers were seeking to tie the trade in London and elsewhere so that the already large capitals needed for buildings, plant, horses, drays and stock were further increased by the necessity of becoming the landlord and creditor of publicans.

Established concerns welcomed into their partnerships bankers and merchants who of necessity brought in the social and political consequences of vast wealth made in other fields. Shipbuilding and East India profits poured into Meux and Meux-Reid with William Wells, Sir Robert Wigram and his son; Gurney cadets arrived at Barclay Perkins from Norfolk; Sir Benjamin Hobhouse, Daniel Clutterbuck, Timothy Brown and William Wilshere brought banking wealth from Bath, Hertford and London to Whitbreads. Buxton and Hanbury wealth sustained Trumans.[23] This wave of recruitment, however, sometimes brought in money more than active partners. Managerially, Whitbreads was brought out of the crisis of a reckless second generation by two salaried clerks, whom the elder Whitbread had enabled to become partners in his will, foreseeing trouble from his son. One of these elderly men then succeeded in bringing an independent brewer, John Martineau, and his two sons, who were operating prosperously in a smaller scale in Lambeth, into the declining firm.

John Martineau and his sons had no partnership articles at all for their firm.[24] Where, as with Meux-Reid, in 1809, no less than twenty partners were required to provide the necessary capital, the problems imposed by those dissociated from active management became acute. Written into the deeds of partnership, therefore, there was a detailed series of formal, institutionalized procedures to regulate the relations between the managing partners and the passive partners. Within the private world of partners, this mirrors exactly the arrangements between the shareholders and the directors of a public company which became formalized in manufacturing industry during the nineteenth century. The partners owning a fairly small fraction of the joint capital in their hands but enjoying the substantial stipend of a managing partner thus, as entrepreneurs, approach in function the salaried clerks of Whitbreads who have a considerable stake in the surplus capital invested, and whose salaries were often calculated to benefit according to the profits by bonuses. At the end of the spectrum, the only serious attempt to break into the London porter market from outside the established firms and without the backing of great family wealth and influence came in 1804 when two men, W.H.R. Brown and J. Parry, raised £300,000 in the open market for a subscription company.[25] It prospered only for six years. With fixed capitals becoming greater and control over local marketing more complete, established concerns absorbed new entrepreneurs, from employees and rich partners, rather than new entrepreneurs establishing new concerns.[26] The names and families of the breweries operating in London in the 1950s bore eloquent testimony to this fact, which a commentator remarked on first in 1747,[27] and which was clearly apparent by 1800. The original founder families, too, showed an astonishingly sustained ability to produce not only sons, but sons who were able businessmen, happy in remaining businessmen and brewers.

Needless to say, in the country at large, each sort of person may be found entering the industry, down to the humblest, while such a precociously mature situation existed in the London porter trade, the position varying with the nature of the urban markets across the country. In some Midland counties there were very few Common Brewers at all in 1800, household brewing in cottages and brewing victuallers still satisfying local demand in a medieval tradition.

V

The importance of kinship in the world of the unincorporate, family or partnership enterprise is a much-told tale, of course, but none the less quite fundamental for this industry. If John Perkin's progress was typical it was because genealogical failure in a family was also typical.[28]

The new cousinhood sustaining the brewery were the relatives of his wife Amelia, who was the widow of the great Quaker merchant and banker, Timothy Bevan. While the immediate family was usually the first source for successors to industrial property, capital for it derived from a wider range, still within the personally known circle of relatives, friends and trusted business associates. The Barclay-Bevan-Gurney-Perkins cousinhood provided both a flow of capital and a succession of able young men which other brewers sorely lacked.

The following pattern might be illustrated at length from several sets of brewers' records: extensive borrowings in the early years of rapid growth, or at purchase, from within the family circle of family and friends; as a substitute for this, perhaps, 'external' sleeping partners, these being paid off as the profits accumulated. Then temporary accommodation from the same group, supplemented by credit from tradesmen and banks in a year of crisis or a year of heavy investment. Often bank loans secured on note for a few months became in effect long-term investments running over several years, for when the note was nearing its term the brewer would ask for its continuance for a further short term, and if the bank was not anxious to call in its investments this might occur several times.

Then, in the case of the London brewery, there came the entry of very large capitals after 1795 for investment in property. For this only the family nexuses behind Barclay-Perkins and Truman, Hanbury and Buxton (which was more explicitly the same clan)[29] were financially and genealogically resilient enough to provide the necessary capital from within; wealth external to the family groups coming into the partnerships at Meux, Reid and Whitbreads. To sum up on a much divided field: on the whole it was talent of varying middle-class origins that entered the industry. The field of recruitment was so diverse that one can only say that the entrepreneur belonged to a *type* not a *class*. There was, however, a more than average strain of dissenting or Quaker stock there.

Whatever the role played by individual religious consciousness — in particular the renowned dissenting ethos — it cannot be dissociated from the social and kinship aspects of the dissenting communities, manifested in such things as the flow of capital and talented succession to partnerships. Perhaps those conscientious in their dissent were kept more free than others from temptations bad for business, for example in education. Possibly more important was the negative utility of keeping youths free of the entrepreneurially debilitating values disseminated at the ancient universities. The second generation of Whitbreads and Hucks[30] show the ill effects

Table 12.4. Barclay-Perkins capital, 1784-1830[1]

Year	Joint partner-ship capital £000 (i)	Surplus capital on private account					
		Partners £000 (ii)	Quaker bankers £000 (iii)	Family & friends £000 (iv)	Others £000 (v)	Publicans, 'clubs', etc. £000 (vi)	Total Surplus Capital £000 (vii)
1784	95.0	—	5.0	8.0	56.0[2]	2.0	71.0
1790	135.0	16.5	71.0	22.5	40.0	17.5	167.5
1800	160.0	56.0	17.0	34.5	21.0	10.5	139.0
1811	200.0	309.0	20.0	56.0	16.0	16.5	417.5
1820	200.0	456.0	5.0	10.0	33.0[3]	80.5	584.5
1830	200.0	556.0	—	4.5	—	142.5	703.0

[1]The bankers in col. 3 are without exception relatives of the partners: Gurney and Bland; R. Bartlett and J. Gurney; J. Gurney, Gurney and Webb; Taylor and Lloyds; Ketts and Back.

The private persons in col. 4 are linked by family and friendship ties as well as by their Quaker stock. They include Timothy Bevan, Priscilla Bevan, Elizabeth Bevan, Elizabeth Kendall, Benjamin Moseley, Ambrose Benning, Thomas Kett, David Springall, S. Fox, Elizabeth Fox, John Breame, Charles Lloyd, Christiana Gurney, Phineas Bond (of Philadelphia); Delaney Barclay, Cadwallader, Rosa Perkins, Mrs Perkins' trustees. Almost all invested above £1000.

Col. 5 includes unidentified names, some of which are undoubtedly tradesmen supplying the brewery with raw materials. These latter, in the 1830 account, appear under col. 6.

Col. 6 is a 'trade list' not given the compliment of being on the 'private account' list of personal friends and the families. It is composed of employees of the brewery, publicans bringing the deposits of clubs and friendly societies at their public houses, and, latterly, tradesmen.

[2]This £56,000 includes £51,000 still owing to Thrale's executors from whom the new partners were in the process of buying the brewery.

[3]£32,000 of this total is a loan from Tompson and Co — in fact a banking-trade debt which was paid off within a year or two.

Source: Rest Books at the brewery. (All figures rounded)

of the dominant value-system associated with a wealthy upbringing in the eighteenth century: the turf, running a pack of hounds, extravagance in building in the country, spending too much time and money in politics, spending too much of both also in the country and the West End rather than in the City. Conspicuous expenditure of money and time outside business, in short, proved inimical to expansion or success in industry. Thrale, too, was thrice pulled back from such disasters of social expenditure of his own making in the nick of time when he attempted, in addition, a reckless policy of expansion to outbrew Whitbread and Calvert, 'two fellows he despises'.[31]

But equally, there seemed to be as many owners of packs of hounds among the brewers who maintained their status as entrepreneurs, and all became landed gentry as fast as it was prudently possible. In the early days of 'heroic' growth, admittedly, the classic virtues of work and thrift and abstinence from unnecessary spending outside the business applied. Whitbread bought no property between 1742 when he entered trade and 1761, commenting when he did begin 'and I borrowed all the money as I could not spare it to be taken out of Trade'.[32] He spoke then for all the ideal entrepreneurs in his predicament. Thereafter, he put over a quarter of a million pounds into land before his death in 1796, and acted for most actual entrepreneurs with his opportunities. Even this was not without its direct business utility. These freehold estates over which the brewing families so assiduously rode to hounds stood always ready to be pledged as security for personal loans when their London breweries stood in temporary need for capital. Nor perhaps is it irrelevant to mention that the Whitbread, Hanbury and Barclay families were rounding out estates in some of the finest barley counties in the kingdom.

VI

Traditional generalizations about the industrial entrepreneur making his name — and his profits — as an organizer, bringing unified control to the management of all factors of production as a manufacturer, and exploiting his markets as a merchant, are fully borne out by the brewing industry. A little has been said above about local markets for the product fashioning the different responses of entrepreneurs in brewing placed in diverse circumstances. Here, a common feature in the success of brewers needs elaboration: it is the importance of merchanting skills in their raw material markets.

The cost of raw materials (malt or barley much more than hops) remained [33] over 50 per cent of the wholesale price charged to the publican by the brewer so that, given the general level of those technical and commercial economies of scale current amongst competitive groups (such as the dozen porter brewers in London or the handful of Burton brewers driving the Baltic market), the margins most immediately variable and vital were those of malt prices and malt quality. In a sense, as productive efficiency improved, and manufacturing costs per unit of production dropped, buying skills and raw material prices became more significant. Certainly, in no quarter could disaster come more quickly than from inefficient buying. When Thrale's business discretion lapsed in the bad years 1772-3 the most immediate effect was that Perkins found himself £18,000 in debt to hop-men and very much more to malt merchants, hence he was tied to his creditors and, needing long credit, unable to gain the best terms in the markets.[34]

Much pivots on this issue of merchanting skills and the industrialist. A theme common to all the surviving letter books of Benjamin Wilson, Samuel Allsopp in Burton, Thomas Greenall in St Helens and Sampson Hanbury in London is their rigid control of the key decisions about the quality of raw materials, the timing and extent of purchasing, and their rigorous comparisons of price and quality between different sources and methods of supply.[35] They held the initiative, sought out the widest range of choice available from samples gathered from widespread regions, were furious and unreconcilable when a consignment failed to conform with its sample. Only very occasionally did they allow a trusted contact to buy a certain quantity at his discretion over price and quality. 'None you know but the most surpassing quality will please me; you have had sufficient experience of me to render anything more on this subject unnecessary', Wilson reminded such a correspondent at the beginning of a new season.[36] The main point, that these buying decisions lay at the centre of commercial success, was supplemented by the more subtle one that variations in quality were commonly more extreme than variations in price (confirmed by the advent of exact measurement by hydrometer in the 1770s).

In course of time, the structure of malt marketing developed partly in response to this trading initiative being kept by the brewer. For London porter brewers this search for quality combined with the problem of ensuring vast and increasing malt supplies to encourage bypassing the open markets and independent malt merchants. Independent malt factors in Hertfordshire collected samples from many small makers, sent them to the brewers, carried out their orders for purchases, organized shipments down the Lea in their own barges, and handled the payments. Apart from their commission as factors, they took the profits of providing both the transport and a cushion of credit between the maltsters and brewers.[37] But the initiative in selecting grain was emphatically not theirs, and they had developed as factors primarily because the merchanting decisions belonged to the industrial entrepreneur. It was the same for active provincial entrepreneurs in the barley market. The Burton brewers bought mainly barley, by sample, from agents in a wide arc of country to the south and east, from Oxfordshire round to Lincoln, occasionally up towards York, supplementing their direct choice of local grain.

Further, the porter brewers themselves developed a partial — and only partial — stake in malting, either permanently by buying malt houses, or temporarily by commissioning maltsters, so that, at a time of hardening prices they could ease the strain by moving into the barley markets but in a year of glut take the greater gains possible in buying malt.[38] Hanbury put off a would-be seller of barley in November 1802 with the comment 'I can still buy cheaper than I can make'. He wrote to his own maltster, John Kemp, 'I can buy the best brown at 44s. therefore I think it madness to make any ... you cannot take the same advantages of the Market in buying Barley as Malt.'[39]

More generally, of course, the insistence of these businessmen in trading only with those who accepted their own strict standards of dealing was an important factor behind success in a business where returns depended on a multitude of small transactions with many customers and where profits came from the translation of very small margins over vast quantities. Efficient control of buying, with efficient control of accounts, as in any modern mass-production concern, were crucial for success.

VII

A further common factor about the brewers, as true for those leading in growth and innovation as for the conservatives in business, has an important entrepreneurial truth lurking behind it.

It is that as businessmen they were usually remarkably active in non-business activities, sometimes, as I have instanced, to the prejudice of business, but not so in the majority of cases. In London and the localities alike there are brewers everywhere as aldermen, sheriffs, mayors, JPs, Lords Lieutenants, governors of hospitals and schools, prisons and almshouses. Between six and a dozen were in the House of Commons throughout the century, Southwark (and to a lesser extent the City) being 'brewers' boroughs' for at least one seat most of the time. They were noted for philanthropy, for their patronage and for the splendour of their hospitality. Did not Richard Meux give 200 people a dinner to celebrate the opening of his huge vat — inside the vessel — and Whitbread entertain royalty in 1787? [40] To take but two examples from among the enterprising: Humphrey Parsons, brewing just east of the Tower of London, inherited a landed estate at Reigate and a seat in Parliament from his father, Sir John, who had been Lord Mayor of London in 1703. The son was a member of the Wax Chandlers Company, then the Grocers and Brewers. He was President of the Bridewell and the Bethlehem hospitals, a City Alderman from 1720 and again in 1740, Sheriff in 1722, Lord Mayor in 1730 and again in 1740, an MP continuously from 1722 to his death in 1741. He obtained a duty-free monopoly of beer exports to France, it is said, by presenting his horse to Louis XV at a hunting party.[41]

On the more modest, provincial scale, three successive heads of the Cobb brewery at Margate were consuls to several foreign courts, pier wardens, Lloyd's agents and Deputy Magistrates to the Cinque Port of Dover.[42] The presidency of institutions, as Humphrey Parsons' more explicit horse-trading, implied a direct business *quid pro quo*, of course, but the main point is that, taken together, these other activities were no less importantly, if less directly, related to business success. The fortunes of the brewing industry, after all, were lapped about by non-economic (or at least non-business) considerations. Duty rates took up 22 per cent of the wholesale price of beer in London in years of peace (rising to 47 per cent in the French wars) and taxation at the point of production implied an intricate excise supervision, and legislative control of all processes of manufacture — both aspects of the excise system, making brewer MPs and their allies in the Commons very useful individuals to the industry. Locally, all facilities for retail sale were subject to annual permission from the licensing justices (at which Brewster Sessions no brewer JP could sit after 1751),[43] which meant that status in local society could pay important dividends. All this was incidental to the informal advertisement of fame and quite apart from the fact that acceptance of office became a natural consequence of property, wealth and social position — as it was for brewers in national politics.

The underlying point is, I think, the same, that the study of business enterprise in the eighteenth century — when the operation of most business was conducted in as personal terms as of most politics — cannot be abstracted out as a purely economic or entre-preneurial phenomenon. The business historian is much concerned with the economic consequences of non-economic factors. Even more, he is concerned with relating the intimate springs of enter-prise in individuals to their differing business circumstances and their differing social circumstances. Some few of these relation-ships, too briefly, have been explored here with regard to the entrepreneur in brewing. Case studies of single families in the industry would illuminate the general truths more pointedly, and investigations in other industries perhaps contrast their applic-ability.

To conclude, about the most forthright of the great London entrepreneurs in brewing during the late eighteenth century, those most aggressive, most dictatorial, there lived an air of greater civility, of status to put it no higher, than about most industrialists. It is reminiscent of the elegance more associated with great wealth in foreign trade or banking. Partly, no doubt, it was that the brewer was recognized as belonging to the same club as the landed interest, whose rents he was directly supporting and whose ranks he was rapidly joining. But as an entrepreneur, too, he was fortunate in the nature of his business. No better 'comments exist than Bagehot's opinion of the London bankers (which are transposed to the terminology of the other mystery):

> The calling is hereditary: the credit of the brewery descends from father to son: this inherited wealth soon brings inherited refine-ment. Brewing is a watchful but not a laborious trade. A brewer, even in large business, can feel pretty sure that all his trans-actions are sound, and yet have much spare mind. A certain part of his thoughts he can readily devote to other pursuits.[44]

Notes

1 I would like to acknowledge with gratitude a grant to help with my research from the Houblon Norman Fund and owners of all MSS. cited who made it possible. They allowed me to study many records still remaining in the breweries whose past they document. See P. Mathias (1959) *The Brewing Industry in England, 1700-1830*, Cambridge.

2 One of the best general discussions remains that of P. Mantoux, (1948 edn) *The Industrial Revolution*, London, pp.374-408. See also C. Wilson (1955) 'The entrepreneur in the industrial revolution', *Explorations in Entrepreneurial History*, VII, pp.129-45.

3 T.S. Ashton (1939) *An Eighteenth-Century Industrialist*, Manchester, pp.71-86. See also P. Mathias (1953) 'Developments in the brewing industry in England: 1700-1830', *Explorations ...*, V, pp.208-24. Statistics from *Excise Statistics, 1662-1805* (MS. at Customs and Excise, London), pp.17, 20-1, 144, 147; *Excise MSS.* 1749, 3069, 3070. London figures are in MSS. at Barclays, being copied from Excise MSS.

4 Brewing Victuallers in London are ignored, being always under 50 in number with an insignificant percentage of production in their hands. The number of brewers declines in London and increases in the country during this period, from the trend towards larger production in individual units of production. In the country this was squeezing out brewing victuallers, in London the smaller Common Brewers.

5 See the Table printed in Mathias, op. cit., p.217. A figure of 100,000 barrels implies almost 15 million retail transactions (at one quart each), a scale of operations from a single unit of production which was not to be met with in many sectors of the economy in the 1780s, when this range was first reached.

6 John Smiths (Oundle), *Sales Book, 1798-1800*; Gardners (Cheltenham), *Ledger, 1800-7*; Palmers (Bath), *D.N.B., Gents Mag. 1818* (II), 276.

7 Information from the Company. I owe this reference to Mr. B. Spiller.

8 P.R.O. *Adm.* 110.

9 Samuel Whitbread II had interests in lime-burning in Essex, and John Martineau in sugar refining (*Partnership Deeds (1812)* at Whitbreads).

10 A. Barnard (1889) *Noted Breweries of Great Britain and Ireland*, I, p.117ff. P. Mathias (1956) *House Journal*, Ind Coope and Allsopp, X, Nos 5-6.

11 *Allsopp Records: Personal Ledger 1779-95, Letter Books*. The shortness of the brewing season also gave these persons time and opportunity to profit by other things.

12 Palmers, op. cit.; Lacons (Yarmouth), *Cash Book 1759-69; Valuations*, 1742, 1752, 1758; Cobbold (Ipswich), *Cliffe Brewery, Ipswich, 1723-1923*. There is a very widespread connection, too, with the wine and

spirit trade, which was a natural extension to supplying publicans with beer. In addition many coastal brewers were 'agents for London Porter.'

13 Mathias, *Explorations* ... for references.

14 M. Combrune (1758) *Theory and Practice of Brewing*; J. Richardson (1784) *Statistical Estimates with the Saccharometer*; J. Baverstock Jr. (1824) *Treatise on Brewing*, Preface and Appendix; P.R.O. Adm. 110/ 37 fol. 359 *et seq*. Baverstock and Richardson in particular were not so circumstanced in the London porter market to have the problems of efficiency and large scale production thrust upon them. It seems to be more professional pride that urged Combrune on, although all of them acknowledged the economic utility of their innovations in print.

15 *London and Country Brewer*, 1742, pp.179, 182; P.R.O. Adm. 110/26 fol. 101.

16 P. Mathias (1954) 'Steam power comes to Chiswell Street', *House of Whitbread* XIV. For Whitbreads' innovation of underground cisterns for storage see Ibid., XII (1952), based on *Southill MSS. Property Book*.

17 *Gents Mag.* 1798 (I), pp.536-7. The brewery was sold by his son for £70,000.

18 Mathias, *Explorations* ... ; also above pp.218-19, 310-15.

19 *Whitbreads Brewery* 1951.

20 *Thraliana* (ed. K. Balderston, 1951), I, 501; Rylands Lib. *Eng. MS.* 600 (7), 600 (II).

21 *Whitbreads Records: Private Ledgers; Gratuity Book, 1798-1850; Southill MSS. Brewery 4638*. In 1781 Mrs. Thrale considered keeping Perkins on a salary, which with bonuses might have reached £1,200 p.a. (*Letters of Samuel Johnson* (ed. R.W. Chapman), II, No. 725).

22 *Whitbreads Records: Gratuity Book*, op. cit.; W.P. Serocold (1949) *Story of Watneys*; *Gents Mag.* 1818 (II), p.83; *Faringdon Diary* (ed. J. Greig) IV, 55; II, 187-8.

23 Partnership Deeds at the breweries; *Faringdon Diary* V, 130, 279; VI, 98; *Gents Mag.* 1830 (II), 563.

24 Herts. C.R.O. *MSS. Nos.* 61134, 61137, Series 61144; *Southill MSS.* 4652-4676, 4727.

25 *Excise MSS. Trials*, 556, 582, 584; Guildhall Library, *Pam.* 3802.

26 Needless to say this feature varied completely over the country in response to the urban markets. For example, there were few public brewers of any kind near Birmingham.

27 *General Description of all Trades* (1747), p.34.

28 J. Boswell (1946 edn) *Life of Johnson*, Oxford, II, p.69.

29 T.F. Buxton's mother was a daughter of Osgood Hanbury. He married Hannah Gurney, daughter of John Gurney of Earlham Hall, Norfolk.

30 The younger Samuel Whitbread gave most of his time, energy and money to matters other than business. He dispersed his own shares of the brewery in partnerships, fell heavily into debt personally and

committed suicide in 1815. Robert Hucks 'spent his money on the turf and sold the brewery ...' (*Notes and Queries*, 12. Ser. II, 93).

31 *Thraliana* I, 333. See chapter 16, pp.311-13.

32 *Southill MSS. Property Book.*

33 This was true until the increase in taxation in the Napoleonic Wars raised the stake which excise had in the price from 20-22 per cent to 45-47 per cent.

34 Rylands Lib *Eng. MS.* 616, Box I, *Note Book*, entry 8 July 1773.

35 In addition to these MSS. at the breweries see T.C. Barker and J.R. Harris (1954) *St Helens 1750-1900*, Liverpool, pp.90-107 where the point is admirably brought out.

36 *Allsopp Records, Letter Books*, B. Wilson to Jackson, 30 September 1791).

37 *Parl. Papers*, 1819, V, *Report ... on Public Breweries*, Evidence of T. Clough, J. Taylor.

38 Whitbread commissioned malting from his entry into trade (*Whitbread Records: Trade Ledger, 1746-52*). Martineau (joined with Whitbreads after 1812) had malt houses in Norfolk at least by 1787 (*Rest Books, 1812-30*), Goodwyns by 1784 at latest (*Charrington Records: Goodwyn Ledger, 1784-6*), Barclays by 1787 (*Barclay Records: Cash Books, 1787*), Calverts by 1818 (*Parl. Papers*, 1818, V, op. cit. Evidence of Calvert, pp.18, 25.

39 *Trumans Records: Letter Books*, S. Hanbury to Wright and Casburne, 18 November 1802; to J. Kemp, 11 November 1802.

40 T. Pennant (1790) *History of London*, pp.278-9; *Whitbreads Brewery*.

41 D.N.B. (Parsons); E.P. Hughson (1805-9) *History of London*, pp.11, 195.

42 See note 7 above.

43 24 Geo. II c. 4; 31 Geo. II c. 29.

44 W. Bagehot (1873 edn) *Lombard Street*, pp.268-9.

13

AGRICULTURE AND THE BREWING AND DISTILLING INDUSTRIES IN THE EIGHTEENTH CENTURY

One of the interesting side issues that arises from a study of the distilling and brewing [1] industries of the eighteenth century is the close connection existing between them and the agricultural economy of the country. The most important feature of this connection is naturally the supply of barley and malt for the raw materials of the industries, but one interesting, if minor, feature of it lies in the use of the waste products as a supply of feeding-stuffs for cattle and pigs, and through that as a contribution to the provisioning of London.

Distillers' waste consisted of the spent 'grains' left after the infusion of the barley and malt and the 'wash' from the resulting first extraction when the spirits had been distilled from it. The brewery [2] waste consisted mainly of the spent grains alone. As the brewing and distilling seasons were from October to May (the warm months being unsuitable for malting and fermentation) the supply of grains and wash came during the winter when the demand for feeding-stuffs was at its height. In Scotland, where the distilleries were more widespread in the country districts than they were in England, this seasonal cycle was important in itself; in the London area it was combined with a geographical importance, for no small part of London's meat and milk supplies were dependent on the stock fattened and the milch cows fed within the confines of the town area on these waste products of two of the city's greatest industries.

The scale on which the breweries and distilleries were conducted in London — especially as the century advanced — accounts for the great quantities of feeding-stuffs produced and the large numbers of hogs, and later cattle, being kept on them. There were eleven 'capital brewhouses'[3] in the Metropolis at the end of the century, of which the largest — Whitbreads — produced 200,000 barrels of porter in a good year, and the least — Cox, King and Co. — about 45,000 barrels. Similarly, there were seven distilleries that produced over 300,000 gallons of spirits in the year 1802-3.[4] The 'length' of a brew of porter — the number of barrels of beer produced from one-quarter of malt — was between three and four barrels per quarter,[5] and there are estimates[6] that a quarter of malt produced about 20 gallons of spirits and 110 gallons of 'wash'. Three-quarters of grain used produced two quarters of 'grains'.[7] These figures are in no sense exact, but they do indicate unmistakably the great amount of material used in this by-product branch of the industry.

The value of the grains of the distillery was greater than of those from the brewery, largely because of the proportion of unmalted barley used in distilling after 1720. The distillers' grains generally sold at 6 to 8s. per quarter in 1808,[8] while the brewers' grains fetched only 3s. The ale grains were reckoned richer than the porter grains. But despite this the quantities involved in the brewery were so vast that there was considerable profit in having them as a perquisite, which was the case for persons in charge of the actual brewing at Whitbreads,[9] and appears to have been the general practice. These were all sold off the premises to the cow-keepers and to cattle dealers, as was the case with the waste from the breweries and distilleries near Edinburgh; so that with this scale of selling the generally assumed picture of the milk-cows of London being driven into the town daily or feeding on the grass of the open districts within London is misleading.

In England the organization of the distilling industry was primarily metropolitan, and, with it, the utilization of the waste products of distilling. This had been encouraged by a deliberate fiscal policy which discriminated against the small producer of both beer and spirits and, in addition, the high rate of duty levied, which was payable before returns from sales were received, told against the small unit of production,[10] throwing the trade into the hands of those people with capital. This applied above all to the brewers and the primary distillers, the rectifiers (redistilling the raw spirit made by the primary distillers) being more numerous and more widespread.[11] The primary distillers kept hogs themselves about their distilleries rather than sell their 'offals' off the premises as did the brewers.

By 1736 the scale of this feeding of hogs at the distilleries, and the low price at which they could afford to sell them was raising opposition[12] amongst the Home County and Shropshire hog farmers. Farmers were having to send unfattened 'stores' to the distilleries in London rather than fattening them themselves and were opposed to giving the distillers the estimated profit of 20s. that the fattening put on the price of each pig. It is difficult to discover the actual numbers involved, because, before the end of the century brought the reports to the Board of Agriculture and the more sober evidence of Parliamentary Papers, the main sources of printed evidence is in pamphlet literature and petitions to Parliament — both highly tendentious. But, at all events, they must have been considerable, and the distilleries were already large units of production.[13] One estimate was of 50,000 fattened annually, and the writer[14] was interested in playing down the claims of the farmers who were exaggerating the menace to their profits. The point at issue was that, since the distillers had begun to use unmalted grain[15] a short time before, they were enabled to feed the hogs completely on their grains and wash without any reliance on beans or pease that were necessary with the grains left over from only malt. Thus they by-passed the farmers completely and were enabled to undercut them in the markets and for the valuable victualling contracts for the navy. These matters were brought before the House of Commons in January 1740, when petitions from the home county farmers were presented, a committee was detailed to investigate the complaints, and a report given to the House in 1745.[16]

It was generally admitted[17] at the time that the 'country-fed' pork was superior to the distillery pork, and this was part of the reason for the difference in price between them — but not entirely, as the petitioners knew. The competition had forced down the prices to a point where it had become uneconomic for the farmers to fatten, and dropping rents in the Fen Lands (largely leased out for hogs it was said), slackening of demand and falling prices for beef and mutton are together blamed on the distillers' hogs. This difference in price was variously estimated to be between 2*s*. 6*d*. per stone (for country-fed) and 1*s*. 6*d*. per stone (distillery-fed), 2*s* and 1*s*. 4*d*., 5*d*. and 3½*d*. per lb.[18] One dealer, after a long tirade about the bad quality of distillers' hogs, admitted that he made but 2*d*. per stone discrimination against them in his buying price and none in his selling price. Since the distillers had entered the market for the victualling contracts it was stated that the Commissioners had 'not dealt with the farmers for many years' and that the West Country hog farmers no longer drove to Portsmouth as they did. Conceivably this driving long distances put the farmers at a disadvantage with the distillers who were enabled to 'fat' near the yards at Deptford, and it was probably advantageous for the naval authorities to deal directly with persons who could guarantee large-scale deliveries at a low price, rather than with graziers and others who would collect the hogs round the farms in the hinterland and drive them to the ports.[19] This had its disadvantages, however, for the distillers were few enough in number to combine together in order to protect their market — much as the 'ring' of timber contracts did at a later period.[20] And in so far as the low price did reflect any difference in the keeping quality of the pork (through the distillery pork being gross and not 'taking' salt in curing as effectively as the country-fed pork), 'saving the public money' partly explains the perennial complaints about rotten provisions in the fleets. John Jennings, one of the contractors buying hogs for the navy described how: 'The Distillers have entered into a combination and advanced a large Sum of Money, in order to prevent other Persons from contracting at the Victualling Office and that because the Witness [i.e. himself] contracted for hogs with some farmers, the Distillers afterwards refused to sell him any.'[21]

Writers in the latter part of the eighteenth century thought that the British distillery reached its peak about 1750. The stoppage of the Corn Distillery from 1756 until 1760 and rising rates of duty from 1751 [22] had further concentrated the industry and limited the number of hogs kept by the distillers while providing an incentive for the exploitation of waste products. The round figure of 100,000 is given [23] for the numbers annually fattened in 1750, with 20,000 to 25,000 in addition sold in a winter to the Victualling Office 'for the use of the Navy, at a low price, deducting the Discount on the Navy Bills'. This account is coloured by the conditions of 1783 being those of a depression year.[24] The writer does emphasize the effect that the distillers' pork has upon the market prices, favouring the abundance of distillers' hogs in order to get the prices down. The farmers had complained of just this in 1740-5 and Burke, pointing out the way a bad grain harvest in 1794-5 increased the prices of country-fed hogs and threw an increased demand upon all other flesh, argued against the stoppage of the corn distillery which increased it '... another cause, and that not of inconsiderable operation.... It is an odd way of making flesh cheap to stop or check the distillery.'[25] Dixon claimed that the high price of Norfolk hogs in 1810 was partly due to the stoppage of the distillery in 1808.[26]

As the distilleries became fewer and larger, so the organization of pig-keeping became scientific, and evidence more reliable than the round numbers of the pamphleteers becomes available. John Middleton, a more independent observer, reported to the Board of Agriculture in 1813, for Middlesex,[27] that the distillers fattened 50,000 hogs for bacon annually, and in doing so increased their value £4 each, making £200,000 each year. And, moreover, he now praised the quality of the pork. Dixon had put the numbers at 'over 41,000' in 1810, and James and Malcolm say that, for Surrey:

> ... the numbers which ... are annually fattened, shews to what an extent it is carried on, and, as a branch of commerce, [it] is of considerable value: it is, besides, of material benefit to those counties from whence they draw their supplies; and inasmuch as it makes a part of agricultural economy, deserves every encouragement that can be given to it. There are also great numbers fed in the starch yards, which we shall distinguish from those of the distilleries....[28]

They continue to give the numbers as 3,000 fattened annually at Messrs Johnson's Distillery at Vauxhall; 3,000-4,000 at Benwell's, Battersea; 2,000 at Bush's, Wandsworth. Stenard's starch manufactory fattened 2,700 yearly, on an average, and Randall and Suter's 600-700. The starch yards, however, were under the disadvantage of having to use a proportion of beans and pease in addition to their offals. All these figures are in excess of the numbers of cattle that the distillers had begun to keep, as described below, and they total for Surrey 11,700 hogs annually, value £46,215.

As with the cattle this was now 'capitalistic' meat production in a systematic way. Finchley Common [29] was the great market, both for the butchers who bought 'fat' and for the distillery feeders who bought the 'lean stores'. Finchley was the selling point for those coming from the Midland counties — Yorkshire, Lincolnshire, Leicestershire, Berkshire, and Shropshire — while the counties to the north-east of London — Norfolk, Suffolk, and Essex — sent their breeds to Romford market after the harvest.[30] At market they were sorted into sizes by the salesmen (the distillers wanted them at about 15 months and they needed too many each to be able to buy all of the same breed) and sent to the various feeders. In 1813 the average buying price was about 55 *s*. and they sold fat, according to weight and quality, in about 18 to 26 weeks time. James and Malcolm print a table of weights and prices showing the great profit obtainable from this business,[31] and comment on the way in which they are kept 'with all imaginable care and cleanliness in one progressive state of increase.... It must be observed that no pains are spared to keep them clean and sweet, which the superior construction of their very extensive premises enables them to do.'

With both meat prices and the rate of duty rising at this time there was every incentive for the distillers to become as efficient as possible in their feeding arrangements. One estimate [32] reckoned upon being able to pay all the running expenses of the concern on the receipts from keeping stock, others supposed the gain to be about 2*s*. per week for each pig and 10-15*s*. a week per head of cattle.[33] This advantage may have been the incentive for the distillers to begin keeping cattle themselves once it had been proved feasible — beef was more in demand and the price was higher. Middleton describes how it began and how a mixed diet which included the distillery offals now had made this side of meat production highly efficient.[34] A certain Mr Man of Bromley first fed meat cattle on the wash and grains in 1789.

During the first three or four years of this practice Mr Man obtained the wash for nothing, the secret then began to extend, and the wash is now fetched from the distilleries to all the environs of the town, and even to the distance of 10 or 15 miles, although it is now sold for 2*s* 6*d*. per butt. The whole quantity of wash used to be drained off into the river as of no value; it is now sold and so desirous are the cow-keepers and cattle feeders of obtaining it that carts to the numbers of 10 or 20 at a time may be seen waiting to be filled up in turn, when the wash is turned on.

On the strength of this Man had, by 1813, enough accommodation to feed 1,000 bullocks at a time; and between 4,000 and 5,000 passed through his hands each year. Cattle on the King's farms at Windsor were also fed on distillery grains; the bailiff considering them a 'very valuable food indeed'.[35] While selling off the premises was still general where there was a market in the neighbourhood for their waste products, it appears that it was becoming general, for the larger distillers to keep cattle themselves on the 'wash' after 1800. Thomas Smith, a distiller of Brentford, thought that about 4,800 to 5,000 were kept by them in 1808, but that the greatest proportion fed by the distillers was still for milk.[36] They themselves, at Brentford, did more fattening than others because they had no cow-keepers near them, and as late as 1808 they found difficulty in selling their grains outside. 570 cattle were kept there in stall.

By 1813, in Surrey, Stephenson writes, that: 'Most of the cattle ... fattened for the butcher in this county are in the hands of the great distillers at Battersea, Vauxhall, etc.... The practice of carrying cattle is adopted by many of the feeders, particularly at the distillery in Vauxhall, and is found to answer remarkably well.'[37]

James and Malcolm note this as being the case at Hodgson's as early as 1794, when special accommodation had lately been built and the management made thoroughly efficient. By 1805 they had begun to fatten 600 each season — from October to May — while at Brentford the distillers' cattle were evidently one of the agricultural sights of the county. At Smith and Harrington's premises there were nearly 500 tied up '... and kept in the highest possible stile; so fine a sight is no where in England to be met with, and these gentlemen take much pleasure in shewing them to persons properly introduced.'[38]

There were, as then, none at Cook's new distillery but Calvert, Clarke, Dunkin and Scott were preparing to keep large numbers and had already 100. William Adam, a farmer at Streatham, had arranged his farm to keep cattle specially on the offals from the distilleries, having the same system of management as Hodgson's but sending the four miles daily to Vauxhall and Battersea for the grains and wash.[39]

This system is itself revealing — and is as efficiently planned and operated as any 'high farming' in Norfolk. At Hodgson's

> ... almost circumscribing their premises a range of houses have been built, of almost 600 ft. in length, by 32 ft. in width for the oxen. These houses are divided longitudinally into separate stalls for each beast.... The oxen are placed in two rows standing with their heads opposite each other, and in the middle between the two rows is a passage 6 ft. wide the whole length, and one at each end of the same width, where the cattle go in and out. Latterly they have introduced an open wooden trellis,[40] or grating, made strong ... to keep the animals from the pavement, that they may not only be kept dry but also that they may with greater facility be kept clean; which, as often as they want to do, the soil is drawn out from under the grating by means of a broad hoe.... For every 100 oxen two men are kept ... the allowance is one bushel of grains put into a triangular trough filled with wash, to each, and one truss of hay per diem to every 15, to which is added sometimes, some of the meal dust that flies from the malt in grinding.[41]

William Adam also had these special houses 'conveniently constructed and sufficiently capacious' to feed 600 bullocks on the same mass-produced, stall-feeding pattern. They bought in September at Kingston and the other West Country cattle fairs, preferring the Welch or the Herefords, for about £5 each, and sold, according to the market, after 14 to 16 weeks to the carcass butchers for about £16 per head. Despite this efficiency there was a certain waste that the reports to the Board of Agriculture regret. The profits were directly from the meat sold to the London market, and the manure resulting was largely wasted in those establishments within the town — 'not for want of a market for it, but because the collecting it in any of the large distilleries would be attended with some trouble, and their premises are too confined and valuable to allow of their affording sufficient room for such an article...'.[42] Here lies one of the big differences in emphasis between England and Scotland — for the keeping of livestock at, or on the produce of, the distilleries was common to both. In Scotland the point always stressed is that the livestock kept through the distilleries provided manure essential for maintaining, and extending, the general fertility of the farms. The connection between the agricultural economy of the country and the distilleries was there more intimate and widespread — for the distilleries were not confined to the towns.

This increasing exploitation of the waste products of breweries and distilleries is concomitant with the development of the parent industries during the same years. They were becoming organized on a large scale, and consequently facing problems of industrial organization more general in the next century — with capitalization, buying policy for stock, pricing and so forth. Because they were functioning on such a large scale it became profitable to use systematically the quantities of valuable by-products remaining from the primary manufacture. And this incentive which arose merely from the scale on which they were working was increased by the opportunity it afforded of off-setting in some degree the rising rate of taxation and spreading a loss in a bad year when raw material prices were high. The long-term influence of the duty was very sharply increased by a bad harvest. It was not customary for retail prices of drink to move in response to one bad harvest, and when the distillers had to bid for barley at a scarcity price, the knowledge that they could command a profit from the sale of their stock which would also be that of scarcity must have been a big compensating factor. Also the move into keeping cattle comes at a time when the greatest fluctuations and difficulties were affecting the breweries and distilleries. It is probably not coincidental that this new phase of livestock keeping comes at the same time as the tied house system was rapidly spreading amongst the brewers. Both are a likely response to bad times. Apart, however, from these more particular questions, the general fact is important. This livestock kept by industries, emerging in their own way through an industrial revolution, made a significant, if unnoticed, contribution to feeding the city population which they supplied with drink.

Notes

1 The grains from brewing had always played a part in the domestic economy of the farm and the country estate. This is mentioned in most of the works on husbandry and agriculture of the time as, for example, Ed. Lisle (1757, 2nd edn) *Observations in Husbandry*, II, 330: 'In managing hogs a gentleman has good advantage above a farmer ... inasmuch as in March (when the corn is almost threshed out) great store of drink may be brewed, with the grains of which many pigs may

be maintained till the middle of May when the broad-clover comes in....'

2 This was not including the yeast of the brewery which was the source of a regular trade to the distillers and the bakers, sometimes direct and sometimes through intermediaries — the Yeast Men. See *Parl. Papers*, 1803-4, IV, Report from Comm. on London Bakers' Petitions, p.8, and 1808, IV, Evidence before the Comm. on Distilling from Sugar, p.51. Benwell and Smith say that the great porter brewers supplied corn distillers, and some Scottish distillers.

It does not include either the sludge from the boilers and vats which was used for manure. (J. Mills (1765) *New System of Agriculture* 1, 94.). Combrune complains that there was as yet no use for the spent hops of the brewery which 'might become an object of private emolument to the brewer, as well as of public benefit to the nation' (M. Combrune (1758) *Essay on Brewing*, p.291), but these are noted as being used with sour grains for manure by 1805 (J. Malcolm (1805) *Agriculture of Surrey*, II, 106-7).

3 Printed estimates for the production of the first twelve houses exist for 1759-60: 525,674 (Annual Register); 1786-87: 978,200 (T. Pennant (1790) *History of London*, p.378, n.); 1794-5: 993,840 (Press Return). These figures are all for the number of 36 gall. barrels.

4 *Parl. Papers*, 1803, VIII, 1039. Papers relating to Distillers. Total numbers in London then were sixteen.

Previous estimates vary greatly. *Corn Distillery stated to the consideration of the Landed Interest* (1783) (Pryme Coll., Marshall Library, Cambridge) gives thirty 'Capital Offices' in and about London in 1750 (p.14), and twelve only after the prohibition of the corn distillery was removed in 1760 (p.16). When the House of Commons called for a return of the stocks of distillers in and near London in 1782-3 there are only eight firms named (*Commons Journals*, XLIII, 505-6.)

5 Whitbread's *Brewing Books*, 1800-50, passim. F.A. Accum (1821) *Art of Brewing*, p.125, gives the length of brew of porter from 2½-3 brls. per qtr. malt. It varied greatly with the quality of the malt.

6 Malcolm, op. cit., I, p.357. See also *Parl. Papers* 1808, IV, 26. Benwell states that 100 gall. of wash can be obtained, on average, from 1 qtr. grain, and 19 gall. of spirits from the 100 gall. of wash. The number of licensed stills and the amount of spirits that paid duty in no sense give total production of spirits, or the total production of these waste products. Fraud was widespread but impossible to estimate.

7 *Parl. Papers*, ibid. p.113.

8 *Parl. Papers*, ibid. pp.26, 113, 164-7. *Parl. Papers*, 1831, VII, Evidence before Committee on use of Molasses, p.69. A discussion of the ratios of malted to unmalted grain used in distilling is also given in *Commons Journals*, 1745, XXIV, 833.

9 Whitbreads: *Gratuity Ledger*, 1800-50, passim. When calculating how

much David Jennings, the brewer, has benefited from perquisites there is the entry (1801) '... for Money received of Cowkeepers and which he has not brought to account — £779, which sums are set against his 2 years Gratuity. Besides which he had perquisites in Hops and Grains suppose between £300 and £400'.

10 See chapter 11, pp.216-17

11 *Parl. Papers*, 1803, VIII, 1039. There were then 133 rectifying distillers of which sixty-one were in the London area. There were only twenty-two licensed primary distillers in the whole country (England) of which sixteen were in London, and the others in Bristol (two), Colchester, Maidstone (Bishop's 'Geneva' distillery), Stanstead, and Worcester.

12 *Impartial Enquiry into the Present State of the British Distillery ...* (1736) (Pryme Coll.), pp.37-8, and *Distilled Spiritous Liquors the Bane of the Nation*, which is on the farmers' side against the distillers.

13 *General Description of all Trades*, 1747, p.79: '... Malt Distilling, which vies with the Brewery for Return of Money and Profit, for most of them are very large concerns indeed, adding to the Distilling Malt Spirits chiefly for the use of Rectifiers, that of fatting Hogs, an Advantageous Article, which together are not to be undertaken without some thousand Pounds in Cash....'

14 *Impartial Enquiry*, p.38.

15 Ibid. This was a measure that profited them fiscally by escaping the malt duty, as well as enabling them to feed their hogs more effectively. James and Malcolm in 1794 suggest that they began to keep hogs in order to recoup some of the excise payments (*State of the Agric. of Surrey*, 1794, pp.33-4).

16 *The Case of the Malsters, Farmers and Graziers in General* (Goldsmith's Library, c. 1750); *Commons Journals*, XXIII, 584, 630; XXIV, 833-6. This latter section includes the evidence of witnesses summoned before the committee.

17 The inferiority of the distillers' meat was the common charge in all pamphlets against the distillery. See *Distilled Spiritous Liquors the Bane of the Nation*, 1736; J. Tucker (1751) *An impartial Inquiry into the Benefits and Damages ... of low-priced Spiritous Liquors; Impartial Enquiry*, op. cit., p.39; *Commons Journals*, XXIV. This evidence includes that of an ex-distiller, Harvest. Jennings, a contractor buying for the naval Victualling Commissioners, says that the distillery-fed hogs could give good keeping pork if they were managed properly and the favourable report of J. Middleton in 1813 (*General View of the Agriculture of Middlesex*, p.486) suggests that this proper management came with experience and experiment — although he is still combating consciously a common opinion.

18 *Impartial Enquiry*, op. cit., p.39. He suggests that the distillers sold at this 1½d. per lb. less because 'they can afford it so cheap'.

19 *Commons Journals*, XXIV, 835. There are few precise references to the

contractors with whom the navy dealt in the printed Calendar of Treasury Books and papers. Reference is made to a grazier who petitioned against a contract that had proved unprofitable through a sudden rise in prices of country-fed hogs (C.T.B. Aug. 1697-8, p.210). And there appear to be regular purchases made in Ireland in 1743 (C.T.B. 1743, pp.260-1, 264, 274).

20 R.G. Albion (1926) *Forests and Sea Power*, Cambridge, Mass., pp.55-60, 320-4.

21 *Commons Journals*, XXIV, 836.

22 'Immediately upon passing the Act (1751) the Distillery was lessened a full Third.' *True State of the ... Distillery* (1760) (Pryme Coll.) 24 Geo II, ch. 40. 2 Geo III, ch. 5. This new duty of 7 guineas per tun meant that when the Corn Distillery was allowed to start again in 1760 the total nominal duty was £24.10s. per tun, increased by £4.18s per tun in 1762. The 1756 stoppage had been partly in response to pressure from the West Indies interest to encourage the sale of molasses and 'low Sugars'. This running fight continued into the nineteenth century, intensifying when the West Indies ran into bad times.
   Corn Distillery stated to the Consideration of the Landed Interest (1783). (Pryme Coll.), p.16, states that, apart from the twelve distilleries that re-opened on corn distilling in 1760, ' ... all the rest (were) shut up or demolished without receiving any recompence or reward from Government under whose sanction they were erected at the expence of many thousands of pounds.'

23 Ibid. pp.43-4.

24 There is the double complaint that fat hogs were too dear for the Victualling Office to buy and that there were too few in the hands of the distillers to be sold. The bad harvest meant less corn for the 'lean stores' on the farms and affected the parent industries of brewing and distilling also in the high grain prices and in the decline of purchasing power through unemployment. The writer emphasizes that the need is for employment, not charity (p.49). Production of malt that paid duty fell from 28 m. bushels in 1782 to 17.23 m. in 1783. (*Parl. Papers*, 1835, XXXI, 15th Report of Commissioners of Excise Enquiry, p.4.)

25 *Thoughts and Details on Scarcity*, 1795, Works, 1834, II, p.243.

26 W. Dixon (1810) *Inquiry into the Impolicy ... of the prohibition of Distillation from Grain,* Liverpool, p.41 (Pryme Coll.). *Corn Distillery stated...*, 1783, p.44, claims that the decline of the distillery was responsible for the increase in the price of hog-fat for the soap boilers from £24 to £34 per ton.

27 J. Middleton (1813) *General View of the Agriculture of Middlesex*, p.579.

28 W. James and J. Malcolm (1794) *State of the Agriculture of Surrey*, p.33.

29 Ibid. pp.36-7; Middleton, op. cit., p.486.

30 D. Defoe (1722) *Tour thro' the whole Island* ... Everyman edn, Vol. I, p.37.
31 Op. cit. p.35. Table of hogs at Messrs Johnson's Distillery:

Breed	Age bt.	Value	Weeks kept	Weight	and value when sold
Salop. Herefd. Glos. Berks.	15 mths.	55s.	18-26	32-5	£4-£5
From Essex	15 mths.	60s.	,,	34-6	£4. 15s.-£5. 10s.
Norfolk. Suffk.	Younger	42s.	,,	21-4	£2. 15s.-£3. 3s.
Yorks	15 mths.	46s.	,,	21-8	£3-£3. 10s.

32 *Parl. Papers*, 1816, IX, Report on Illicit Distilling in Ireland, p.143. The reference is to a large distillery.
33 James and Malcolm, op. cit., p.35. W. Stephenson (1815) *Agriculture of Surrey*, p.522.
34 Middleton, op. cit., pp.579-90.
35 *Parl. Papers*, 1808, IV, Evidence before the Comm. on Distillation from Sugar, p.120, N. Kent, the King's Bailiff.
36 Ibid. p.29. One of the main issues raised by this Committee and argued by the witnesses is the potential dislocation of the cattle-feeding branch of the distillery if distilling from corn should be prohibited. The wash from distillation from molasses could be utilized if need be, but it would not be feasible to keep stock without the grains that were produced only from corn distillation. Beans and pease would have to be purchased from other sources if the corn distillery were closed, pp.33, 135. Also *Parl. Papers*, 1806-7, II, Report from Comm. on distilling from Corn and Sugar, Report, p.6, and Evidence, pp.24-6.
37 Stephenson, op. cit. p.522.
38 J. Malcolm (1805) *Agriculture of Surrey*, I, 355-9.
39 James and Malcolm, op. cit., p.32; Malcolm, ibid.
40 This was discontinued in 1805 because of the trouble it caused to the feet of the cattle. The stalls had then been entirely paved with brick. Malcolm thought that some of the cattle kept by the other distillers were cleaner than Hodgson's, being well strawed. Malcolm, op. cit.
41 James and Malcolm, op. cit. p.31.
42 Malcolm, op. cit., II, 26.

14

SWORDS AND PLOUGHSHARES: THE ARMED FORCES, MEDICINE AND PUBLIC HEALTH IN THE LATE EIGHTEENTH CENTURY

I

The present chapter explores the links between one area of military commitment and developing knowledge, skills and innovations which were not without effect in the country more widely, though with certain time-lags: the relations between the armed forces, medicine and public health in the later eighteenth century. It deserves to be documented more systematically than space allows in the present volume, if only because historians of naval and army medicine have not considered these wider effects of the developments they have recorded, while economic and social historians, in this case no less than in many others, have not given the army and navy in the eighteenth century the attention which their importance deserves.[1]

The numbers of professional medical men in the armed services, when mobilized for war after 1793, suggest the scale of the commitment within which these influences have to be considered. By 1794-5 there were 500 naval surgeons and hospitals at all five of the main naval ports, and over 700 by 1800. Forty-five ships in the channel fleet carried surgeons (thirty-two ships of the line, eight frigates and five lesser vessels) with a hospital ship. Over sixty physicians served the army and the position of surgeons was, if anything, on a greater scale than for the navy with every regiment of over 500 men being attended by a surgeon and two assistants (with the 'completest equipment of medicines and hospital bedding'). The artillery had a separate medical establishment. In the navy most medical regulations had been within the authority of individual physicians to the fleet, acting under the authority of the admirals of different squadrons who had appointed them, as Rodney had appointed Gilbert Blane, his personal physician, to be physician to the West Indies squadron in 1780. However, in 1797 the Admiralty established a medical board under the first Sea Lord with Blane and Dr Robert Blair as Physicians to the Fleet. General Admiralty orders then gave more centralized, generalized authority for imposing medical standards throughout the navy, as general orders had required the universal distribution of specific anti-scorbutics for the first time in 1795 (see p.270).

This large establishment and its progressive institutionalization within the armed services conditioned the influence of the professional medical personnel within it. The sense of professional identification and status became much enhanced by the growing presence of doctors within the armed services: their presence in a formally organized hierarchical society with precise allocations of seniority, authority, status and reward meant that their interests, as a professional group, were determined in all these respects. Not accidentally much discussion took place during the Napoleonic wars, as before, on these matters, with demand for professional equality in status and pay for doctors in the navy compared with the army. Thomas Trotter, the most obdurate spokesman for naval surgeons, on much lower *per diem* payments and with much lower degrees of entitlement to half pay, argued always in terms of the professional importance of the surgeons to naval strength. 'A medical establishment', he wrote, 'can alone prescribe those means of prevention from sickness which has often, and may again, unnerve the naval arm.' Naval doctors served 'the vital part of the machine that is our glory.'[2] His own publications represent, for a serving officer subject to the orders of the commander in chief and the Admiralty, astonishingly outspoken claims for the professional authority of medically qualified practitioners in all that had to do with the health of seamen — and earned him savage rebuke from St Vincent, for example, who accused Trotter of suborning his authority and threatening his strategic plans by ordering captains not to put to sea before taking on their full complement of anti-scorbutics.[3] Trotter also demanded that the physicians of all naval hospitals should be fully qualified, university MDs in accordance with expected professional standards.

The connections between military medicine and the wider national context existed at various levels. The transference of doctors between the army and navy (as the East India Company ships) and civilian practice is the most obvious, and must have been amongst the most significant, given the numbers involved, in time of peace. With skills embodied, above all, in the persons of practitioners this link brought inter-relationships in a two-way traffic. It was particularly important in a field which this paper does not consider — surgery. In the eyes of naval doctors, army physicians had a great advantage. The army doctor could live in towns with 'polished society' taking advantage of the 'gay manner of life peculiar to the army' which kept him in touch with advances in civilian medicine and his prospective clientele, while the naval doctor was isolated, away from books and civilian preferment. 'Many of the Physicians in London and other great towns of England', commented Trotter, 'began the practice of Medicine in the army … but there are few of the navy list that have been so fortunate in their career.'[4]

The effectiveness of the services as a training ground for preventive medicine owed much to the greater premium given to health in this specialized environment as well as to the greater medical hazards faced by troops and seamen. In civilian life physical effectiveness was not of such immediate concern to government or employers, save in the rare communal emergencies imposed by plague or equivalent catastrophe, which could invoke dramatic public response. As long as epidemic disease was accepted as inevitable, its visitations unpredictable, its causes unknown (or interpreted as divine retribution upon the wicked), and treatment ineffectual there was little likelihood of public resources being mobilized against it. Public costs stood in the way of private benefits as long as no immediate public gain could be captured. The political imperatives of a 'minimum' state in the eighteenth century also stood against public action. City councils and merchant interests in England, for example, stood out against effective quarantine laws in municipal action against plague because the siege economy this entailed imposed high costs, with authoritarian controls, and interrupted trade. Continental countries, where such local libertarian principles did not obtain, could implement *cordons sanitaires* more effectively.[5]

These constraints lost much of their influence when countered by the urgency of improving the effectiveness of the armed forces in the emergencies of war, where sanctions were much greater. One of the central dynamics of the nation — its ability to win wars in a bellicose world — was put at risk by such a failure. The increase in the scale of warfare, with larger communities of men living at close quarters in barracks, encampments, naval ports and fleets increased the hazards of disease. Colonial expansion (particularly in the West Indies and India), which kept fleets and troops in hot climates, added a further dimension to medical risks. And, from the mid-seventeenth century, naval strategy had become much dependent upon how long a fleet could stay at sea. This, in turn, depended very much upon the number of seamen in good health. As levels of incapacity in troops and seamen from sickness became major constraints upon military effectiveness, in that measure were incentives for medical improvements enhanced. It is noticeable, for example, that little attention was paid to discovering counter-measures against scurvy in the merchant marine (where it certainly existed in the more distant trades) or in the civilian population, where the disease was said to be rife in the seventeenth century.[6] In those contexts, the structure of incentives for devoting resources to its cure was absent. In contrast two of the most celebrated, or notorious, military and naval expeditions of the period tell their own story: 1,051 out of 1,955 seamen died during Anson's navigation of the globe in 1740-1, mainly from scurvy; while the 'Walcheren fever' (malaria, dysentery, typhoid and typhus) incapacitated over half the troops on this fatal venture and killed forty times more men than the enemy. The context in which these disasters befell was such that very energetic enquiries were held to investigate the matter, followed by urgent demands for action and the mobilization of resources and effort to effect it.[7]

If incentives and sanctions within the armed forces were more effective in promoting investigations into infectious and deficiency diseases than in civilian life, the institutional conditions of the army and navy greatly helped the physicians in charge of them. Financial resources which could be mobilized for investigation and experiment were not limited by the prospects of short-term profitability in a commercial context. The whole concept of 'cost-effectiveness' in a military context is not evaluated in commercial terms. Because of the incentives to discover a cure for the scurvy the Admiralty put much effort into commissioning research. A long sequence of experiments was conducted into producing a beer concentrate which could provide an easily stored antidote for ships' crews long on foreign station. Cook's circumnavigation of the globe was, in effect, a multi-purpose scientific expedition, with high priority given to an experimental search for antidotes against scurvy. Malt, 'sourkrout', salted cabbage, 'saloup' (conserve of oranges and lemons), 'portable broth', mustard, 'marmalade of carrots', and spruce beer were tried out, with systematic testing in the fleets during the war of American Independence.[8]

Circumstances allowed much greater scope for comparative testing and experimenting under controlled conditions than in civilian medicine. The army and navy (particularly ships' companies when afloat) were very tightly controlled authoritarian communities. The same was true of military hospitals ashore, to a greater extent than civilian hospitals. Other authoritarian communities such as orphanages, schools, prisons and poor houses were not so concerned with medical innovations. The influential naval doctors took full advantage of these opportunities. James Lind, whom Trotter called the 'father of nautical medicine', demonstrated conclusively that scurvy was a specific deficiency disease responding most effectively to oranges and lemons by undertaking a controlled clinical trial of comparative diets, conducted by rational observation and experiment. 'Several medicines [were] tried at sea in this disease', he reported, 'on purpose to discover what might promise the most certain protection.... The following are the experiments. On the 20th May 1747 I took twelve patients in the scurvy on board the *Salisbury* at sea. Their cases were as similar as I could have them.' He then administered different diets and medicaments to these seamen, in pairs: a quart of cider, elixir of vitriol, vinegar, sea water, oranges and lemons and other mixtures. His conclusion: 'the consequence was that the most sudden and visible good effects were perceived from the use of the oranges and lemons.'

He worked within assumptions that were deliberately and articulatedly committed to empirical, comparative, experimental, controlled, observations. 'The true causes of the disease' were to be determined 'from observations made upon it.'[9] Thomas Trotter, as its Physician, deliberately used the Channel Fleet as his laboratory after 1793. Ships' surgeons were required to report observations regularly on diet, clothing, the incidence of infection and incapacity. 'The operations of a large Fleet in Channel service offer a field for observation of the first importance to the medical enquirer', he wrote, and he backed up his demands to the Admiralty for regular distributions of fresh meat, fresh 'sallad', oranges and lemons and vegetables against scurvy with the systematic reporting of observations from ships' surgeons and captains in 'this immense field for observation which the Channel Fleet has afforded.' Scurvy was now (at long last) conquered. The stock of facts about it were great beyond all precedent; prevention and cure had been brought to such a certainty by recent experiments 'as to suspend the utility of future investigations'. General Admiralty orders to all ships for issuing oranges and lemons in 1795 (issued on the authority of Sir Gilbert Blane) meant that no general outbreak occurred again.[10]

Typhus was the next problem and Trotter held great hopes of preventive measures being worked out 'from the advantage of having attended an immense number of cases in very diversified situations'.[11] He also proposed a systematic vaccination campaign for all seamen as ships successively arrived in port, once convinced of the efficacy of Jenner's new method.[12]

II

Efforts to utilize the opportunities afforded for experiment in authoritarian communities depended, not only upon the incentives to achieve results, but also upon this prior and associated belief in the efficacy of the scientific method. Lind was praised for ignoring as irrelevant and unscientific the intellectual authority of ancient authors. Sir Gilbert Blane and Sir John Pringle, the most prestigious of military medical authorities, both argued forcibly for the experimental method.[13] Sir Gilbert Blane praised Bacon as 'the great author and leader in the employment of inductive reasoning': he held that medicine advanced by ascertaining the agencies of nature 'by observation and experiment'. 'By the former,' he wrote, 'we may be said to listen to nature, by the latter to interrogate her.'[14]

Paradoxically the advocacy of preventive measures in personal and public hygiene did not spring from any exact awareness of the intrinsic nature of the main infectious diseases involved or their carriers. No bacilli or viruses were identified during the eighteenth century, and even in the case of scurvy and smallpox, where specific medical remedies had been evolved, this was without benefit of scientific knowledge. The essence of the matter was scientific method, rather than formal scientific knowledge, a scientific procedure of systematic observation and experiment. Such empiricism, without formal scientific knowledge, greatly widened the area of awareness in associating infectious diseases with their habitat, of what associations increased the likely incidence and what measures reduced it. It was much more effective in preventive action than in proposing cures, once a disease had been caught, because effective cures depended rather more specifically upon (or the probability of discovering a cure was increased by) formal knowledge about the intrinsic nature of the disease. The chapters in Pringle, Blane and Trotter analysing the medical causes of infectious fevers and their formal transfer mechanisms are still almost medieval, as are the remedies proposed for those having caught the diseases.

Fevers are not separately identified in a scientific way. Typhus, typhoid and malaria, for example, are not distinguished by their different modes of infection: the vocabulary remains that of distempers, fluxes, remitting, continued and intermittent fevers, although dysentery has its modern connotation. 'Putrid exhalations' and variants of the 'miasmic' theory of infection dominated views of infective mechanisms, with a heavy medieval overlay. For example, Pringle's analysis of the incidence of hospital and gaol fevers made shrewd remarks about the predispositions of infection — 'the quantity of the contagious matter, the closeness of the air and crowds of people' — but he identified the mechanism of infection as 'corruption of the air ... deprived of its elastic parts ... vitiated with the perspirable matter, which, as it is the most volatile part of the humours, is also the most putrescent'. Similarly, the symptoms of the diseases are accurately described, being immediately responsive to observation, but the medical therapy directed at the infected patients was essentially medieval: vomiting agents, bleeding, purging and blistering.[15] References to Galen, Hippocrates, other less famous classical commentators and medieval writings are made up into a witch's brew of explanation.

Blane was very clear about the medical ignorance of curing, as distinct from preventing, fevers and the other main infectious diseases. It was a moot point, he wrote, 'whether recoveries have been effected by *virtue* of medicine or in *spite* of it ... we must frequently run the risk of congratulating ourselves on a great *cure* where there may have only been a happy escape.'[16] This was, in effect, the continuance of the medieval and immediately post-medieval pattern of the response to the plague. Preventive measures, based upon observation, were rational and effective as far as they went: the isolation of victims, fumigation and cleansing of infected premises, destruction of the clothing, etc. of those infected, the attempt to isolate the plague-ridden communities by a *cordon sanitaire*. But this was combined with ignorance of the medical nature of plague, with its carriers, and virtually irrelevant medications for its victims.[17] Medical ignorance, of course, blunted the edge of preventive measures, as well as preventing cures; but the observed association between diseases and their environment did lead to much greater rationality in prevention if not in cures, despite the ignorance of carriers and vector mechanisms.[18]

The experimental method itself, advocated so vigorously by those eighteenth-century doctors concerned with preventing .the spread of infectious diseases, embodied a motivational structure, a mentality, itself encouraging activism in the search for new knowledge and new measures. The assumption was that the secrets of nature would yield to the efforts of man through observation and experiment and that control over nature could be enhanced by such deliberate efforts. This was true despite the scientific ignorance about the main diseases which prevailed well into the nineteenth century until the development of the new science of bacteriology — with the carriers of typhus and typhoid separately identified only in 1861, the cholera bacillus discovered in 1883 and that of plague in 1894.[19]

In this sense generalizations concerning the relations between scientific knowledge and innovations in medicine fit into a wider tradition. Even though it may be argued that formal scientific knowledge did not provide a main stimulus to innovation in Western Europe until well into the nineteenth century, scientific attitudes and the experimental tradition, reflecting a changing intellectual consciousness, had an influence of their own.[20] When the incidence of disease was mysterious, or taken as the hand of divine providence striking the dissolute, public effort would be less engaged in diagnosing a more material explanation or devising appropriate preventive measures (particularly where the dissolute in question happened to be of the lower income groups). In the army and navy the premium upon improvements, as well as the intensity of the problem, was greater, particularly in time of war, but a call for action was created in much more insistent terms by evidence explaining scurvy as a specific deficiency disease than by older traditions of explanation embodied in Cockburn's *Sea Diseases* which provided the main rationale up to that point, where scurvy was put down to congenital laziness, bad air and indigestible food. They were doubtless more a response to medical ignorance than its cause, as the reactions to plague had been five centuries earlier (and a rational psychological response to such ignorance), but such a response in turn reinforced the structural logic of the intellectual world of which that scientific ignorance was a part. When the historian investigates disease, the investigation is not into an autonomous medical problem. Disease is a medical phenomenon given significance (even medical significance) by its environment and by the contemporary consciousness of the disease and its environment, because human reactions are conditioned by such consciousness.[22]

III

Hospital practice and preventive medicine were two important areas where military example led innovations and strongly influenced national practice (although interactions also moved in the other direction). There was no question about the work of naval and military doctors feeding a common pool of professional knowledge and skills. Sir Gilbert Blane became Physician of St Thomas's Hospital, after the peace of 1783, one of the most prestigious and influential medical posts in the country, where he energetically implemented the practices and standards he proposed for naval hospitals. He then attained the senior medical post in the navy, as Physician to the Fleet, after the outbreak of war once more in 1793 — a sequence which symbolises the links between military and civil practice at the highest level. Sir John Pringle, the leading army physician, attained the eminence of being President of the Royal Society. Their writings were of justified renown in their professional world, military and civilian, in specialised periodicals and independent publications. Thomas Trotter's declared intention was that his writings should translate knowledge from the naval service 'to medical readers in general'.[23] The fame of such men as Lind, Blane, Pringle, Robert Blair, Robert Robertson, William Farr and Thomas Trotter ensured a wide professional audience for their publications. Sir John Pringle's *Observations on the Diseases of the Army*, first published in 1752 had reached its fifth — cumulatively revised — edition by 1815. The essence of the work had appeared in the *Philosophical Transactions* in 1750, gaining a wider currency from there in the *Gentleman's Magazine* in the following year.[24] A similar transmission belt brought the experiments of James Lind and James Cook from a professional to a wider audience. By the early nineteenth century specialized medical journals, such as *Medico-Chirurgical Transactions* (1809) were supplementing general scientific journals in London, quickly followed by equivalent periodicals in the main provincial centres.

Knowledge of preventive measures was transferable from naval and military experience over infectious and deficiency diseases to a wider context because the worst medical problems faced by the fighting services were exactly those of the urban poor; although experienced in an intensified form through the greater intensity of conditions facing seamen and soldiers. Moreover improvements in medical practice concerning hygiene were demonstrable. Although mortality rates for the navy during the Napoleonic wars were twice that of comparable civilian age groups, over time the gain was substantial. Sick rates fell from 1 man in 2.45 of those serving in 1779 to 1 in 10.75 by 1813 and death rates fell over the same period from 1 in 42 to 1 in 143. Blane saw these improvements adding one-third to the effective naval manpower.[25] Trotter argued that not less than 100,000 seamen had been saved from death by scurvy during the wars since 1795; comparing the rate of mortality from the disease in the preceding war with the total numbers of seamen in 1795-1814.[26] This came primarily from the success of preventive rather than curative measures. Only scurvy and smallpox had been eliminated (or could be eliminated) by specifically medical therapy: none of the epidemic fevers was yet responsive to effective medication.

Hospital practice had the most direct parallels with civil experience — and Sir John Pringle prefaced his main book with the mordant observation 'Among the chief causes of sickness and death in an army, the reader will little expect that I should rank, what is intended for its health and preservation, the Hospitals themselves.' The principal aim of his book was to show how to prevent infection, 'the common and fatal consequences of a large and crowded hospital'.[27] Coupled with this were conditions of overcrowding, privation, lack of ventilation and warmth, dirt, insanitary habits, inadequate (or unbalanced) diets, filthy clothing and bedding, bad water supplies, and the other conditions which were more generally the lot of the poor throughout the land, and more particularly the lot of the urban poor. Sir John Pringle explicitly projected the relevance of his treatise on 'hospital and jayl fevers' from military to civilian hospitals, and from hospitals to the fevers 'more frequent in large and populous cities than elsewhere', and Trotter also drew attention to the links between typhus in ships and 'in great towns, among poor people in low, dirty, ill-aired and damp houses towards the fall of the year and particularly in times of scarcity or during long and rigorous winters'.[28] Blane emphasized repeatedly the predisposing conditions for fevers and enteric diseases: 'circumstances of personal filth and want of ventilation, frequently combined with hardships and privation'.[29]

The importance of the preventive measures advocated by these famous military doctors is exactly that they spoke for the poor as a whole, and it was no accident that their main research into preventive measures against infectious diseases should have been initiated from the very specialized environment of ships, army camps and hospitals. Their efforts were particularly aimed at mitigating 'crowd' diseases, even though they were made without specific knowledge of the intrinsic nature of these diseases, or their carriers, and despite the fact that contemporary curative medicine was largely irrelevant. Collectively, these diseases were the worst demographic killers of the eighteenth century, and their incidence was not alone amongst urban dwellers, although the intensive living conditions of insanitary towns provided the best context for their propagation. The 'dismal' peaks of the crude death rates curve, occurring every few years, occasioned by epidemic disease, particularly fevers and enteritis, were an important demographic phenomenon. It was just this range of infections which contemporary doctors thought preventive measures might check. The measures they proposed — which appear enlightened commonsense for the most part to our later view — were not specific to the diseases, none of the principal vectors or carriers being known, apart from the special cases of scurvy and smallpox. Perhaps because of that, paradoxically, they could have a wider effect upon improving health and survival rates. A consequence of holding a generalized rather than specific view of the nature of infectiveness of different diseases was that the preventive measures proposed were also generalized, and could be of wider effect than specific prophylactics. Rationality was to be judged by results even if not by the test of formal knowledge.

IV

The measures advocated in chorus by this group of eminent military and naval doctors, and implemented wherever the emergencies of active campaigning did not prevent it, amounted to a systematic programme of social medicine — ranging from public health measures to household hygiene, from personal hygiene to questions of diet and clothing. They were aimed at specific problems of their specialized constituencies — communities of adult men for the most part, healthy, sick and wounded, in conditions of privation but not, in normal circumstances, of deprivation of the essentials of food, clothing, warmth and shelter. The range of issues and the range of diseases which received their attention were limited, for this reason, and did not touch important branches of family medicine, midwifery, the care of babies and infants directly (although much of their work became of indirect relevance). Thus, in matters of public, domestic and personal hygiene their influence was complementary to the work of such famous civilian doctors as William Buchanan and his influential *Domestic Medicine* (1769) which had gone into twenty-two editions by 1826.[30]

The centre of the military doctors' concern lay with public health measures for community health in densely occupied institutions, particularly hospitals. All wards in naval and military hospitals were to be whitewashed, scrubbed, and fumigated regularly. All dirt, and particularly excrement, had to be cleared away, privies had to be kept clean, bedpans washed and water supplies isolated from pollution. Thomas Trotter's rigorous visitation and report on conditions in the Haslar Naval Hospital (with the subsequent regime imposed with his new authority as Physician to the Fleet) went beyond these measures. He ordered that 'W.C.'s ... should be in a separate building so as not to endanger the drinking water.' He refused to allow visitors to the fever wards and segregated patients with infectious fevers. Dispensers, apothecaries and physicians were required to *end* their rounds with the smallpox and fever wards, to reduce the spread of infection.[31] For army camps Pringle advised the sterilization of faeces (as a main source of infection), placing privies on the leeward side of camps, covering them daily with earth, clearing all rotting straw from tents and the like. Blane brought iron bedsteads into St Thomas's on hygienic grounds.

All put very great emphasis on ventilation. Hospitals were to have airy rooms of good height, with windows and doors opened daily in strict routine. Barrack rooms and wards were to have open chimneys and fires rather than enclosed stoves: the ventilation caused by the fire was more important than the warmth created. Blane, in particular, believed that much infection arose from want of fuel and warmth in the winter, which led the poor to close up their windows and remove all sources of ventilation. He thought that the greater availability and cheapness of fuel, by increasing both warmth and (of necessity) ventilation in open fires, very important indeed in reducing infections and mortality in the populace at large.[32] Captain Cook had ventilated the lower decks of HMS Resolution by lighting 'portable fires' to create draughts.[33]

A logical progression took the analysis forward from institutional measures to questions of personal hygiene, clothing and diet. When Blane was appointed Physician at St Thomas's in 1783 he took immediate measures to improve hygiene, quoting the tag about cleanliness being next to godliness. Patients were washed regularly and had regular changes of clean clothes. Their hair was cut. Dirty clothing (particularly that of infected patients) was to be burned or fumigated.[34] Equivalent measures were advocated by Pringle, Lind, and Trotter as part of the regime to ensure good health and low mortality rates.[35] The health regime established by Captain Cook in his circumnavigation of the globe, which recommended 'close attention to cleanliness', fresh water and regular washing was widely reported.[36]

A similar point was made about clothing: it should be adequate for warmth in winter but, more particularly, undergarments should be of cotton and linen so that they could be washed and changed regularly. Trotter gave full publicity to a disagreement he had had with the traditionalist martinet Admiral Earl St Vincent over clothing. St Vincent had issued a general memorandum to the fleet, without reference to his Physician (there had been earlier rows over diet and scurvy), requiring all captains to enforce the wearing of flannel shirts or waistcoats 'next the skin' and ordering pursers to provide them. Trotter delivered a furious rebuttal to his commander in chief, whom he accused of turning seamen, without the possibility of changing their clothes regularly, into 'walking stinkpots'. 'If British seamen are to wear flannel next the skin,' he wrote with the full force of professional authority, 'they... must soon lose the hardihood of constitution that fits them for duty. Clothe them as warm as you please but in the name of cleanliness give them linen or cotton next the skin.'[37] Such sustained advocacy of soap and water, cotton and linen garments (regularly washed) began in the mid-eighteenth century, but there is good reason to doubt whether cotton cloth became a commodity in mass demand at home until after 1780. What percentage of the nation wore linen, or clothes of cotton mixes, which could be (and were) washed regularly remains a matter of speculation.

Scurvy had shown one specific association between diet deficiencies and disease. In the search for antidotes much useful dietary advice had been proposed, with particular emphasis on fresh (rather than salt) meat, salad and green vegetables. Pringle, Blane and Trotter all noted the importance of vegetables in diet from continuous observations reported from ships and army camps; and both Blane and Pringle argued that considerable improvements had taken place in this respect in the feeding habits of the nation during the eighteenth century.[38] Blane, in common with Adam Smith and many other non-medical observers, praised potatoes particularly as an 'invaluable auxiliary' item of diet.[39] In general terms the fact that the mortality rate from many diseases (as distinct from the rate of infection) was strongly influenced by the nutritional standards of those infected was quite clear to these contemporaries, although compounded with other attributes of the lives led by their potential patients — overcrowded, poor housing, insanitary conditions.[40] Enteric diseases, with lethal fevers, were directly associated with bad harvests, high food prices, and the poor eating bad food by these contemporaries as well as by modern scholars.

V

It is not easy to assess the wider significance of the new knowledge and improved practices being developed by military doctors in the late eighteenth century. Other influences upon changes have to be acknowledged. Advances in knowledge have to be distinguished from its implementation. The implementation of improved practice has to be considered according to the scale of change. To use the terminology more familiar in discussions of innovations in technology: invention has to be distinguished from innovation; increases in the capital stock of knowledge follow a different logic to the incentives which determine the putting into practice of selections from that stock of knowledge. The diffusion of innovations, and the incentives which govern the choices of technique within a known technology, requires a different analysis from that concerned to understand advances at the frontiers of technology. The extent of diffusion of new techniques, the time-lags involved with the process of diffusion, the distribution between 'best practice' technology and traditional technology in an industry all govern the significance of an innovation.

Space permits only a general consideration of some of these issues here, but all of them, where operative, imply a certain narrowing of the general significance to be afforded to the work of these military doctors, whether judged in the context of the social groups directly influenced by them, or the period in which their influence has to be judged. It is difficult to come to anything more than subjective conclusions when seeking to judge the long-term, indirect effects of their professional contribution or to place it in an order of priority with other influences.

Their work has to be seen in terms of a contribution to knowledge as much as to improved practice in the first instance — although, in larger perspective, advances in the first conditioned progress in the latter. In these terms, the special conditions prevailing in the institutional context in which they worked created particularly effective incentives for the advancement of knowledge and the deployment of improved knowledge — as earlier pages have sought to argue. The army and navy were not the only institutions promoting the development and professionalization of medicine in eighteenth-century England, of course, nor was England unique in Europe in this regard. The most comprehensive schema of social medicine published in the eighteenth century, for example, is that of Johann Peter Frank, the great Austrian doctor.[41] But the contributions to advances in knowledge of the association beween diseases and environment made by doctors in the armed forces has not been sufficiently acknowledged.

Within their own world these advances in medicine (particularly the conquest of scurvy) were not without effect. As we have seen, Sir Gilbert Blane and Thomas Trotter believed that the gains in the effectiveness of seamen from improved health could be quantified. Blane was also proud of the fact that the regime he introduced into St Thomas's Hospital after 1783 considerably reduced cross-infection and mortality there, death-rates for in-patients falling from 1 in 14 in 1773-83 to 1 in 16.2 by 1803-13.[42] But the practical success of the measures proposed presupposed, in many cases, an authoritarian community, whether that of a ship, barracks, army camp or hospital, and could not be applied to the institutional conditions of the populace at large. One petty, but important, regulation proposed by Sir John Pringle for the layout and use of privies in an army camp is evidence enough: 'let there be some slight penalty, but strictly inflicted', he ordered, 'upon every man that shall ease himself anywhere about the camp but on the privies.'[43]

Much of the success of the measures advocated depended upon an authoritarian regime required to enforce them: very precise instructions laid down for all controllers of hospital wards; regular inspections and systems of report to ensure compliance; general orders imposed upon all subordinate commanders (as when Blane, on his appointment as a Commissioner, made lemon and orange juice a compulsory general issue to all ships, whereas it had depended upon more individual initiative up to that time) and like measures. Even here practice could fall well short of advocacy, particularly in the emergencies of campaigning, as the disasters of the Walcheren expedition and the initial circumstances of the Crimean war revealed. No equivalent controls were possible over the civilian population, whether by magistrates, civil servants or doctors, although local government regulations by city ordinance evidently did embody rising standards of expectations to a degree during the eighteenth century. The gap between knowledge and effective, compulsory action remained very wide, with local authorities resisting centralizing forces and the authoritarian pressure of professional opinion, as Edwin Chadwick found to his cost forty years into the nineteenth century.

When considering improvements in mortality more generally, during the eighteenth century (which he certainly assumed) Gilbert Blane listed many of these general measures: 'the use of linen and soap, the greater facility of procuring fuels and the more ample supply of water', less filth accumulating in London streets in the eighteenth century compared with the seventeenth ('the improved state of agriculture having rendered it very valuable as manure'), wider streets and brick houses, more effective statutory control in providing common sewers in London. He argued, on the evidence of the bills of mortality, that infant mortality had almost halved between 1728-50 and 1800-20, putting this down partly to specific measures against smallpox, but more generally to 'ventilation and cleanliness and more judicious management ... such as greater warmth in appartments and clothing and the correction of the vulgar error that the exposure of children to the open air at all seasons is salutary'. 'It is a question', he concluded, 'how far improved medical treatment has had any share in it.'[44]

Even though these assertions remain unquantifiable, much of this contemporary optimism has to be discounted, at least for eighteenth-century conditions. Blane had London principally in mind when he spoke of improvements in paving and street cleansing (but not when he was considering the benefits of cheaper fuel, because he singled out Lancashire for comment) and with only 10 per cent of the total population in the metropolis this was clearly an unrepresentative sample, both for certain improvements in hygiene and because the spread of high density living in urban conditions increased morality for many of the main causes of death. The increase in the proportion of population living in towns intensified the problems of sanitation, sewerage and public health down to the mid-nineteenth century in a context where the administrative framework for coping with a mass urban society had yet to be evolved (if the relative death rates between large towns and country districts be a guide). Equally, certain other improvements noticed by contemporaries, such as the increased use of healthier cotton clothing, spread more slowly down the social pyramid than contemporaries assumed. Rational responses by individuals, in questions of personal hygiene, and effective family response for household hygiene, were always dependent to a degree upon income levels — a minimum critical level of incomes set a threshold to adopting many of even the most elemental improvements in diet, clothing, shelter, warmth and cleanliness — whereas some of the most important attributes of hygiene, such as sanitation and water supplies, in practice lay beyond the power of rational action by individual families in rapidly growing towns.

The general preventive measures rather than specific medical therapy (save in the case of scurvy) advocated by military and naval doctors probably had the greatest potential significance. These were promoted in the light of a general awareness of the association between the context (personal, household and environmental) and disease rather than from specific medical knowledge. But carriers of many main infectious diseases — whether lice, fleas or contaminated food and water — would have had their effect removed or reduced by the adoption of such hygienic standards.

It may also be argued that only a demographically insignificant percentage of the population ever saw the inside of an institution to which the standards of public health and hygiene being propounded by military doctors were applied — whether ship, army camp or hospital — which were most unrepresentative habitats for the population at large. But this is not the whole point. Much of the new knowledge, and the measures, born within these highly specialized habitats, where mortality was intense and the premiums on reducing it very high, were of more general applicability. Personal hygiene, a better balanced diet and cleaner clothes had universal relevance; so did household and family hygiene with cleaner water, better heated and ventilated rooms. Overcrowded, ill-ventilated, unsanitary accommodation was the universal lot of poor families, not just those living in towns. Equally, even if most improvements depended upon access to higher family earnings, not all did; while the attainment of higher purchasing power does not, of itself, ensure the allocation of extra resources to promote healthier living without change in habits and patterns of spending. Some improvements required only changed practice on the basis of new knowledge and advocacy; others presumed changes in priorities of spending rather than incremental purchasing. It is demonstrable, at the other end of the social scale, that adopting a healthier life-style was not simply a function of a minimum critical level of income.

New knowledge, new priorities, new fashions were influential determinants of cultural change for the upper classes, who also adopted higher standards in these respects during the eighteenth and nineteenth centuries. It is also salutary to remember how dramatically certain cultural changes could spread down the social scale during the eighteenth century, without changes in living standards always being a critical variable — fashion in clothing, innoculation after 1750, the potato and tea drinking amongst them.

The influences which combine to affect levels of health, morbidity and mortality (quite apart from fertility) are manifold and their interactions still largely unravelled and certainly unquantified. However during the nineteenth century, improvements in public health, hygiene, preventive measures (particularly against infectious diseases), improved diet and clothing are considered collectively to be principal agents in the decline in national death rates. The contributions of doctors in British fleets and armies in the eighteenth century form one of those influences and have a place in the interactions. Their full effect came much later than in the lifetimes of the individuals whose work has been considered here. But to study that work is to stand in the hills observing streams from which great rivers were eventually sustained.

Notes

1 For a general survey of military medicine see C. Lloyd and J.L.S. Coulter (1961) *Medicine and the Navy*, Edinburgh; N. Cantlie (1974) *A History of the Army Medical Department*, Edinburgh.

2 T. Trotter (1801) *Medicina Nautica*, III, pp.37-8.

3 Ibid., pp.74-5.

4 T. Trotter (1797) *Medicina Nautica*, II, p.14.

5 Of course, the fact that Britain was an island reduced the need for such measures. See C.M. Cipolla (1972) *Christophano and the Plague*, London, and 'Origine et developpement des bureaux de santé en Italie', *Medicina Economia e Societa nell'Esperienza Storica*, Pavia, 1974; G.E. Rothenberg (1973) 'The Austrian sanitary cordon and the control of bubonic plague, 1710-1781', *J. History of Medicine and Allied Sciences*, XXVIII. The effectiveness of these measures was another matter.

6 G. Blane (1822) *Select Dissertations*, p.121.

7 C. Lloyd and J.L.S. Coulter, op. cit., chapter 18; R.M. Feibel (1968) 'What happened at Walcheren: the primary medical sources', *Bulletin of the History of Medicine*, XLII, with full bibliography. Detailed evidence on medical organization in the Walcheren expeditionary force is given in *Parl. Papers*, 1810, VII, 1.

8 See PRO/Adm. papers and other authorities listed in P. Mathias (1959) *The Brewing Industry in England, 1700-1830*, Cambridge, pp.204-9; J. Cook (1777) *A Voyage towards the South Pole*; J. Cook, *Phil. Trans.*, DXVI (No. XXII), p.402; A. Sparrman (1953 edn) *Voyage Round the World*, London, pp.26, 112,.

9 J. Lind (1753) *A Treatise on the Scurvy*, pp.118, 119-23.

10 The dramatic resurgence of the disease in 1794 had provoked a 'crisis' administrative response which determined the definitive preventive measures.

11 T. Trotter (1797) *Medicina Nautica*, I, pp.405, 426; II, pp.304.

12 Ibid., III, p.78.

13 Sydenham, long before, had seen the obligation of a physician as the 'industrious investigation of the history of diseases and of the effect of remedies, as shown by the only true teacher — experience.'

14 G. Blane (1821) *Elements in Medical Logic*, pp.17-18.

15 Sir John Pringle (1750) *Observations on the Nature and Cure of Hospital and Jayl Fevers*, pp.2, 4, 8-33; (1815, 5th edn) *Observations on the Diseases of the Army*, pp.126 ff., 149-56, 183-5.

16 G. Blane (1822) *Select Dissertations*, p.147.

17 L.F. Hirst (1953) *The Conquest of Plague*, Oxford; C. Cipolla, op. cit.

18 Examples of medical ignorance countering the effectiveness of preventive measures are manifold: amongst them the 'shutting up' of houses against plague, where the infected were isolated with the uninfected; the general absence of 'isolation' wards or 'isolation hospitals' for infectious diseases; Lind advocating the near-boiling of citrus fruits to produce a 'rob' for taking against scurvy; Chadwick flushing out sewers into rivers (a main source of drinking water) to clear 'miasmas' in the cholera epidemic of 1848.

19 See W. Budd (1861) *Typhoid Fever*; L.F. Hirst, op. cit.; M. Greenwood (1935) *Epidemics and Crowd-Diseases*, London.

20 The debate is summarized in chapter 3.

21 W. Cockburn (1696, 3rd edn 1736) *Sea Diseases*.

22 This is the essential point of Charles Rosenberg's study of the reactions to cholera epidemics in the nineteenth century. He remarks: 'A disease is no absolute physical entity but a complex intellectual construct, an amalgam of biological state and social definition' (*The Cholera Years*, 1962, Chicago and London, note to p.5).

23 T. Trotter, *Medicina Nautica* II, p.2.

24 *Phil. Trans. Royal Society*, XLVI, 1750; *Gentleman's Magazine*, XXI, 1751.

25 C. Lloyd and J.L.S. Coulter, op. cit., pp.183-4.

26 T. Trotter (1819) *A Practical Plan for Manning the Royal Navy without Impressment*, pp.26, 45.

27 Sir John Pringle (1752) *Observations on the Diseases of the Army*, preface.

28 Sir John Pringle (1750) *Observations on the Nature and Cure of Hospital and Jayl Fevers*, p.51; T. Trotter, *Medicina Nautica*, I, pp. 252-3.

29 G. Blane, *Elements in Medical Logic*, p.209.

30 See T.C. Smout (1969) *A History of the Scottish People, 1560-1830*, London, pp.257-9.

31 T. Trotter, *Medicina Nautica*, I, pp.27-34.

32 Sir John Pringle, *Observations on the Nature and Cure...*, pp.33, 46-51; *Observations on the Diseases of the Army*, pp.84-5, 96-7, 101-3, 107-9; G. Blane, *Select Dissertations*, pp.91, 125, 127, 137-40, 172-3; *Elements in Medical Logic*, p.209.

33 Sir John Pringle (1776) *Discourse upon some late Improvements...* p.28.

34 G. Blane, *Select Dissertations*, pp.122, 125-6, 136-7, 140, 172-3.

35 Sir John Pringle, *Observations on the Nature and Cure ...*, pp.46 ff.; *Discourse upon some late Improvements...*; J. Lind (1757) *An essay on the most Efficient Means of Preserving the Health of Seamen*; (1763) *Two Papers on Fevers and Infection*; T. Trotter (1786) *Observations on the Scurvy*.

36 J. Cook, 'Methods taken for preserving the Health of the Crew of H.M.S. Resolution', read to the Royal Society in 1776.

37 T. Trotter, *Medicina Nautica*, III, pp.93-4. See also T.C. Smout, op. cit., p.258.

38 Pringle, *Observations on the Diseases of the Army*, p.111; (1776) *Discourse upon some late Improvements of the Means for Preserving the Health of Mariners*, pp.11-13; Blane, *Select Dissertations*, pp.121-2; Trotter, *Medicina Nautica*, I, pp.405-25; III, pp.74-6, 387-402. For a Scottish parallel see Smout, op. cit. pp.250-2.

39 Blane, *Select Dissertations*, pp.161-2. He added 'but by no means as a staple article, far less as an exclusive constituent of national subsistence'.

40 Greenwood, op. cit., pp.139, 175, 178-9.

41 J. Peter Frank (1784) *System einer vollständigen medicinischen Polizey*, Vienna.

42 Blane *Select Dissertations*, p.141. He was very aware, in recording these improvements, that improved medical techniques did not necessarily reduce death rates, but extended the range of patients being treated. 'The comparative mortality of different hospitals', he commented, 'is a most fallacious test of the success of practice, unless the nature and intensity of the several diseases are taken into account. A large mortality may even be considered as a presumption of a hospital being well conducted in as far as it indicates that the most severe disorders have been admitted' (p.140).

43 Pringle *Observations on the Diseases of the Army*, p.101.

44 Blane, *Select Dissertations*, pp.122-3, 126-8.

15

THE FINANCES OF FREEDOM: BRITISH AND AMERICAN PUBLIC FINANCE DURING THE WAR OF INDEPENDENCE

Most of the retrospection, in the Bicentennial Year of 1976, rightly focused upon the political and military aspects of the War of Independence. But the finances of the war — for both parties — have an interest of their own; not least for those concerned with the financial options facing beleaguered economies two centuries later. In some ways, the contrasts between the policies adopted by Congress and Westminster in that fateful struggle embody choices which still affect us all, for good or ill. The various strategies of public finance invariably reveal political no less than economic constraints facing governments.

On the British side, war finance followed an already traditional pattern, determined for almost a century by a radical and unprecedented innovation of seventeenth-century England — the unredeemable, permanent funded debt. Taxes were raised, to the extent that the country gentlemen in Parliamnent and elasticities of demand for commodities suffering customs and excise impositions would tolerate — but borrowing met the gap between this and the financial demands of war. Such military costs grew continuously — one of the few general laws in history seems to be that war always gets more expensive. An annual public expenditure of £10.4m. in 1775 had grown to £29.3m. by 1782 — and of the cumulative total of £114.6m. over the seven years of war finance 1776-82, no less than £91.8m. (80 per cent) was the direct military spending of the army, navy and ordnance, which averaged £13m. per year of war.

Against this great weight of public expenditure new resources from taxation were limited. The land tax (at 4*s* in the pound) and the window tax were at their politically effective limits. A suggestion for a realistic re-assessment of property valuations (which could have revolutionized the yield of the land tax) was received in horror at Westminster; as was the rumour of an income tax. It needed Napoleon to sufficiently frighten Parliament to institute that. Instead there was window-dressing. Lord North announced, with unaccustomed sensitivity to the dictates of social conscience, that 'luxuries ought to be taxed ... because the first weight ought to fall upon the rich and opulent'. Hence his taxes on carriages, cards, dice, newspapers, inhabited houses, and male servants — 'taxes laid on luxuries and elegant conveniences of life'. But when it came to the point, he had to acknowledge, as always, that to get large revenues taxes had to be laid upon articles in mass demand. So the malt tax, affecting the staple beverage of the poor, sustained much of the increase in revenue from taxation, by being raised from 9½*d* per bushel to 1*s*4½*d*, with other increases in customs and excise rates, including those on wine and tobacco. The latter proposal provoked the comment from Lord North: 'If he knew what luxury was, tobacco came within that description', although the poor paid most of the tax.

All these stratagems really signified the political impossibility of taxing incomes and wealth effectively. Almost half the costs of the American war were covered by borrowing, which increased the permanent National Debt from £127 m. in 1775 to £232 m. in 1783. The entire debt was virtually a creation of war finance in the eighteenth and nineteenth centuries, added to only in war, but not being retired significantly in peace, despite much concern with sinking fund schemes. Thus a cumulative burden of interest charges faced succeeding generations as a financial heritage of wartime borrowing on the basis of a cumulative National Debt. Before the American War of Independence no less than 45 per cent of total net government expenditure was mortgaged to paying interest on the National Debt. By 1786, when peacetime finance schedules again ruled, the proportion had risen to 55 per cent.

Even more surprising, perhaps, is that the level of central government taxation in Great Britain was almost twice as high as in France and a much higher proportion of this revenue was raised by indirect taxes falling upon the 'bulk of the people' — that is, the poor. In Britain three-quarters of the total tax revenue came from levies on commodities and outlays; less than a fifth from direct taxes on income and wealth. Direct taxes on wealth sustained half the revenues of the central government in France of the *ancien régime*.

What did *not* happen in England during wartime was the over-issue of paper currency covering government expenditure, subsequently redeemed at a fraction of its nominal value — there was no *assignat* inflation, no land banks, no 'system' such as John Law's. Bank of England notes were still issued in large denominations, under conditions of convertibility into gold on demand, and issued only in response to 'genuine' needs by a cautious institution reflecting the conservative, established interests in the City. The Bank accommodated the Government as its most important customer, but only within its usual strict rules. The only raid on it by North during the war was to extract a ransom of £2m. as a *quid pro quo* for renewing its monopoly Charter.

The financial resources which Britain could deploy to fight a war in North America reflected great economic resilience: extensive and expanding foreign trade (which provided a basis for customs revenue); a large internal mass market almost fully 'monetized' (which enabled excise taxation to yield almost twice as great a revenue as the customs); a strong unitary political authority which could vote new taxes effectively (where internal political constraints allowed), and — above all — guarantee public credit. This immaculate credit-rating had been supported by an unblemished record since the temporary aberration of Charles II 'stopping the Exchequer' more than a century before in 1672. When a temporary closure was made five years earlier Samuel Pepys, hard-pressed to maintain supplies for the Admiralty in the Dutch war, had at once noted that this would 'spoil the credit of all his Majesty's service, when people cannot depend on payment anywhere.'[1]

Against this, what financial resources could the American colonies — in particular the Continental Congress — deploy to fight a war where the full weight of British armies and fleets was to be turned against them?[2] Very little could be hoped for from taxation. Internally, much of the economy of the colonies was primitive, with a great deal of self-subsistence limiting the market-ability of resources which was a pre-condition for effective excise taxation. Where British forces occupied territory, or loyalist sentiments prevailed, no tax revenue at all would result. Most American foreign trade had been within the imperial system — particularly with Britain and the West Indies. That would be cut off and any alternative commerce swept from the seas by the Royal Navy. Evidently, Congress could not look to customs revenue either for salvation.

The individual states had long found difficulty in raising significant amounts of revenue by taxation; and this was their continuing response to requests by Congress during the war for requisitions based on taxes levied by the state legislatures. Before 1780 only $2.4m. (in specie terms) arrived from such requisitions; and the individual states stubbornly refused to grant Congress any rights of levying federal taxation. The war was being fought, amongst other things, to challenge the rights of Westminster to impose central taxation on the colonies, who had no intention of substituting one Leviathan for another. Yet, without the powers to tax, Congress had no possibility of raising long-term loans either. Mobilized savings were scarce in the colonies; without taxation receipts under its own control there was no security upon which to guarantee interest payments on loans (all British government stocks were secured on specific taxes). Nor did precedents exist for the issue of saleable government securities. In any case, selling government securities and raising loans depended on creditors (at home or abroad) believing that the colonists would win the war.

Without taxes or borrowing powers — the two staples of British war finance — what could Congress and the States do? The answer, essentially, was to print money — at least until the tide of war had turned against Britain in 1780. This had been the only feasible tradition of public finance amongst the States for a long time before 1776 and supplemented a motley range of private barter and paper credit arrangements for providing the means of payment.

$12m. in bills or notes were probably in circulation in 1774, following a chequered history. Pennsylvania managed its issues responsibly but those of Rhode Island and the Carolinas, in particular, were notorious. In 1750 Massachusetts bills had depreciated by nine-tenths of their nominal value; at which point the Westminster Parliament outlawed further issues of legal-tender bills of credit by the New England colonies, and by all colonies thirteen years later. The restriction did not apply to treasury notes (issued in anticipation of taxes) which were not legal tender. The tradition was clear, however: of creating means of payment by paper emissions of different kinds; of settling formal obligations subsequently in depreciated paper; using depreciation rather than taxation as a principal instrument of financial policy; of not carrying any permanent debt; of using taxation to retire debt (in conjunction with depreciation) rather than to pay interest on a permanently funded debt.

The first emissions of paper began in June 1775 when the Continental Congress authorized $2 m. in bills of credit. It was the beginning of a flood: $6 m. by the end of 1776 (on the hopeful assumption that they would be retired by the States through taxes at the end of a very short war); $19 m. in 1776 (with depreciation to 70 per cent of the nominal value); $13 m. in 1777; $63 m. in 1778 and $140 m. in 1779. By 1780, with over $240 m. issued in bills by the Congress and a further $200 m. by the States, nemesis had arrived and the paper currency was 'not worth a Continental'. A 'dirty tricks' agency of the British forces had sought to help the process by introducing counterfeits. The index of wholesale prices, which had stood at 78 in 1775, reached 598 in 1778 and 10,544 in 1780, with the collapse of the currency on an almost Weimar scale.

But the Continental bills had brought in the equivalent of $41 m. in specie and had been the only means of raising finance to fight the war. The voices of orthodoxy — as when Henry Adams supported the view that 'to diminish the quantity of metals in coin is to steal.... A theft of greater magnitude and still more ruinous is the making of paper money' — were silenced.[3] Indeed, many virtues were discovered in necessity. A member of a state legislature commented cheerfully: 'Do you think, gentlemen, that I will consent to load my constituents with taxes when we can send to our printer and get a wagon load of money, one quire of which will pay for the whole?' (By April 1779, ironically, an army contractor was complaining that a wagon-load of money would scarcely purchase a wagon-load of supplies.)

Tom Paine, who had a clear perception of the consequences which different modes of financing the war had upon the people, argued that depreciation was equivalent to taxation — and the fairest form of tax for the people. 'As while they pay the former they do not suffer the latter,' he wrote, 'and as when they suffered the latter they did not pay the former the thing will be nearly equal....' 'The natural unavoidable tax of depreciation', went another comment, 'is the most certain, expeditious and equal tax that could be devised. Every possessor of money has paid a tax in proportion to the time he held it.' In retrospect the result was acknowledged as remarkable — representatives from the States to Congress were self-congratulatory. 'I would ask the best financier amongst us', commented one, 'whether in four years he could have levied a tax of 43 millions of hard dollars in a more equal or less expensive way' — without commissions, embezzlement, appeals or public defaults.

As the value of bills of credit fell in terms of specie desperate expedients were made by legislators to defy gravity. Congress and the States declared that bills were legal currency and that creditors must accept them at par, or be considered enemies of America. Pennsylvania farmers demanding hard cash for wheat were denounced. Simple soldiers did not understand the true cause for the fall in the value of money, not being paid in coin and facing an inexorable rise in prices. But, when some members of Congress proposed to pay half their bounties in coin, Washington remonstrated that after such an object lesson in reality the troops would insist on being paid entirely in specie.[4]

The emergency even invoked primitive forms of 'indexation' of wages. In January 1779 four battalions of Massachusetts soldiers petitioned the legislature that they were losing seven-eighths of the real value of their pay, the Massachusetts 'paper' dollar having fallen to 3.5 per cent of its par value since 1776. A joint committee from the army and the legislature thereupon agreed on a 'table of depreciation' — based on the changing prices of beef, Indian corn, sheeps' wool and sole leather — which was to cover the terms of repayment of 'Depreciation Notes' compensating the soldiers (and some civilians, such as the resigning President of Harvard College) who continued to be paid in paper.

But these stratagems could not hold up the value of the paper — and, indeed, in some respects they encouraged its further depreciation. During the severe winter of 1779-80 reports flowed in of the terrible conditions facing Washington's ragged army; with 'near half' the troops at West Point on the Hudson barefooted and a great proportion 'entirely destitute of Hatts, Stockings or Blankets' and on the point of deserting. Paying for the war by the printing press had come to the end of the road.

Fortunately by this time changing circumstances were opening up other financial options — in particular the ability to borrow. Such new policies demanded new standards, and the rake discovered the advantage of the bourgeois virtues in the aftermath of his progress. Military successes raised the credit-worthiness of Congress — writing cheques now had a greater credibility because the odds were improving that they could be cashed in the future. After Yorktown, in October 1781, the rate of military expenditure fell sharply. Outright impressments continued but, above all, loans from abroad, with France and other European countries in the war, demonstrated the new possibilities of borrowing. A scheme for retiring the depreciated bills was agreed between Congress and the State legislatures, in conjunction with new taxes and consolidation arrangements which brought in the paper bills at a discount of 40 to 1 against specie dollars. $119m. old bills were liquidated and further paper issues stopped, in what must have been the first funding scheme of its kind in monetary history to be so successfully implemented while war still continued. The old bills were driven out of circulation, as the new money became the sole legal tender. Taking the monetary system firmly in hand also brought out much specie from hoards.

After frantic lobbying in Europe loans of $174,000 were raised in Spain; $1.3m. from Holland and $6.4m. from France. Most of these sums were used to offset deficits with Europe but $462,862 actually arrived from France in cash, which evidently had a greater effect than the sum might suggest; and it is clear that a proportion of British military expenditure in North America also found its way indirectly into improving the financial liquidity of the American economy. Internal borrowing then became easier — and such loans now formed the basis of a continuing debt which, with various other military and civilian claims derived from the war falling to the responsibility of Congress, made up a thriving young national debt of $28m. Although depreciated when traded during the 1780s, this nominal total had grown with accumulated interest to $42m.

Launching Congress and the States upon a 'sound money' policy had been the responsibility of Robert Morris, appointed Superintendent of Finance on 7 May 1781. Part of his strategy was to found the first real bank (and the first proto-central bank) in America — the Bank of North America — for deposits, discount and note issue, which opened its doors in Philadelphia in January 1782. This was designed as an important instrument for

the most religious of men and formidable of scholars, showed in his own life. A typical moral reaction of Johnson's is his comment upon Mandeville's *Private Vices Public Benefits*: 'Poverty takes away so many means of doing good and produces so much inability to resist evil that it is by all virtuous means to be avoided.'[8] Considering Johnson's own position in the early part of his life, his views on poverty and riches provide an 'especially graphic example of the balance and purity of his thinking', in Jackson Bate's words. He does not rationalize on the bitterness of poverty; or compensate for this by an embittered view of wealth.[9] Indeed, his own interest in the economic foundations of society was not merely a negative awareness bred from poverty by resentment. He had a positive zest for these things in life, as observer and participant.

The part of London society which he adorned and later domina-ted was itself an easy meeting ground for those of status in intellectual matters, art, and letters with men of wealth from land and trade (although not much from industry in Johnson's time). Here was the most fluid social scene of any European capital (except possibly for Amsterdam); that least hardened by formal caste categories setting boundaries to status and social intercourse. Every continental visitor reacted to the importance of the middling groups in that society. It was above all, as Johnson observed many times, a great *commercial* society where the wealth of a great commercial city and nation mingled freely with a county-based aristocracy living part of their year and spending most of their money in the world of affairs and fashion. In no other country did politics respond so sensitively to the material interests of such a diverse establishment, or did a 'titled and untitled aristocracy'[10] find itself so committed to fortunes other than agricultural rents. In Johnson's immediate circle, apart from the world of learning, literature, and publishing, which were intrinsically his own as a writer and intellectual, there was a Moscovy merchant, John Rylands; Joseph Banks, explorer, President of the Royal Society, adviser to excise authorities, admiralty, and industry; Topham Beauclerk, son of a duke; Richard Clark, one attorney among several and Lord Mayor of London. Boswell's brother ('a very agreeable man and speaks no Scotch') was a merchant based in Valencia; Garrick's brother was a wine merchant; Adam Smith, sanest of economic philosophers, was a customs commissioner. There was Robert Adam, architect and entrepreneur in building. The vast circle of those whom Johnson felt he knew well enough to approach varied from Warren Hastings to General Oglethorpe. It was as true a microcosm of the larger London society in its own way as was that greater club, the House of Commons. Such a varied society bred sanity in those it did not corrupt by wealth and leisure.

To observe Johnson as himself the observer of the animated economic scene he saw around him in London and on his travels would involve a long journey through his writings, taking always his words rather than Boswell's. Johnson's own comments on travel set the tone for his eye and his brain: 'The use of travelling', he once said, 'is to regulate imagination by reality and instead of thinking how things may be to see them as they are.'[11] Wherever he went he visited manufactures, whether it was silk and porcelain factories at Derby[12] or kelp collecting in the Hebrides.[13] In such expeditions Boswell was the reluctant companion. Johnson reported assiduously to London the prices of malt, barley, and the level of rents in the country he was passing through on his travels and he described in detail financial panics afflicting London for the benefit of his country friends.

The following excerpt is noteworthy as an observation on the depression in 1779: 'All trade is dead, and pleasure is scarce alive. Nothing almost is purchased but such things as the buyer cannot be without, so that a general sluggishness and general discontent are spread over the town. All the trades of luxury and elegance are nearly at a stand' (Johnson to E. Aston at Lichfield, 5 November 1779). On the 1772 panic he wrote: ' ... the failure of Fordyce has drawn upon him a larger ruin than any former Bankrupt. Such a general distrust and timidity has been diffused through the whole commercial system that credit has been almost extinguished and commerce suspended.... It can, however, be little more than a panick terrour from which when they recover, may well wonder why they were frighted' (Johnson to J. Taylor at Ashbourne, 15 August 1772). This was also an extremely perceptive comment.

Johnson remained an active member of the Society for the Encouragement of Arts, Commerce, and Manufactures. On many occasions he astonished his friends by near-professional standards of knowledge about such technical matters as coining, the trade of a butcher, granulating gunpowder, brewing spirits, tanning, malting, the various operations of processing milk for whey, cheese, and butter. His active and erudite curiosity is also shown in the detailed review of Home's *Experiments on Bleaching*. Johnson's assistance to Zachariah Williams compounded technical competence with charity. He was already caring for William's blind daughter. Then, with the old Welsh physician sick and demoralized over his failure to gain the reward offered by Parliament for an improved method of finding longitude at sea, Johnson energetically took up the problem, making a special study of navigation theory, expanding Williams's ideas, and writing up the account for him in an effort to win the prize. His preface to Rolt's *Dictionary of Trade and Commerce* did not reveal such a specific commitment. 'The booksellers wanted a preface...', Johnson is reported as saying, 'I knew very well what such a dictionary should be and I wrote a preface accordingly' — without having read the book or seen Rolt.[14] There seems little doubt that some of Johnson's interest in chemistry, with the experiments he carried out in the brewery, were linked with Thrale's own attempts to improve the brewing process and his confidence in the work of Humphrey Jackson. However his commitments were wider than this and he also dabbled in experiments in porcelain manufacture.[15]

When famous, Johnson refused to withdraw from this worldly and commercial scene himself, whether as professor at Oxford, as cleric, or as library keeper, even declining to use the title by which he has become known to the world. He belonged to the world at large, above all, to London. Here lie the roots of one aspect of 'the vigorously inquiring mind', the 'mind which was always ready for use', which Reynolds and his other friends admired so much.[16]

II

This is not to say that Johnson ever formulated, or attempted, a systematic, articulate, economic philosophy. He had no complete vision of an economic system as had Adam Smith or Hume or Quesnay, and it is exceedingly doubtful if the fragments of such a system could be dug out of his writings and pieced together without much interpolation and much omission of awkward opinions.[17] Johnson was just not an economist: in writing he was concerned exclusively with the folly of Hume's religion, or lack of it, rather than with the sanity of his economic judgements. Nor does he seem to have commented in writing on Smith's *Wealth of Nations* beyond the general defence in conversations that a person who had never been engaged in trade might undoubtedly write well upon the subject, and that nothing required more to be illustrated by philosophy than trade.[18] If Boswell is to be believed — and he was a little jealous of Smith — Johnson did not get on very well with the great economist, who criticized Oxford too much and was altogether too bookish in his conversation.

As a layman, however, Johnson shows the unmistakable drift of his economic opinions. He took for granted and viewed with favour, on the whole, the commercial society which made London the richest city in Europe which was not at all as usual in his circle as enjoying it while condemning the degeneracy of times when wealth accumulated and men decayed.[19] When he travelled through backward, poverty-stricken, subsistence-farming districts in Scotland and the islands he knew which type of society benefited its people most. Part of his condemnation of Scotland and things Scottish, even when jocular, was the condemnation of material poverty and a way of life at the margin of subsistence. The clan system there lay broken in pieces by the aftermath of the '45' and a market economy was penetrating some regions hitherto innocent of cash crops. With it came the full implications of rigorous commercial attitudes in landowners, tenants, and labourers for the first time. The passing of a way of life Johnson regretted, but not the material effects of the change upon the people: 'The admission of money into the Highlands', he wrote to Boswell in 1777, 'will soon put an end to the feudal modes of life by making those men landlords who were not chiefs. I do not know that the people will suffer by the change, but there was in the patriarchal authority something venerable and pleasing.'[20] The quality of his perceptions into the rapidly changing economy of the Highlands and Western Isles is remarkable. The following passage is typical of his insight:

The payment of rent in kind has been so long disused in England that it is totally forgotten. It was practised very lately in the Hebrides, and probably still continues, not only at St Kilda, where money is not yet known, but in others of the smaller and remoter Islands.... It were perhaps to be desired that no change in this particular should have been made. When the Laird could only eat the produce of his lands he was under the necessity of residing upon them; and when the tenant could convert his stock into no more portable riches, he could never be tempted away from his farm, from the only place where he could be wealthy. Money confounds subordination, by overpowering the distinctions of rank and birth, and weakens authority by supplying power of resistance and expedients for escape. The feudal system is formed for a nation employed in agriculture and has never long kept its hold where gold and silver have become common.[21]

Apart from vivid curiosity about things economic, this passage also reveals the romanticized nostalgia of an observer from a sophisticated society towards the primitive. Johnson is typical of his age in such an attitude. More interestingly, and more significant in relation to his economic opinion, was Johnson's defence of the 'tacksman', condemned almost universally as a parasitic middleman between Laird and tenants. He complained to Mrs Thrale on 6 September 1773: 'The improvements of the Scotch are for immediate profit, they do not yet think it worthwhile to plant what will not produce something to be eaten or sold in a very little time.' Johnson maintained firmly that the specialized, trading intermediary was a necessity and an asset to any society. Without them 'all must obey the call of immediate necessity, nothing that requires extensive views or provides for distant consequences will be ever performed'.[22] This at bottom is Adam Smith's own defence of the division of labour, specialization of function, and an expanding market which implies, too, as a social consequence of the process, a more differentiated society. In fact, we may claim that it is all of a piece with his love of London, of the city life. For his own society, Johnson similarly defended wealth, trade, and luxury (by which he meant conspicuous expenditure); not the most natural opinions at first glance for the hammer of the Whigs, then commonly identified as the party of commercial wealth opposing a Tory squirearchy of land unsullied by commerce. This dichotomy of wealth in politics was always a myth, as research makes plainer each year, but yet the opinion was abroad in the eighteenth century and was itself a political weapon. One might well tax Johnson, with his Whig economic doctrines. At all events, however, Johnson is far from the Physiocrats in these general sentiments although, when writing about agriculture, he saw trade as a subordinate activity.

Trade, he asserted, produced pleasure directly from the increased enjoyment of commodities, and intermediate good by giving employment, although it was possible for trade (particularly some branches of foreign trade) also to be associated with undesirable results. He sought to distinguish between 'real' and 'monetary' transactions whén commenting about the advantages of trade, but compounded the difficulties of definition and distinction between the two. 'As to mere wealth, that is to say, money, it is clear that one nation or one individual cannot increase its store but by making another poorer,' he wrote, 'but trade procures what is more valuable, the reciprocation of the peculiar advantages of different countries.'[23] However, he was not completely consistent, even though the remarks above give the general tenor of his opinions. In another context he wrote: 'Trade is like gaming. If a whole company are gamesters play must cease for there is nothing to be won. When all nations are traders, there is nothing to be gained by trade, and it will stop first where it is brought to the greatest perfection. Then the proprietors of land only will be the great men.'[24] This is an odd compound of certain traditional mercantilist ideas and a quasi-Ricardianism, which anticipates a long-run declining rate of profit and an increasing proportion of the economic surplus accruing to rent.

The extension of this argument to the defence of luxury (in the face of a widespread pious condemnation of it) was not alone the view 'Depend upon it, sir, every state of society is as luxurious as it can be. Men always take the best they can get' but a reasoned challenge developed from Bernard Mandeville.[25] Johnson once said the author of the *Fable of the Bees* opened his 'views into real life very much'.[26] Behind it lay the conviction that unwilling destitution — what we should now call chronic involuntary unemployment — was one of the worst social evils of a pre-industrial society. Here, perhaps, is the unconscious echo of the relative poverty of the agricultural economy about the Lichfield of his childhood — the economic aspect of which his love for London society and awareness of the poverty of provincial social life is the obverse. For Johnson, luxury continued the benefits which trade began: 'as far as it reached the poor it would do good to the race of people; it will strengthen and multiply them'.[27] You cannot spend in luxury', he wrote, 'without doing good to the poor. Nay, you do more good to them by spending it in luxury than by giving it: for by spending it in luxury you make them exert industry, whereas by giving it you keep them idle.'[28]

This is the familiar argument against saving, which was growing in the eighteenth century, equivalent to that of Keynes in more recent times of depression, repeated upon the banners of the unemployed, 'work not charity'. Johnson elaborated his meaning: the luxury of building produced elegance of accommodation and exertion in industry. 'A man gives half a guinea for a dish of green peas. How much gardening does this occasion, how many labourers must the competition, to have such things early in the market, keep in employment.... As to the rant that is made about people who are ruined by extravagance, it is no matter to the nation that some individuals suffer.'[29] But this is Johnson beginning to argue for victory, pushing a partial truth towards dogmatic completeness.

Such attitudes are more appropriate in a non-industrial setting. For the industrial entrepreneurs of this same generation saving (that is abstinence from extravagant personal expenditure) to allow profits to be reinvested in the business to sustain its expansion was a major economic virtue which had Johnson's strong approval. His argument, like that of Keynes, was really an argument against hoarding, certainly not one against increasing investment. Increased spending for Johnson, just as increased investment, would generate increasing employment.

Johnson is not consistent in his views about the economic system, despite the drift of his opinions outlined above.[30] He also argued strongly for a balanced economy at times, in favour of protecting agriculture to support farmers' incomes and agricultural rents, while wanting the ports to be open in times of scarcity to protect the poor from famine prices. He claimed that agriculture produced the chief assets of a nation 'its only riches which we can call our own and of which we need not fear either deprivation of diminution'. This occasional piece 'Further thoughts on Agriculture' (*The Visiter,* March 1756) certainly smacked of the Physiocrats. While not wishing to deter Englishmen from commerce, Johnson nevertheless argued vigorously that trade was subordinate to agriculture, and industry arose from it. 'Traffic ... ', he wrote, 'must owe its success to agriculture; the materials of manufacture are the produce of the earth ... Agriculture, therefore, and agriculture alone can support us without the help of others in certain plenty and genuine dignity.' Government, therefore, clearly had an obligation to protect agriculture and Johnson argued equally forthrightly about the benefits of the policy of granting export bounties on corn.[31] Far from being responsible for scarcity and higher prices, Johnson saw the bounty as encouraging the extension of cultivation by creating an export surplus (which could always be restrained by legislation in a year of scarcity). The bounty 'certainly and necessarily increases our crops and can never lessen them but by our own permission'. He cut quickly to the real cause of high prices: 'The true reason of the scarcity is the failure of the harvest; and the cause of exportation is the like failure in other countries where they grow less, and where they are, therefore, always nearer to the danger of want.'

He accepted, almost instinctively one feels, many of the basic postulates of mercantilism; that is to say he did not oppose many of the current assumptions traditional before Adam Smith, and he recommended students to Thomas Mun, Josiah Child, Locke, Davenant, and Gee.[32] But this is just the list of all the eminent commentators (except for the arch-Whig dissenter Defoe) and in his later years, when new winds began to blow, he spoke favourably of Dean Tucker, Bernard Mandeville, and Adam Smith. Part of Johnson's support for a mercantile society can undoubtedly be traced to the broad acceptance of the assumptions of the mercantile state. He thought that dependence on imported food and raw materials from areas of the world not under British political control was casting hostages to fortune. Foreign trade, as opposed to imperial trade, was fickle: 'one of the daughters of Fortune, inconstant and deceitful as her mother … every trading nation flourishes, while it can be said to flourish, by the courtesy of others. We cannot compel any people to buy from us or to sell to us.' Colonies therefore should be strictly controlled and their economies brought into complementarity with that of the mother country. An economically independent colony was for Johnson a denial in terms. Hence his scorn for any view of British relations with the Americans which was not in favour of total independence or total control.

But there is another side to the matter. Johnson's economic beliefs, as all his other beliefs, were shot through with moral judgements. Views which are contradictory in economic logic, may sometimes be explained, if not reconciled in economic consistency, by the moral position they represent. Johnson was fundamentally opposed to slavery, to settlement by conquest of inferior peoples, to wealth made by cheating ignorant natives, or exploiting labour in conditions of serfdom or slavery. He opposed much foreign trade on these grounds, and was antipathetic to much colonialism for these reasons. These were the real foundations for his dislike of the Americans. Here are grounds for disliking some big business and lucrative foreign trade which he felt was based on exploitation. He argued against specious advertising.[33] He approved of trade which was not dependent on one man getting the better of another, or of one people or society getting the better of another. He liked small business and individual enterprise, he approved of making money through inventions and discoveries and enterprise. Internal improvements, the extension of enterprise within Britain, industrial advance, in principle benefited everyone. But there were other kinds of enterprise where this was not so, and he maintained this interesting and significant split attitude throughout his life. Johnson became involved himself most completely with business of the former kind.

Johnson's objections to *The Fable of the Bees*, despite his acknowledgement that luxury might serve a purpose, also had a moral basis because of the deliberate confusion of virtue and vice which Mandeville's paradoxes of 'public vices and private benefits' implied, but he condemned it 'not without adding that it was the work of a thinking man'.[34] A characteristic transcendent moral imperative about the justification and use of wealth is contained in one of his many dedications ' ... no motive can sanctify the accumulation of wealth, but an ardent desire to make the most honourable and virtuous use of it, by contributing to the support of good government, the increase of arts and industry, the rewards of genius and the relief of wretchedness and want'.[35] There are many passages where he approved of the 'bourgeois virtues' — the Puritan virtues — of honest work, thrift, sobriety, 'redeeming the time', and spoke against idleness and extravagance.[36]

If Johnson always tried to relate economic activity to moral criteria, to its effect upon the nation, he was always aware that the 'condition of the nation' implied concern for the well-being of the anonymous multitude of the humble. A further extract from the *Journey to the Western Islands* illustrates exactly Johnson's keenness of observation, defended by a general attitude towards concern for these practical details of life:

The art of joining squares of glass with lead is little used in Scotland, and in some places is totally forgotten. The frames of their windows are all of wood. They are more frugal of their glass than the English, and will often, in houses not otherwise mean, compose a square of two pieces, not joining like cracked glass, but with one edge laid perhaps half an inch over the other. Their windows do not move upon hinges, but are pushed up and drawn down in grooves, yet they are seldom accommodated with weights and pulleys. He that would have his window open must hold it with his hand, unless what may be sometimes found among good contrivers, there be a nail which he may stick into a hole, to keep it from falling....

These diminutive observations seem to take away something from the dignity of writing, and therefore are never communicated but with hesitation, and a little fear of abasement and contempt. But it must be remembered, that life consists not of a series of illustrious actions, or elegant enjoyments; the greater part of our time passes in compliance with necessities, in the performance of daily duties, in the removal of small inconveniences, in the procurement of petty pleasures.... The true state of every nation is the state of common life. The manners of a people are not to be found in the schools of learning, or the palaces of greatness, where the national character is obscured or obliterated by travel or instruction, by philosophy or vanity; nor is public happiness to be estimated by the assemblies of the gay, or the banquets of the rich. The great mass of nations is neither rich nor gay: they whose aggregate constitutes the people, are found in the streets, and the villages, in the shops and farms; and from them collectively considered, must the measure of general prosperity be taken. As they approach to delicacy a nation is refined as their conveniences are multiplied, a nation, at least a commercial nation, must be denominated wealthy.[37]

As Mrs Thrale remarked, 'Dr. Johnson's knowledge and esteem for what we call low or coarse life was indeed prodigious.'[38]

III

Such opinions were not merely those of an eminent literary figure who glimpsed the business world of his day from his study, in the conversations of his clubs or through chance observations on his travels. Samuel Johnson found himself in close touch with certain of the technical innovations which marked the onset of industrialization in England, and he tried to encourage innovation as far as it lay in his power to do so. Such efforts were tangential to his literary life, in the same sense that his economic opinions were tangential to the general matrix of his system of values, but they emphasize even more that here was an eighteenth-century literary figure with a difference.

If, before 1800, the technical revolution in textile production was, above all, a revolution in cotton spinning, then its central feature was the technical mastery of spinning mechanically under power in large mills, and one of the vital technical innovations lay in spinning a thread stretched out through a series of rollers each moving at progressively increasing speeds. The first persons to formulate this principle, to build machines to demonstrate it and to occupy factories to profit by it were Lewis Paul, the feckless Huguenot genius, and John Wyatt, an English carpenter.[39] Paul came to Birmingham in 1732 to develop a file-cutting machine and he met there John Wyatt, who was working on machinery with a gun-barrel forger named Heeley. This was the traditional eighteenth-century machine-building combination of woodworking skills in alliance with metalworking skills. John Wyatt had come from Lichfield, where his family and brother remained. His mother had some connection with Johnson's mother, whether of friendship or cousinhood being unknown, and the two boys, although eight years separated them in age, had probably attended the grammar school there together. Here was one, perhaps inconsequential, contact. By 1736-8, Lewis Paul was just completing his first spinning machine, under the guidance of Wyatt's better technical skills as a mechanic. His workshop was in the Upper Priory, Birmingham, a house Paul had rented, just adjacent to the house of Johnson's friends the Lloyds whom he often visited. Then in February 1737/8 Paul took as apprentice for a shroud-making project a young girl, Miss Swynfen, whose father had just died. That father was Samuel Johnson's godfather, with whom the family and Johnson kept in close touch after the Swynfens had gone to live in Birmingham in 1729. Swynfen acted at that time as physician to Johnson, and his daughter some years later, when widowed as Mrs Desmoulins, lived in Johnson's household on his charity. In 1738, clearly, Johnson had two personal, if indirect, links with Paul and his constructor mechanic, and by this time the machine was finished, patented, and awaiting, it seemed, only backers with capital to bring it into commercial production.

Transition from invention to innovation is the crucial translation of individual genius and creation to commercial action; the move from the laboratory of technology to the arena of economic history. The initial barrier to this process of innovation is often one of capital. In the case of roller-spinning, the first backers of the Wyatt-Paul project were Edward Cave, Thomas Warren, and Dr Robert James — plus one small cotton manufacturer in Spitalfields called James Johnson (no relation to Samuel), who used the machine intermittently for a few years, and one or two Lancashire backers who came in after the others. Robert James came from Lichfield. He was a schoolfellow and friend of both Wyatt and Johnson. Johnson helped with James's medicinal dictionary. Thomas Warren was the Birmingham printer to whom Johnson had first gone for employment on his newspaper, the *Birmingham Journal*, in the autumn of 1732 when he left Lichfield to earn his living. He remained his good friend in these early years, staying at Warren's house. Edward Cave, the wealthiest backer of them all, was the editor of the *Gentleman's Magazine*. He had published Johnson's first important poem; he had been his first employer when he commissioned the struggling writer of Grub Street to report Parliamentary debates for his magazine, and thereafter he published for Johnson and Johnson edited for him. Although it seems clear that Johnson had no hand in introducing Paul to Wyatt in 1732, or in the actual construction of the machine, [40] thereafter he is the only common link between the London, Birmingham, and Lichfield backers which determined the projection of the invention. He was a projector without capital himself — as always, amongst his friends, the honest broker.

Paul's first factory in Birmingham of 1740, backed by Cave and Warren failed in 1743, and when revived, failed again in 1756. Johnson's attempt to get help for Paul by persuading William Cave (the legatee of Edward who had died in 1754) to let the rent lapse and his attempt to get more capital into the venture through his friend Charles Hitch both failed. At the start, in 1739, all the backers had received the reward for their investments in licences to set up spindles themselves under the patent. All three had quarrelled by 1741, and as Lewis Paul became shifty and truculent, experiencing the difficulties which were to beset all these first factory owners, so Johnson had to appease as arbitrator those whom he had first brought together as broker for Paul. A series of letters shows his concern for Paul (with whom he stayed) and his intense desire to further the project. Of Johnson's initiative in bringing the backers to Paul there is little doubt: when urging Paul to settle their differences he spoke of 'my assiduity in expediting the agreement between you ... '.[41]

Warren went bankrupt, and James nearly so. Cave meanwhile had converted a warehouse into a factory himself in London but failed to keep his working force together. He tried again with 250 spindles (for his £1,000 investment) at Northampton in 1742 — the first power spinning mill to receive yarn from its spindles. Another attempt by the Lanchashire backers at Leominster launched in 1744 had failed by fire within ten years, although one of them, Samuel Touchet, had faith enough to persevere with Cave and Warren in Birmingham. Behind all of them, save the Lancashire men, stood Johnson as intermediary, friend, and supporter. In the event, all failed commercially. There were many problems: a mounting incidence of petty difficulties over labour, the unreliability of wooden machines working at speed, the unfulfilled need for mechanizing the processes up to spinning before mechanized spinning could itself succeed commercially. Perhaps the greatest problem lay in the character of Lewis Paul himself. At the end of his life, Johnson drafted for him a petition to the Duke of Bedford, pleading that his machine would abolish idleness in the Foundling Hospital (an ugly portent) and that its inventor deserved a pension.[42] But, in 1759, death arrived before charity and Johnson's link with the textile industry was over. It had been a near thing: even Matthew Boulton said that the mill would have got money had it been in good hands. Only ten years later, a man of a very different stamp, Richard Arkwright, took out similar patents and made his fortune.[43] When Sir John Hawkins was describing Johnson's great knowledge of manufactures and mechanical devices he mentioned that Arkwright pronounced him to be 'the only person who, in a first view, understood both the principle and powers of his most complicated piece of machinery'.[44] From what we now know of the similarity of Arkwright's patents to those of Paul this is scarcely surprising.

Having been the go-between for an affair which ruined two of his friends temporarily and almost caused the bankruptcy of his employer and publisher, Johnson had cause to ponder on the mutability of business fortunes. In 1765, however, he had met Henry Thrale and become involved with a very different industrial world: a world of an assured market, a single staple product, great technical efficiency, vast capitals and large profits — brewing. Nothing could have contrasted more with the struggles of Lewis Paul and his projectors. Into this new world Johnson entered with alacrity and soon found himself helping Mrs Thrale to run her husband's great porter brewery at Southwark whenever there was a business depression.

During Johnson's childhood, when Henry Thrale's father, Ralph, had bought the Anchor Brewery at Deadman's Place, Southwark, from his uncle for £30,000 there had come a great innovation in the brewing industry: the brewing of porter.[45] Upon the technical efficiency of the new product, from the multitude of innkeepers who brewed and sold their own beer, and from the many tiny London breweries which sold to publicans within a narrow market, there emerged the gigantic 'capital houses' brewing beer upon a scale unknown elsewhere in England, making their owners amongst the wealthiest and most influential industrialists in the land and their breweries a target for every foreign visitor in London. The drays from a single porter brewery might serve four hundred publicans and a thousand private customers in 1780, holding to account perhaps ten million retail transactions from the annual production of a single industrial plant.

Such a scale of industrial enterprise was scarcely rivalled elsewhere in the industrial economy of Britain or elsewhere in the world save in an ironworks or a dockyard or two, until these few breweries were surpassed by the Lanchashire spinning mills in the decade after Johnson's death. It was with such a concern as this — one of the half-dozen whose owners had in their hands almost three-quarters of the annual production in London of a million barrels of beer — that Johnson found himself involved after 1765 through his friendship with Henry Thrale, one of the 'great fermentators' of London (as Sydney Smith once called Samuel Whitbread). The brewhouse, its contents and stock might be valued at nearly £200,000. Raw materials might cost £100,000 in a single season if the harvest was poor and prices high.

It is not possible to claim that Johnson's familiar definition of 'Excise' in the Dictionary was influenced by his connection with the brewing industry (which post-dated it by a decade).[46] Quite certainly his hostility to the tax derived from his belief in Common Law jurisdiction and fear of inquisitorial methods of administration, which were old Tory shibboleths. His father had also been in trouble with the excise authorities over tax obligations for a tanning business.[47] But his subsequent refusal to withdraw his initial definition, which was hostile enough to threaten him with a legal action by the Commissioners, may have been reinforced by his friendship with Thrale and his direct involvement with the tax when helping in the counting house of the Anchor Brewery. Intimately associated with the business Johnson certainly became, as with the cotton spinning project, but being a man still without capital, he remained without any final responsibility. Hence, given the temperament he had, Johnson's judgements were over-sanguine. Hope of gain always influenced his assessment of possibility too strongly. Living in Thrale's household at Southwark and Streatham, Johnson eagerly supported his hosts' ambitions and problems, trying to hold a balance between the policy of heedless expansion pursued by Thrale and the restraint urged upon him by his wife. Henry Thrale's entry into his heritage in 1758-9 had been the sign for immediate expansion. The total valuation of plant and utensils doubled in that year, as old equipment was sold off and new coppers, 'backs', piping, and mill-work of increased capacity were installed. These sustained the increase in production at least until 1767, when a new burst of expansion once more doubled the value of the utensils and fixed goods by 1780.[48] Production leapt from the level of 32,000 barrels at which Henry Thrale had found it at his father's death to 75,000 in 1776 and 87,000 in 1778, under his great drive to obtain the personal leadership of the London trade.[49] In fact, he succeeded in gaining only third place, for both Whitbread and Felix Calvert remained ahead (to his chagrin) but this was vastly better than the eighth position the Anchor Brewery had held in 1760, and Sir Benjamin Truman, at least, had been surpassed.

Johnson's help in the active management of the brewery at the elbow of Mrs Thrale came exactly during the times of trouble common to all business in London during years of financial crisis and trade depression. For the Anchor Brewery, the difficulties of such periods were exacerbated by Thrale throwing all available financial resources into the trade and operating without adequate cash reserves. The reason for the timing of Mrs Thrale's and Johnson's rescue operations was that the strain of coping with business problems during depressions induced apoplexy in Henry Thrale. He thereupon retired to Brighton, leaving his wife and Johnson, with John Perkins the salaried manager, to cope as best they might. In 1772-3, therefore, we have acute descriptions of a money panic and commercial crisis from the pens of both Mrs Thrale and Johnson, who was in constant attendance at the counting house. He esteemed Perkins's abilities highly and Perkins hung a mezzotint of the Doctor up in his country house — I conceive in good faith — because he said he wished to have a wise man always present.[50] Despite this panic, however, when the good years came back again, Johnson soon forgot the dangers in which his master's recklessness had placed the brewery. Mrs Thrale's comments and his own on the new burst of expansion in 1777 tell significantly different tales. Mrs Thrale, in her diary for 11 July 1778, commented:

> Mr. Thrale overbrewed himself last winter and caused an artificial scarcity of money in the family, which has extremely lowered his spirits. Mr Johnson endeavoured last night and so did I to make him promise that he would never brew a larger quantity of beer in one winter than 80,000 barrels. *Note.* If he got half a crown by each barrel 80,000 half crowns is £10,000 and what more can mortal man desire than £10,000 per annum — half to spend and half to lay up…. But my master mad with the noble ambition of outbrewing Whitbread and Calvert two fellows he despises could scarcely be prevailed on to promise even this….[51]

Johnson, a few months before had been writing to her as follows:

> I have no doubt of a most abundant harvest, and it is said that the produce of barley is particularly great. We are not far from the great year of a 100,000 barrels, which, if three shillings be gained from each barrel will bring us fifteen thousand pounds a year. Whitbread never pretended to more than thirty pounds a day, which is not eleven thousand a year. But suppose we shall get but two shillings a barrel, that is ten thousand a year. I hope

we shall have the advantage. Would you for the other thousand have my master such a man as Whitbread?

Next year will, I hope, complete Mr. Thrale's wish of a hundred thousand barrels. Ambition is then to have an end.... When he has climbed so high, his care must be to keep himself from falling.[52]

The next depression of 1779-80 was more intense than the last. Thrale's apoplexy was more severe and he died after a prolonged bout on 4 April 1781. Now from close advice and active help Johnson was projected for the first time into joint responsibility for the fortunes of the vast concern. Mrs Thrale found herself in a double predicament. Firstly, she had only daughters and no male heir to take on the trade, yet active management, involving regular attendance at the brewery, would be vital if the business was to remain profitable.[53]

At first when Thrale was prostrate but still alive Johnson encouraged Mrs Thrale to take on the management herself with his aid, writing to her:

The Trade must be answerable for the debts contracted. This can be none but yourself, unless you deliver up the property to some other agent, and trust the chance both of his prudence and his honesty. Do not be frighted, Trade could not be managed by those who manage it if it had much difficulty. Their great books are soon understood and their language.... The help which you can have from any man as Trustee you may have from him as a friend....[54]

In the event he became an Executor and still did not wish to sell. But the second predicament was now fully revealed. Of the five Executors, only two, Johnson and Mrs Thrale, knew anything about the trade, standing virtually alone, yet with the responsibility of their decisions being shared amongst the five. And — the crux of the matter — neither Johnson nor Mrs Thrale actually *knew* how to brew. For this critical technical skill, the hub of commercial success, they were firmly in the hands of John Perkins, who had been pressing for a partnership (and hence for a share in the profits) with Thrale long before his death. This was his chance to bid for the whole. Without his wholehearted co-operation the Executors could not carry on. When being conducted on such a scale as this brewing was a very highly skilled business and no set of persons unfamiliar with the trade on this scale would lightly throw £200,000 into the venture. The Executors received legal advice that they should reduce the capital to £70,000-80,000, confine the sales to London and its environs, and abandon the export and country trade as 'an uncertain business and not for an Executor or Trustee but only for a Principal who can act as he wishes'. They were then to look for an opportunity to sell the business conducting it 'not in prospect so much of Gain as preservation'.[55]

Perkins's first trump was that he had been at the centre of operations, the real architect of technical success for a lifetime: his second was that he had recently married the widow of Timothy Paul Bevan one of the richest Quaker apothecary-bankers of Lombard Street, whose extensive Quaker cousinhood stood ready to bring capital in plenty for the purchase, and able men for partners. What was she to do? Calamity might come within a season, and the risks were overwhelming. The other Executors knew only too well the laws of unlimited liability. She agreed with them and slipped her golden millstone from her neck:

> Will it surprise you now to hear that, among all my fellow executors none but Johnson opposed selling the concern? Cator, a rich timber merchant was afraid of implicating his own credit as a commercial man. Crutchley hated Perkins ... Smith cursed the whole business and wondered what his relation Mr. Thrale could mean by leaving him £200 he said, and such a burden on his back to bear for it. All were well pleased to find themselves secure and the brewhouse decently though not very advantageously disposed of, except dear Dr. Johnson, who found some odd delight in signing drafts for hundreds and for thousands, to him a new, and so it appeared delightful occupation. When all was nearly over, however, I cured his honest heart of its incipient passion for trade, by letting him into some and only some of its mysteries.[56]

Thus John Perkins, as the industrious apprentice who lived to take over his master's business (even if he did not marry his master's daughter or widow) fulfilled the traditional success story of the eighteenth century. Even here it seems there was a suggestion that a kinship bond was in prospect, despite the wide social gap: Mrs Thrale was furious when she caught a rumour that Perkins had once entertained a hope of acquiring control of the business by aspiring to marry her.

Johnson invested his executor's fee of £200 in the business at 5 per cent, borrowed money occasionally, and got the brewery to supply him with coal.[57] Once more, this time with the entry of a new social world into the project he had concerned himself in so much, he became dis-associated from the business world. This time it was for good. His exit here is a suitable point at which to take leave of him. While Executor, he had been diverting Boswell by talking in a pompous manner of his new office and particularly of the concerns of the brewery. Finally, at the sale over which he presided, we know that he was bustling about 'with an ink-horn and pen in his button hole like an excise man'. His celebrated remark on this occasion underlines once again his awareness of the advantages of wealth: 'We are not here to sell a parcel of boilers and vats but the potentiality of growing rich beyond the dreams of avarice.'[58] It was, in its way, an appropriate ending for a man who at no time had been fully responsible for the conduct of any business enterprise, but who had remained from his youth intensely intererested and actively concerned on the edge of several. Such interest and concern were not unreflected in the field of letters which he made his own.

Notes

1 J.L. Clifford (1955) *Young Samuel Johnson* London and New York, p.173. I benefited from the advice of Dr Clifford when preparing an earlier draft of this article.
2 W.J. Bate (1961) *The Achievement of Samuel Johnson,* New York, p.v.
3 A recent comprehensive bibliography of Johnsonian scholarship shows only four items of recent scholarship on his economic views, compared with sixteen on science, twenty-two on the law, and over thirty (including a clutch of books and theses) on his views about politics. J.L. Clifford and D.J. Green (1971) *Samuel Johnson: Survey and Bibliography of Critical Studies*, Minneapolis.
4 Mrs Piozzi, 'Anecdotes...' in *Johnsoniana*, ed. R. Napier, 1884, p.6.
5 See 'Johnson in Grub Street' in S.C. Roberts (1930) *An Eighteenth Century Gentleman ...*, Cambridge.
6 Murphy in *Johnsoniana*, op. cit., p.381.
7 J. Boswell (1946) *Life of Johnson*, Oxford; *Johnsoniana*, p.80.
8 *Life*, ii. p.448.
9 Bate, op. cit.

10 This apt epithet occurs, as well it might, in a *Directory of the County Families*, London, 1881.

11 Johnson, *Letters*, ed. R.W. Chapman, 1948, London.

12 *Life*, ii. pp.124-5.

13 Johnson, *A Journey to the Western Islands of Scotland*, ed. R.W. Chapman, 1924, London, pp.73, 108; J. Boswell, *Journal of a Tour to the Hebrides* ... ed. R.W. Chapman, 1924, London, p.316. Johnson's report of this journey has few rivals of its kind in the eighteenth century, and has perception of a higher order than Defoe's *Tour*. See pp.300-1.

14 Johnson (1825) *Works*, Oxford, V, p.254.

15 See J. Baverstock Jr. (1824) *Treatise on Brewing*, Preface and Appendix; H.L. Thrale (Piozzi), *Thraliana* ed. K.C. Balderston, 1951, pp. 309-12; A. Hayward (ed.) *Autobiography of Mrs. Piozzi*, ii. 25-26; *Johnsoniana*, p.95; (1829) Faulkner *Chelsea*, ii. p.273.

16 J. Reynolds (1952 edn) *Portraits* ... Yale, p.67. Murphy speaks of his mind 'quickened by necessity', op. cit., p.378.

17 G. O'Brien (1925) 'Dr. Johnson as an economist', *Studies*, March.

18 *Life*, i. p.647; J.H. Middendorf (1961) 'Dr. Johnson and Adam Smith', *Political Quarterly*, xl, pp.281-96.

19 *Life*, ii. pp.138, 190, 199, 243, 287; i. p.567; *Adventurer*, no.67 (26 June 1753).

20 *Letters*, Johnson to Boswell, 22 July 1777.

21 *A Journey to the Western Islands*, p.103.

22 Ibid. pp.78-80.

23 *Life*, i. p.647.

24 *Journal of a Tour*, p.315.

25 *Life*, ii. 213; E.R. Miner (1958) 'Dr. Johnson, Mandeville and "public benefits"', *Huntington Library Quarterly*, February.

26 *Life*, ii. pp.221-2.

27 *Life*, i. p.487.

28 *Life*, ii. p.222.

29 *Life*, ii. p.37.

30 J.H. Middendorf (1965) 'Johnson on wealth and commerce', in M.M. Lascelles *et al.* (eds), *Johnson, Boswell and their Circle*, London, pp.47-64; J.H. Middendorf (1960) 'Samuel Johnson and mercantilism' *Journal of the History of Ideas*, xxi, pp.66-83.

31 Johnson (1766) *Considerations on the Corn Laws*.

32 D.J. Greene (1960) *The Politics of Samuel Johnson*, pp.280 ff.

33 *Idler*, no. 40 (20 January 1759), ' ... every art ought to be exercised in due subordination to the public good'.

34 *Johnsoniana*, p.730.

35 *Works*, V, pp.450-1. Dedication written for J. Payne (1758) *New Tables of Interest*.

36 *Idler*, no. 16 (29 July 1758); no. 26 (14 October 1758); no. 47 (10 March 1759).

37 *A Journey to the Western Islands*, pp.18-20.
38 *Johnsoniana*, p.64.
39 S. Smiles (1868) *The Hugenots*, pp.416-24; A.P. Wadsworth and J. de
    L. Mann (1931) *The Cotton Trade and Industrial Lancashire*, Man-
    chester, chapter 21, and appendix C; R.K. Dent (1917) in *Central Litera-
    ture Magazine*.
40 J.J. Brown (1946) *Modern Language Review*, January pp.16-23;
    Wadsworth and Mann, op. cit., pp.410-11.
41 *Letters*, Johnson to Paul, 31 January 1741. Boswell evidently did not
    know of Johnson's connection with Lewis Paul.
42 Ibid.
43 Wadsworth and Mann, op. cit. pp.447-8.
44 *Johnsoniana, Apophthegms, Sentiments etc.*, collected by Sir J. Haw-
    kins, p.137.
45 For a general description of the development of the London brewing
    industry at this time see above chapter 11 and P. Mathias (1959) *The
    Brewing Industry in England 1700-1830*, Cambridge, chapter 8.
46 His definition was 'Excise — a hateful tax levied upon commodities
    and adjudged not by common judges of property but by wretches hired
    by those to whom excise is paid'.
47 Clifford, op. cit., p.69.
48 Records of Barclay Perkins's Brewery: *Rest Books*, 1758-9, 1764, 1767,
    1780.
49 Records of Barclay Perkins's Brewery: *Brewery Statistics* (MSS).
50 *Life*, i. p.539, n.1.
51 *Thraliana*, i. p.333.
52 *Letters*, ii. 538, of 23 August 1777; ii. 548, of 18 September 1777.
53 *Life*, ii. p.69.
54 *Letters*, ii. 647, of 16 November 1779.
55 Rylands Library: Eng. MS. 600, f. 33.
56 Hayward, op. cit.
57 Barclay Perkins Records, *Rest Books,* 1781-82; *Letters*, ii. 738, John-
    son to J. Perkins, 6 August 1781; 779, Johnson to Perkins, 7 May
    1782; 1147, n.d., Johnson to Perkins.
58 *Life*, ii. p.397.

INDEX

Figures in italic refer to complete chapters.